Understanding the Holocaust

ISSUES IN CONTEMPORARY RELIGION

Series Editors: Christopher Lamb and M. Darrol Bryant

The volumes in this series are interdisciplinary and present their subjects from global and cross-religious perspectives, examining issues that cut across traditions and emerge in distinctive ways in different religions and cultural settings. Based on sound scholarship, the books are intended for undergraduate courses and for professionals involved in inter-faith dialogue.

Also available in this series:

Christopher Lamb and M. Darrol Bryant (eds),
Religious Conversion: Contemporary Practices and Controversies

Understanding the Holocaust

An Introduction

Dan Cohn-Sherbok

Cassell
London and New York

Cassell
Wellington House, 125 Strand, London WC2R 0BB
370 Lexington Avenue, New York, NY 10017–6550

First Published 1999

British Library Cataloguing in Publication Data
A catalogue record for this book is available from the British Library.
ISBN 0–304–70442–3 (hardback)
     0–304–70443–1 (paperback)

Library of Congress Cataloging-in-Publication Data
Cohn-Sherbok, Dan.
    Understanding the Holocaust: an introduction/Dan Cohn-Sherbok.
       p.   cm. — (Issues in contemporary religion)
    Includes bibliographical references and index.
    ISBN 0–304–70442–3 (hardcover). — ISBN 0–304–70443–1 (pbk.)
    1. Holocaust, Jewish (1939–1945) 2. Jews—Germany—
History—1933–1945. I. Title. II. Series.
D804.3.C649 1999
940.53′18—dc21   99–11715
                                                                        CIP

Typeset by Bookens Ltd, Royston, Herts.
Printed and bound in Great Britain by Biddles Ltd, Guildford and King's Lynn

Contents

CONTENTS

Acknowledgements

In writing this study I would like to acknowledge my indebtedness to two seminal works from which I have obtained a wealth of information and source material which I have used throughout this book: M. Gilbert, *The Holocaust*, London, 1987 and J. Noakes and G. Pridham (eds), *Nazism 1919–1945*, vols 1–3, Exeter, 1995. I am also indebted to other important books which have provided information and source material: R. Landau, *The Nazi Holocaust*, London, 1992 in Chapters 1, 8, 11, 22 and 23; Leon Poliakov, *History of Anti-Semitism*, Vol. III, London, 1975 in Chapter 1; Michael Burleigh and Wolfgang Wippermann, *The Racial State: Germany 1933–45*, Cambridge, 1996 in Chapters 1, 5, 20 and 21; Klaus P. Fischer, *Nazi Germany*, London, 1995 in Chapters 3–6; Robert Wistrich, *Who's Who in Nazi Germany*, London, 1995 in Chapter 6; Michael Marrus, *The Holocaust in History*, London, 1993 in Chapter 11; Lucy Dawidowicz, *The War Against the Jews*, London, 1990 in Chapter 13; Wolfgang Sofsky, *The Order of Terror: The Concentration Camp*, Princeton, 1997 in Chapter 17; Deborah Lipstadt, *Denying the Holocaust*, New York, 1993 in Chapters 18 and 25; Robert Jay Lifton, *The Nazi Doctors*, New York, 1986 in Chapter 19; Ann and John Tusa, *The Nuremberg Trial*, London, 1995 in Chapter 24. I would also like to express my grateful thanks for permission to reproduce some of the maps from my book *Atlas of Jewish History* (London, Routledge, 1994). I would like to acknowledge that the photographs are used in this book with the permission of the Trustees of the Imperial War Museum, London; the reference number for each photograph is given at the end of the caption.

For Lavinia

Chronology of the Holocaust

1919

16 September Hitler joins the German Workers' Party

1920

24 February Proclamation of the Party's 25-Point Programme
8 August Founding of the National Socialist German Workers' Party (NSDAP)

1923

8–9 November Hitler's Beer Hall putsch in Munich fails

1924

1 April Hitler sentenced to five years' imprisonment
20 December Hitler released from prison where he wrote *Mein Kampf*

1925

26 April Re-establishment of the NSDAP
26 April Hindenburg elected President of the Weimar Republic
11 November Founding of the SS

1928

20 May Nazis poll 810,000 (2.6%) in the *Reichstag* elections

1929

29 October Stock market collapses in the United States

1930

14 September Nazis poll 6,409,600 (18.3%) in the *Reichstag* elections

1931

December — 5.6 million unemployed in Germany

1932

13 March and 10 April — Hitler defeated by President Hindenburg in two presidential elections

13 April — Chancellor Brüning prohibits both the SS and the SA

30 May — Brüning is replaced as Chancellor by Papen

16 June — Ban on the SA and SS lifted

31 July — Nazis poll 13,745,800 (37.4%) in the *Reichstag* elections, making the NSDAP the largest party

13 August — Hindenburg turns down Hitler as Chancellor

6 November — Nazis poll 11,737,000 (33.1%) in the *Reichstag* elections

2 December — General Schleicher becomes Chancellor

1933

4 January — Meeting between Hitler and Papen

30 January — Hitler appointed Chancellor and in the following months the Nazis assume control of the state

27 February — *Reichstag* fire

28 February — Protection of the People and State decree suspends civil liberties

5 March — Nazis poll 43.9% in *Reichstag* elections

20 March — Dachau concentration camp set up on Himmler's orders. First prisoners include Communists, Socialists, homosexuals and Jews

24 March — Enabling Law establishes Hitler's dictatorial control

1 April — Nazi boycott of Jewish businesses and professions

7 April — Restoration of the Professional Civil Service Act dismisses Jews and others from the Civil Service

22 April — Jews disqualified from working in hospitals

25 April — Law Against the Overcrowding of German Schools begins policy of eliminating teachers and students from schools

10 May — Book burning in Berlin directed at works by Jewish authors

14 July — Law banning all existing parties and prohibiting the creation of new parties

August	Zionist organization arranges large-scale emigration of Jews to Palestine
29 September	Hereditary farm law bans Jews from owning land. Another law bans Jews from cultural life and sport
12 November	First *Reichstag* election in the one-party state. Nazis poll 95.2%

1934

1 May	Der Stürmer revives ritual murder accusation against the Jewish community
30 June–2 July	Röhm purge during the Night of the Long Knives
20 July	SS becomes independent
2 August	President Hindenburg dies and Hitler merges offices of Chancellor and President and declares himself 'Führer'

1935

13 January	Reincorporation of the Saarland into the Reich
16 March	Introduction of military conscription
26 June	Compulsory labour service for young men aged 18–25
15 September	Nuremberg Laws
1 November	Supplement to Reich Citizenship Law disqualifies Jews from citizenship
14 November	Further supplement defines *Mischling* (part-Jew)

1936

7 March	Hitler marches into demilitarized Rhineland
20 March	Plebiscite on Hitler's policies
17 June	Himmler becomes *Reichsführer* and chief of the German police
1 August	Hitler opens Olympic Games in Berlin
8 September	Party Congress approves Four-Year Plan
25 October	Rome-Berlin Axis comes into effect

1937

30 January	Extension of the Enabling Law
14 March	Papal encyclical *With Burning Concern* denounces Nazi policies towards the Church
19 July	Buchenwald concentration camp established
25–29 September	Visit by Mussolini

26 November	Schacht resigns as Reich Economics Minister and is replaced by Walther Funk

1938

12 March	Annexation of Austria
26 April	Personal property of German Jews over 5000 Marks to be registered
4 May	Numerus Clausus restricting Jewish entry into professions introduced in Hungary
14 June	Jewish firms in Germany to be registered
6–15 July	Evian Conference fails to find a solution to the Jewish refugee problem
25 July	Licences of Jewish doctors revoked
August	Eichmann opens an office in Vienna for Jewish emigration
17 August	Jewish women to add 'Sarah' and Jewish men 'Israel' to their names
27 August	Chief of the army general staff (Ludwig Beck) resigns
27 September	Licences of Jewish lawyers revoked
29–30 September	Munich Conference
5 October	New passports issued to Jews with the suffix J
28 October	Polish-born Jews in Germany expelled
7 November	Herschl Grynszpan assassinates German official in Paris
8–9 November	*Kristallnacht*
12 November	Göring convenes Nazi officials to plan the Aryanization of Jewish businesses
16 November	Jewish children forbidden to attend German schools

1939

24 January	Heydrich assigned by Göring to remove all Jews from the Reich through emigration
30 January	Hitler delivers *Reichstag* speech in which he predicts that Jews in Europe will be annihilated
21 February	Decree orders that Jews surrender all gold and silver
14–16 March	Germany invades Czechoslovakia
23 March	Germany invades the Memel region
22 April	Pact of Steel between Germany and Italy

30 April	Revocation of tenancy protection for Jews
May	British White Paper restricts entry of 75,000 Jewish refugees into Palestine over the following five years
23 August	Nazi-Soviet Non-aggression Pact
1 September	Germany invades Poland
3 September	Britain and France declare war against Germany
27 September	Reich Main Security Office established under Heydrich
October	Euthanasia programme initiated
8–12 October	Hitler divides Poland and creates the Government General
8 November	Assassination attempt by Georg Esler against Hitler
23 November	Jews in Nazi-occupied Poland ordered to wear Star of David
28 November	Jewish Councils created in German-occupied Poland
12 December	Labour camps established throughout German-occupied Poland

1940

9 April	Germany invades Denmark and Norway
1 May	Lodz ghetto sealed off
10 May	Hitler invades Holland, Belgium, Luxemburg and France
22 June	Franco-German armistice
July	Proposal that European Jews be deported to Madagascar
October	Deportations to Warsaw ghetto
3 October	Vichy government debars Jews from public offices and interns foreign Jews
28 October	Mussolini attacks Greece
18 December	Hitler formalizes plan to invade Russia

1941

January	Anti-Jewish pogrom in Bucharest
February	Deportations of Dutch Jews to Buchenwald and Sachsenhausen concentration camps
1 March	Hitler plans to expand Auschwitz
6 April	German invasion of Yugoslavia and Greece

May	Foreign-born Jews interned in Paris
10 May	Hess flies on secret mission to Scotland
4 June	German army order to troops about to invade the Soviet Union to eliminate all resistance
22 June	Nazi invasion of Soviet Union
22 July	Vichy government begins expropriation of French Jewish business establishments
31 July	Heydrich receives orders from Göring to begin preparations for the Final Solution
August	Romanians expel Jews from Bessarabia and Bukovina
23 August	Hitler cancels euthanasia programme
26 August	Massacre of Hungarian Jewish refugees by SS units
1 September	Jews forced to wear yellow Star of David in Germany
3 September	Zyklon B gas tested at Auschwitz
6 September	Vilnius Jews ghettoized
29–30 September	Massacre at Babi Yar, Russia
14 October	Deportations of Jews from Greater Germany to the east
23 October	Nazi emigration policy ends
24 November	Ghetto created at Theresienstadt
30 November	Executions of Riga Jews
December	Plan for the East formulated to deport non-Germans
8 December	Gassing of Jews and gypsies in mobile killing vans
11 December	Germany declares war against the United States
16 December	Hitler assumes command of the army

1942

January	Jewish resistance organized in Vilnius and Kovno
20 January	Wannsee Conference
24 January	The *Struma* carrying Jewish refugees from Romania refused permission to sail to Palestine and sunk
16 March	Liquidation of Polish Jews begins
24 March	Deportation of Jews to Auschwitz from Slovakia
27 May	Heydrich assassinated

2 June	BBC broadcast of extracts from a report about murder of Jews at Chelmno and elsewhere
June	Mass gassings at Auschwitz
14 July	Mass deportation of Dutch Jews to Auschwitz followed by Jews from Belgium and Luxemburg
22 July	Deportation of Jews from Warsaw to Treblinka
28 July	Formation of Underground Jewish Combat Organization in the Warsaw ghetto
15 October	Murder of Jews by SS in Brest-Litovsk South Russia
25 October	Deportation of Norwegian Jews to Auschwitz
2 November	Round-up of Jews in Bialystok region of Poland
16 November	Deportations of gypsies to Auschwitz
19 November	Soviets launch counter-offensive at Stalingrad
27 November	Expulsion of Poles from Zamosc region of Poland

1943

January	Jewish transport to Treblinka attacks guards
8 March	Deportation of Greek Jews to Treblinka
13 March	Failed plot against Hitler
14 March	Cracow ghetto liquidated
17 March	Bulgarian parliament votes for deportation of Jews
5 April	Massacre of Lithuanian Jews
19 April	Warsaw ghetto uprising
12 May	Liquidation of Warsaw ghetto completed
21 June	Lvov ghetto liquidated
1 July	All legal protection of Jews in Germany removed
25 July	Fall of Mussolini
2 August	Attempted revolt in Treblinka crushed
16 August	Bialystok ghetto liquidated
September–October	Danes sabotage Nazi deportation plan
23 September	Vilnius ghetto liquidated
16 October	Deportation of Italian Jews to Auschwitz

1944

22 January	President Roosevelt sets up War Refugees Board
19 March	Nazis occupy Hungary
May	Proposals from Jewish leaders to Allies that they bomb railway lines to Auschwitz

15 May	Deportation of Hungarian Jews to Auschwitz
6 June	D-Day
8 June	Eichmann negotiates with Jewish leaders to exchange Hungarian prisoners for war armaments
20 July	Bomb plot to assassinate Hitler
23 July	Majdanek concentration camp liberated
6 August	Remaining Jews in Lodz deported to Auschwitz
7 October	Revolt at Auschwitz
15 October	Arrow Cross stages coup in Budapest
2 November	Raoul Wallenberg saves Hungarian Jews

1945

January	Death marches of Jewish and non-Jewish slave labourers towards Germany
27 January	Auschwitz liberated
11 April	Buchenwald liberated
15 April	Bergen-Belsen liberated
28 April	Dachau liberated
30 April	Hitler commits suicide
2 May	Red Army captures Berlin
1–5 May	Death marches continue
8 May	Germany surrenders

Key names

Anielewicz, Mordechai Young Zionist who led the Warsaw ghetto uprising of April-May 1943.

Baeck, Leo German reform rabbi who became president of the *Reichsvertretung der deutschen Juden* after the Nazi takeover in 1933.

Bormann, Martin Hitler's personal secretary. After Hess's flight to Scotland, he was appointed Director of the Party Chancellery, Reich Minister and a member of the Cabinet Council for Defence.

Braun, Eva Hitler's mistress and bride.

Chamberlain, Houston Stewart British racial philosopher whose *Foundation of the Nineteenth Century* powerfully influenced the ideology of National Socialism.

Darré, Richard Walther Expert on animal husbandry, who became Nazi head of the Race Office.

Eichmann, Adolf *SS-Obersturmbannführer* who, as a specialist in Jewish affairs, oversaw the expulsions of Jews from Greater Germany and subsequently the transportation of Jews for the implementation of the Final Solution.

Eicke, Theodor Head of German concentration camps.

Frick, Wilhelm Reich Minister of the Interior.

Funk, Walther Economist, journalist and subsequently Minister of Economics under Hitler.

Goebbels, Joseph Hitler's Minister of Propaganda.

Göring, Hermann Early associate of Hitler who had wide powers over Germany's economy and war preparations. His titles included Reich Minister, Aviation Minister, Commander-in-Chief of the Air Force, Reich Forest Master, Reich Hunting Master, General Plenipotentiary of the Four Year Plan, and Reich Marshal.

Hess, Rudolf Hitler's deputy and leader of the Party.

Heydrich, Reinhard *SS Obergruppenführer.* Together with Himmler, the creator of the Nazi police state and the concentration camp system. He also served as chief of the *Einsatzgruppen.*

Himmler, Heinrich Head of the SS and Nazi police organization. After 1943 Minister of the Interior. Organizer of the concentration camps and the architect of the Final Solution.

von Hindenburg, Paul Head of the German army in World War I and President of the Weimar Republic.

Hitler, Adolf Leader of the Nazi Party and later Führer of Germany.

Hoess, Rudolf Commandant of Auschwitz.

Jodl, Alfred General and chief of staff of operations in the German High Command.

Kaltenbrunner, Ernst *SS Obergruppenführer* and successor to Reinhard Heydrich as chief of the Security Service of the SS.

Kaplan, Chaim Polish writer and author of a diary about the Warsaw ghetto.

Keitel, Wilhelm General Field Marshal and head of the High Command of the Armed Forces.

Kesselring, Albert General Field Marshal.

Mengele, Josef SS physician at Auschwitz where he conducted medical experiments.

von Papen, Franz Conservative Catholic politician and Weimar Chancellor.

Pope Pius XII Head of the Catholic Church during the Nazi period.

von Ribbentrop, Joachim Foreign Minister after 1938.

Riefenstahl, Leni German film-maker.

Röhm, Ernst Head of the SA.

Rommel, Erwin General Field Marshal during World War II.

Rosenberg, Alfred Nazi racial philosopher and politician.

Schacht, Hjalmar Financial expert during the interwar period. Later he served as president of the *Reichsbank.*

Speer, Albert Architect and later Minister of Armaments.

Streicher, Julius Editor of *Der Stürmer.*

Wirth, Christian Participated in the euthanasia programme and was later responsible for Belzec, Treblinka and Sobibor.

Glossary

Anschluss Annexation of Austria by the Nazis in February 1938.

Blitzkreig Lightning war.

Concentration camp Camp for prisoners during the Nazi period.

Death camp As distinct from a concentration camp, a centre where Jews and others were killed. The main death camps were Auschwitz, Belzec, Chelmno, Majdanek, Sobibor and Treblinka.

Death marches Forced marches of camp inmates during the latter part of the war.

Deportation Process whereby people were removed from their place of residence to a concentration or death camp.

DAF German Labour Front.

Der Stürmer Anti-Semitic newspaper published by Julius Streicher.

Einsatzgruppen Mobile killing units.

Einsatz Kommando Unit of the Einsatzgruppen.

Enabling Law Law on which Hitler's dictatorship was based.

Freikorps Non-governmental military group.

Führer Leader.

Gauleiter Party district leader.

General Government Administrative area in Poland created by the Nazis.

Genocide Plan to eliminate all Jews in Europe.

Gestapo Terrorist police force.

Ghetto Quarters in towns where Jews were compelled to reside.

Hasidim Jewish pietistic sect.

Hitler Youth Organization established to inculcate social and military values into young Germans.

Judenrat (plural **Judenräte**) Jewish Council.

Kapo Concentration camp prisoner in charge of other prisoners.

Kristallnacht Night of Broken Glass.

Labour camp Camp designed to contribute to German production through slave labour.

Lebensraum Additional living space to be colonized by Germans in the east.

NSDAP Nazi Party.

Reichsgericht Highest court of the Reich.

Reichsleiter Reich leader.

Reichstag German parliament.

Reichsvertretung National Jewish body during the Third Reich.

SA Storm detachment. Hitler's private army.

SD Security Service.

SDP Social Democratic Party.

Seder Passover first night celebration.

Sonderkommando Special mobile task forces.

SS Protection squads. Paramilitary organization that began as a party police force, becoming a terrorist Reich police force, and a regular army within the army (*Waffen-SS*).

Strength through Joy. Government programme to support recreational activities for German workers.

Völkisch Ethnic or national, referring to German ethnocentrism.

Völkischer Beobachter Official newspaper of the NSDAP.

Volksgemeinschaft Community of the people.

Waffen-SS Fighting branch of the SS.

Wannsee Conference Conference which took place on 20 January 1942 under Heydrich and planned the Final Solution.

Wehrmacht Armed Forces.

Weimar Republic Democratic regime established in Germany after World War I.

Yeshivot Rabbinical academies.

Plates

Maps

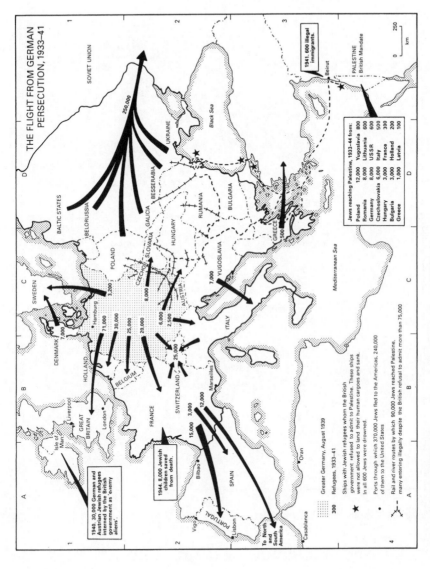

Map 1   The flight from German persecution, 1933–41

Map 2 Concentration camps

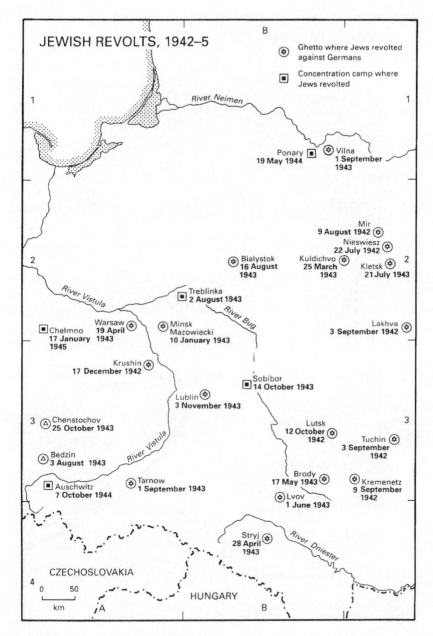

JEWISH REVOLTS, 1942–5

Ghetto where Jews revolted against Germans

Concentration camp where Jews revolted

River Neimen

Ponary
19 May 1944

Vilna
1 September
1943

Mir
9 August 1942
Nieswiesz
22 July 1942

Bialystok
16 August
1943

Kuldichvo
25 March
1943

Kletsk
21 July 1943

River Vistula

Treblinka
2 August 1943

River Bug

Warsaw
19 April
1943

Chelmno
17 January
1945

Minsk
Mazowiecki
10 January 1943

Lakhva
3 September 1942

Krushin
17 December 1942

Sobibor
14 October 1943

Lublin
3 November 1943

Chenstochov
25 October 1943

Lutsk
12 October
1942

Tuchin
3 September
1942

Bedzin
3 August 1943

River Vistula

Tarnow
1 September 1943

Brody
17 May 1943

Kremenetz
9 September
1942

Auschwitz
7 October 1944

Lvov
1 June 1943

Stryj
28 April
1943

River Dniester

CZECHOSLOVAKIA

0   50

km   A

HUNGARY   B

Map 3   Jewish revolts, 1942–5

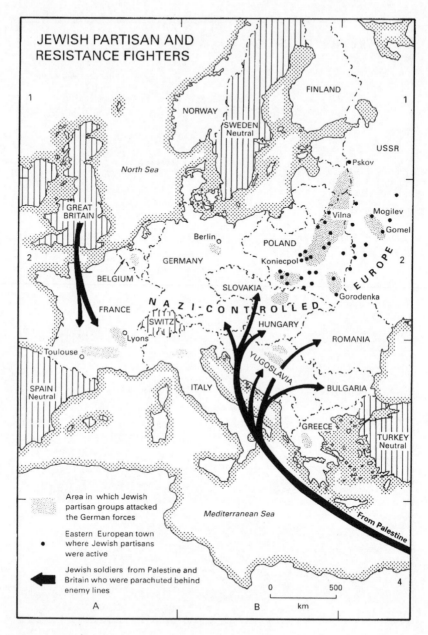

Map 4   Jewish partisan and resistance fighters

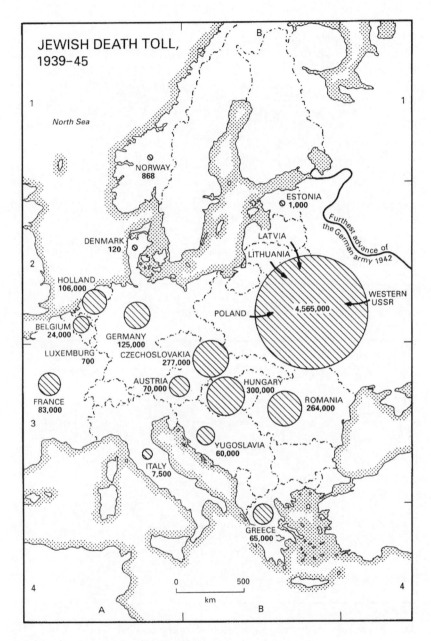

Map 5 Jewish death toll, 1939–45

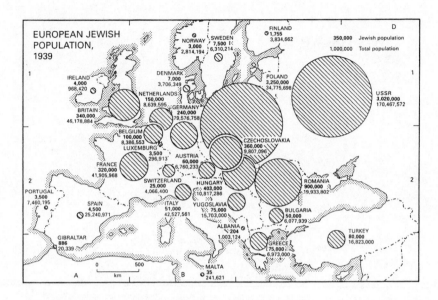

Map 6 European Jewish population, 1939

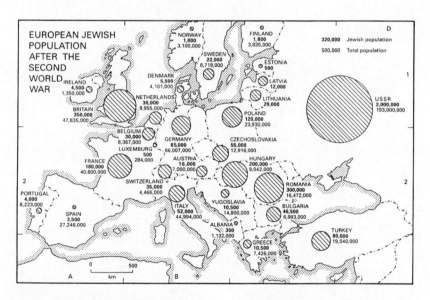

Map 7 European Jewish population after the Second World War

Introduction

On a recent trip to the United States, I went with friends to the United States Holocaust Memorial Museum in Washington. Crossing the streets in downtown Washington, we came to an ordinary-looking government building. Yet, as we quickly discovered, this was not a typical museum. It is rather a profoundly disturbing introduction to horror and death. Dedicated to the millions of victims of the Holocaust, the Holocaust Museum provides an overwhelming experience of barbaric murder. Moving from room to room, the visitor is bombarded by photographs, videos, oral histories, maps, documents, film and music, all designed to present the full terror of the Holocaust.

Beginning with the American encounter of the camps at the end of the war, photographs relate the experience of troops in front of calcined corpses. Starved, emaciated prisoners, dressed in striped uniforms drink from tin bowls. Standing among scattered bodies, Generals Dwight D. Eisenhower and George Patton look on with disbelief. Witnesses to these scenes later expressed their sense of dismay. When asked how she could photograph such atrocities, *Life* magazine photographer Margaret Bourke-White stated: 'I have to work with a veil over my mind. ... In photographing the murder camps the protective veil was so tightly drawn that I hardly knew what I had taken until I saw prints of my own photographs'.[1]

How could one of the most civilized nations in the world have perpetrated such crimes? Were Hitler and his executioners sadistic psychopaths? Were ordinary Germans morally culpable for murdering millions of innocent victims? This volume seeks to explore these and other questions within a historical context. Unlike other studies of the Holocaust, each chapter first deals with a particular period; this is followed by a discussion of the implications of these events.

Hence this volume is not simply an introduction to the horrors of the Holocaust, but an extensive reflection on the social, moral, ideological and religious issues raised by the emergence of the Third Reich and its impact on subsequent history.

Commencing with a survey of anti-Jewish attitudes in the Graeco-Roman world, Chapter 1 traces the evolution of Judaeophobia through the ages. Chapter 2 continues this narrative with a discussion of German hatred of the Jews in the nineteenth century. The writings of such figures as Wilhelm Marr, Heinrich Treitschke and Houston Stewart Chamberlain are examined, as are the growing anti-Semitic attitudes in Germany prior to World War II. This is followed by a discussion of Nazi Judaeophobia and the 25-point racial programme adopted by the Nazi Party.

Chapter 3 continues with an account of Hitler's antipathy towards the Jews, developed through his exposure to Jewry in Vienna. The chapter outlines the growth of his virulent anti-Jewish attitudes as well as his analysis of the Jewish problem; this is followed by a discussion of Hitler's psychological make-up and possible sources of his hatred of the Jewish people. Chapter 4 briefly sketches the nature of the Weimar Republic and surveys the history of this period and the rise of the Nazi party, emphasizing the economic factors in German instability.

Chapter 5 then depicts the nature of Nazi racism, and charts the development of racial theory in the eighteenth and nineteenth centuries and its crystallization in Nazi policy. As the next chapter illustrates, for Hitler life was conceived of as a struggle. This ideology became the guiding principle of the Nazi leaders most intimately involved in the onslaught against the Jews. As Chapter 7 demonstrates, the SS was instrumental in implementing the anti-Jewish ideology of the party. Acting within the Nazi state as a separate organization, the SS began as a small bodyguard which protected the Führer; eventually it became a Reich police force with its own military apparatus, the *Waffen-SS*. This chapter focuses on the role of Heinrich Himmler and the organization he created.

Once Hitler was sworn in as Chancellor of the Reich in 1933, the attack against Jewry was intensified. Chapter 8 provides an overview of the development of anti-Jewish legislation during the early years of the Nazi reign of terror. Here the doctrine of racial purity became a guiding principle of the state. From an early stage the Reich Interior Ministry had contemplated altering regulations concerning

Reich citizenship. Yet, as the next chapter points out, it had not proceeded far largely because of the desire not to affect the economic situation in the country and also because of the legal complexities of such legislation. This chapter describes the Nuremberg laws which were promulgated in September 1935, and ponders their ethical implications.

As Chapter 10 shows, hostility towards the German Jewish community intensified. Such attitudes were reinforced by an attack on a German civil servant. Seeking revenge for the persecution of his parents as well as other Jews, a young Polish Jew fatally wounded this official. This led to *Kristallnacht*: during this attack fires were ignited throughout Germany and the shattered glass of synagogues and Jewish businesses was scattered throughout the streets. Chapter 11 proceeds with a description of the conquest of Poland. In the view of many Germans, the loss of the Polish corridor was a calamity. Hitler's non-aggression pact with Poland was welcomed by Polish citizens, but Germany had no intention of honouring this treaty. Following the *Anschluss* of Austria in 1938 and the victory over Czechoslovakia in the same year, the Nazis invaded Poland as the first step in the quest for *Lebensraum*, living space for Germans, in the underpopulated areas of Eastern Europe. This narrative continues in Chapter 12 with a description of the subjugation, humiliation and murder of Polish Jewry.

In 1940 the first ghetto was established in April in Lodz. Chapter 13 portrays the largest ghetto created by the Nazis in Warsaw; inhabitants there had to survive on a food allocation of 300 calories a day. Heating materials were limited, and those who did not have access to the black market were not able to survive long. This chapter also explains the nature of ghetto life, and explores the interaction between captors and victims as well as the attitudes of non-Jews who observed ghetto life.

As Chapter 14 illustrates, the next stage in the plan of extermination of European Jewry began with the invasion of Russia in 1941. This was designed to destroy what was first described by the Nazis as the Jewish-Bolshevik conspiracy. At first mobile killing battalions of 500–900 men (the *Einsatzgruppen*) under the supervision of Reinhard Heydrich began the slaughter of Russian Jewry. This chapter provides an account of these events, and the attitudes of those who carried out such victimization.

Mercilessly the Nazis deported Jews to their deaths. As the next

3

chapter indicates, the round-up of Jews was frequently undertaken with lightning speed. This chapter examines the actions of the Nazis and the suffering of those who were taken to the camps. Of particular interest here was the passivity of those who were victimized. Chapter 16 continues with an account of the transportation to the camps. This chapter offers a detailed description of the journeys endured by victims of Nazi harassment, persecution and murder. In addition, the attitude of bystanders is critically examined.

Chapter 17 delineates the nature of the concentration camps. The creation of these institutions was initially a consequence of the burning of the *Reichstag* on 27 February 1933. The following day the Emergency Decree for the Protection of the Nation and State abrogated the civil rights enshrined in the Weimar Constitution. The SA and the SS were empowered to exercise protective custody without permission of the courts. As this chapter demonstrates, from this period until the end of the war, inmates were incarcerated in the most horrific conditions. Chapter 18 continues this discussion with an examination of the gas chambers, and the process of extermination administered by the SS.

Paralleling the determination of Germans to implement the Final Solution, the Nazis relentlessly instituted a programme of medical experimentation on those imprisoned in the camps. Chapter 19 provides an account of such experimentation, and explores the motives of those who engaged in such investigation. Alongside such medical activities, the Nazis instituted a euthanasia programme designed to eliminate over 100,000 mentally-ill and handicapped persons. Chapter 20 examines this programme. As this chapter indicates, the aim of this policy was to rid society of those persons who were deemed to have no value to the community.

As part of their racial programme, the Nazis adopted harsh measures against gypsy communities living in their midst. Chapter 21 looks at the policy which became a central feature of Nazism. In addition, the chapter examines the policy against the asocial as well as homosexuals. With the Nazi seizure of power, both these groups were put at risk. This chapter describes the ideology of such a practice, and illustrates the ways in which both the asocial and homosexual communities were put at risk. In addition the chapter explores the ways in which the Nazis attempted to modify the sexual inclinations of those living in Germany.

By September 1942 the German armies had conquered most of

Europe. Yet, as Chapter 22 demonstrates, resistance increased during this period. This chapter surveys the uprising of Jews throughout the countryside and in city centres. Of particular interest was the mass uprising in the Warsaw Ghetto and the attitudes of those who witnessed this revolt. The next chapter examines the reactions of those who witnessed the onslaught against Jewry. With few exceptions the churches within Nazi Germany accepted the policy of the State and its attitude towards the Jewish community. This chapter surveys the views of Church leaders in the various Christian denominations within Germany as well as outside the Third Reich. The chapter also examines the attitudes of the Allies to German atrocities during the war.

In the aftermath of the war the Allies were anxious to bring those who had perpetrated atrocities to trial. On 20 November 1945 the Nuremberg Tribunal interrogated members of the Nazi regime. Chapter 24 provides an account of the trial and the sentences given by the judges. After nearly a year, twelve defendants were sentenced to death, three to life imprisonment, four were given prison sentences, and three acquitted. Despite the testimonies given at the trial, Holocaust deniers have disputed the historical evidence provided by both victims and perpetrators of Nazi terror. Chapter 25 surveys the arguments used by these individuals, and provides a critical evaluation of Holocaust denial.

The book concludes in Chapter 26 with a discussion of the religious implications of the Holocaust. The murder of six million Jews in the most horrific circumstances raises serious questions about God's nature and activity in the world. If the God of Israel has established a covenantal relationship with his chosen people, how could he have allowed such terror to occur? Such questions have haunted Jewish theologians since the end of the war, and this chapter outlines the views of a number of Holocaust theologians who have grappled with this issue. On the threshold of the twenty-first century, the Jewish people now need to come to terms with this most pressing religious perplexity.

This volume thus provides a framework for understanding the history of the Holocaust. The main task of the student of these events is comprehension. As the philosopher Hannah Arendt commented, the Holocaust is the burden of this century. In her view, the quest to come to an understanding of the Holocaust calls for personal involvement and heightened sensitivity:

Comprehension does not mean denying the outrageous, deducing the unprecedented from precedence, or explaining phenomena by such analogies and generalities that the impact of reality and the shock of experience are no longer felt ... it means, rather, examining and bearing consciously the burden which our century has placed on us – neither denying its existence nor submitting meekly to its weight.[2]

This is the challenge posed by this book. Its aim is to enlighten readers about this most horrifying tragedy of the modern world, and to stimulate them to ponder the questions it raises about human nature and moral responsibility in contemporary society.

Notes

1 Michael Berenbaum, *The World Must Know*, Boston, 1993, p. 9.
2 *Ibid.*, p. 20.

1. The history of anti-Semitism

For thousands of years Jews have been persecuted and murdered: arguably anti-Semitism is humanity's longest hatred. Given such widespread antipathy, the Holocaust should not be seen as a modern aberration, but rather the last link in a long chain of history stretching back to ancient times. The German onslaught against the Jews is a catastrophe that might well have been predicted.

The origin and growth of anti-Jewish hostility

The long history of such Judaeophobia begins in the Graeco-Roman world. Living among pagans, both Jews and Judaism were subject to persecution and discrimination. Living in a Hellenistic culture, the typical view was that anything non-Greek was barbaric. Hence the Jewish tradition was viewed with suspicion and contempt. Later when Christianity emerged as a dominant force in the ancient world, Jews came to be regarded as contemptible and demonic. In its advocacy of anti-Jewish attitudes, the Church drew upon Hellenistic ideas.

Continuing this tradition of hostility to Jewry, the early Church believed itself to be the authentic heir to the promises given by God in Scripture. Jesus' messiahship ushered in a new era in which the true Israel would become a light to the nations. Such a vision of the Christian community evoked hostility against Jewry, who were viewed as apostate and unrepentant. Such hatred was fuelled by the Gospel writers who depicted Jesus attacking the leaders of the Jewish nation. The Church taught that what is now required is circumcision of the heart rather than obedience to the law. In proclaiming his message, Paul emphasized that the Jewish nation had been rejected by God, and the new covenant had taken the place of the old.

Following New Testament teaching, the Church Fathers evolved an *Adversos Judaeos* tradition which vilified Jewry. According to the writers, the Jewish community is lawless and dissolute. For this reason all future divine promises apply only to the Church. It is the Church who constitute the elect, rather than the Jewish people. Appealing to Scripture, the Fathers sought to demonstrate that the conflict between the Church and the Synagogue was prefigured in Scripture. Separated from the Christian message of salvation, the Jews were rejected and are subject to God's wrath. Destined to wander in exile, they find no peace on earth.

The tradition of anti-Semitism created by the Fathers of the Church continued into the Middle Ages. During the centuries of the Crusades, Jews were killed throughout Western Europe. During this period a number of charges were levelled at the Jewish nation. Repeatedly Jews were accused of murdering Christian children to incorporate their blood into unleavened bread for Passover; such allegations of ritual murder spread from country to country and Jews were victimized for supposedly condoning such atrocious deeds. Jews were also accused of blaspheming the Christian faith in their sacred literature, and as a consequence copies of the Talmud were burned. In addition, the Jewish population was accused of bringing about the Black Plague by poisoning wells.

During this period the stereotype of the demonic Jew became part of Western culture. Repeatedly Jews were accused of possessing attributes of both the Devil and witches. As the personification of evil, they were relegated to a sub-species of the human race. In addition Jews were perceived as magicians, able to work magic against the Christian community. This belief served as the basis for the charge that Jews desecrated the Host and committed acts of ritual murder. In the wake of these allegations, the masses attacked Jews in their pursuit of the demons, and in this onslaught thousands of innocent victims lost their lives.

In the post-medieval period such attitudes were perpetuated throughout Western Europe. Although the Jewish community was expelled from France in the fourteenth century, negative images of Jews continued to play a role in French culture. Catechisms, lives of Jews and canticles portrayed the Jewish people as tools of Satan.

Further, tracts abounded which denounced the Jews in terms reminiscent of the Middle Ages. In England, Jews were vilified even though the Jewish nation was expelled in 1290. German Jews were also regarded with contempt – such hostility was powerfully expressed in Martin Luther's *Against the Jews and their Lies*. Such publications were followed by a wide range of tracts which denigrated both Judaism and the Jewish people.

Although Spanish Jewry flourished during the Middle Ages, Jews eventually came to be regarded with suspicion and contempt. Measures were taken against the Jewish population, and as a result many Jews embraced the Christian faith to escape attack. Such apostasy, as well as the Christian onslaught on Jewry, led to the decline of the Jewish communities, a trend which was resisted by Jewish leaders. During the fifteenth century the Church initiated a new form of Jewish persecution. The Inquisition was established to purge *conversos* or New Christians – Jewish converts to Christianity as opposed to Old Christians of pure blood – who were suspected of practising Jewish customs. Tribunals were created throughout Spain which applied torture to extract confessions from the guilty. Those who refused to confess were cast into the flames. Finally at the end of the century, an Edict of Expulsion was enacted to rid the country of the Jewish race.

When the Inquisition intensified its efforts to root out Christian heresy in Spain, Marranos (Jewish converts to Christianity) fled to other countries for safety from their Christian persecutors. Many sought refuge in Portugal, where they led a Christian way of life while observing Jewish practices. Following Spanish precedent, the Portuguese Inquisition was established in the next century and sought to discover Marranos. Other Marranos were driven to find homes in other lands. Both Turkey and Salonica constituted Marrano refuges from Christian oppression. Others went to Antwerp, Venice, Ancona and Bordeaux. In the next century Marranos settled in Amsterdam, Hamburg and London. Although in these centres *conversos* returned to Judaism, they nonetheless retained many of their former cultural characteristics. Some Marranos, however, broke away from traditional Judaism, and advanced heterodox religious opinions which unintentionally became the basis of further Christian anti-Semitism in later centuries.

Unlike their co-religionists in Western Europe, Jews in Poland enjoyed considerable tolerance and were granted numerous privileges. They were not confined to ghettos, nor restricted in their occupations. Under such conditions, the Jewish community created an elaborate form of local and national self-government, and rabbinic scholarship reached great heights. Yet despite such general prosperity, the country was subject to Christian anti-Jewish hostility in the late medieval period, and in the seventeenth century Polish Jewry was massacred by Cossacks under Bogdan Chmielnicki. In the wake of this Christian onslaught, the Hasidic movement encouraged religious pietism, but was severely criticized by the traditional rabbinical establishment. As the community was torn by this conflict, attacks were directed against the Jewish population by Gentiles. Such hostility in Poland was paralleled in Russia. Initially Jews were prevented from settling in the country, and with the annexation of Polish territories to Russia in the nineteenth century, Jews were viewed by Christians with suspicion and contempt and eventually expelled from the villages where they resided.

During the early modern period the commercial interests of the bourgeoisie, coupled with centuries-old prejudice against Jews and Judaism, evoked considerable hostility towards the Jewish population in western countries. In Germany, merchants protested against the infidels living in their midst. Jewish trade, they believed, would destroy the economic life of the country and pollute the Christian population. Similar attitudes were expressed in France where the bourgeoisie resisted Jewish settlement despite the fact that the nobility regarded Jews as financially useful. In Great Britain, Jews were also subject to virulent criticism, and attempts to simplify procedures for Jewish naturalization and to authorize Jews to possess land were met with considerable resistance. In the United States, however, Jews gained a broad measure of freedom as the country struggled to achieve its independence from England. Nonetheless, despite many advances made in the seventeenth and eighteenth centuries, Jewish life did not alter radically from medieval patterns of existence. Stereotyped as foreign and strange, Jews were subject to discrimination and persecution during the early modern period.

Under the banner of the Enlightenment, English free thinkers sought to ameliorate the condition of the Jews. Such attempts, however, were countered by other writers who attacked Jewry on grounds consonant with the spirit of a rationalist and scientific age. In France, Protestants influenced by the Enlightenment attempted to refute charges against the Jewish population. Yet despite such progressive attitudes, they were unable to free themselves from traditional Christian assumptions about Jewish guilt and divine retribution. In addition, many of the major thinkers of the age encouraged Judaeophobia. In Germany an attempt was made to present Jews in a more positive light, but here as well the rise of national self-confidence provoked antipathy towards the Jewish populace. Such philosophers as Kant, Fichte and Hegel wrote disparagingly of both Jews and Judaism. In order to escape such hostility, a number of enlightened Jews – primarily in Berlin – dissociated themselves from the Jewish way of life, and others sought to gain acceptance by becoming a new Jewish-Christian sect.

At the end of the eighteenth century the spirit of the Enlightenment stimulated Christian Europe to seek the amelioration of Jewish life. With the establishment of the Napoleonic era, Jewish existence was revolutionized. The summoning of a Great Sanhedrin in France paved the way for Jewish emancipation and the position of Jewry improved throughout the continent. In the midst of such social upheaval, German Jewish reformers such as Israel Jacobson attempted to adapt Jewish worship to modern conditions. To the consternation of the Orthodox, Reform Temples appeared throughout Germany. Yet ironically, many enlightened Jews influenced by the Romantic movement were uninterested in what Reform Judaism had to offer. Instead of providing a basis for the resurgence of Judaism, the movement undermined confidence in traditional belief and practice and intensified Christian antipathy to the Jewish way of life.

In Russia, the aim of emancipation was to bring about the assimilation of the Jewish population – the programme of the Tsars was driven by centuries-old Christian hostility to the Jews. From the Jewish side, responses to these moves throughout Europe to improve the plight of Jewry were mixed: traditionalists tended to fear that such steps would undermine Torah Judaism, whereas progressives enthusiastically welcomed new freedoms and opportunities. The Gentile reaction was equally ambivalent. Although liberals ardently campaigned for equal rights, many Christians feared the consequences of such agitation, and at the end of the second decade of the nineteenth century outbursts against the Jewish population spread from country to country.

In the enlightened environment of the nineteenth century, Jewish apologists sought to ameliorate the conditions of the Jewish population. In England Benjamin Disraeli, the Tory Prime Minister, formulated a theory of the Jewish race which served as the basis for his quest to grant civil rights to British Jewry. His advocacy of Jewish emancipation, however, provoked a hostile response from such critics as Robert Knox, who denigrated Jewry in terms reminiscent of previous centuries. Such disparagement was similarly a central feature of French life, as evidenced by the Damascus Affair in which the President of the French Council sided with the French consuls in Damascus who accused Jews there of ritual murder. Despite the peaceful conclusion of this affair, this medieval charge gave rise to widespread anti-Jewish sentiment in France. In addition, the Christian myth of the Wandering Jew who was driven from his homeland for having rejected Christ became a predominant image in French literature of the period and stimulated French Judaeophobia, as did the anti-Jewish allegations of French socialists. In Germany the advocates of German racism as well as metaphysical writers critical of Jews and Judaism generated considerable ill-will. Such hostility reached its climax in the diatribes of the composer Richard Wagner, whose critique of Judaism paved the way for the Nazi onslaught in the following century.

Discussion: The legacy of anti-Semitism

As we have seen, the Jewish people have been detested by those among whom they lived for nearly twenty centuries. What have been the causes of what is arguably humanity's most virulent and sustained hatred? There appears to be a variety of answers to this vexing question. First, the Jewish population, as a small, distinct minority community, has continually been regarded by their host countries as alien and strange. Determined to remain faithful to their religious traditions, Jews generally remained unassimilable. In addition, Jewry regarded itself as God's chosen people. Of all nations, the Jews were selected to be God's special servants; they were to be a light to the Gentiles. It is not surprising that such a sense of religious superiority outraged their Gentile neighbours.

In the view of some modern Jewish thinkers, such a minority status has inevitably rendered the Jews vulnerable. The father of the Zionist movement, Theodor Herzl, for example, was convinced that the problem of anti-Semitism could only be solved if Jews emigrated from the countries where they lived to create a Jewish homeland.

'We have sincerely tried everywhere to merge with the national communities in which we live,' he wrote, 'seeking only to preserve the faith of our fathers. It is not permitted us. In vain are we loyal patriots, sometimes superloyal; in vain do we make the same sacrifices of life and property as our fellow citizens; in vain do we strive to enhance the fame of our native lands in the arts and sciences, or her wealth by trade and commerce. In our native lands where we have lived for centuries we are still decried as aliens.'[1]

Was Herzl right? Modern historical events – the Holocaust in particular – have for many proved the truth of his analysis of the Jewish question. Germany, as one of the most culturally and intellectually advanced nations in the modern world, unleashed the most terrible mechanized apparatus of murder to eradicate Jewry from Europe. In its quest to carry out a policy of annihilation it violated the fundamental canons of human decency. The war against the Jews has arguably demonstrated that no minority people which holds fast to its ancient ways can escape the wrath of host nations with their own xenophobic convictions.

But, it was not simply the minority status of Jewry which fuelled the flames of hatred. The conflict between the Church and the Synagogue led to bitter rivalry and contempt. As Christianity emerged triumphant in the Roman Empire, its leaders denounced the rival tradition from which it had sprung. Typical among the critics of Judaism was the fourth century Patriarch, John Chrysostom, who denounced Jewry for its rejection of Christ. The Jews will be crucified throughout history, he declared, because they crucified Christ:

It is because you killed Christ. It is because you stretched out your hand against the Lord. It is because you shed the precious blood, that there is now no restoration, no mercy any more, and no defence.[2]

Such a tradition of contempt continued from century to century. Repeatedly the Church alleged that the Jews were to suffer because of their rejection of Christ. They were blamed for deicide, and accused of the most heinous crimes against humanity. Demonized in the Middle Ages, they were perceived as the scourge of European society, corrupters of Western civilization. In this light, the great reformer of the Church, Martin Luther, continued to vilify the Jewish nation. Initially he had hoped to convert Jewry, but when they failed to heed his call, he was incensed. In *Against the Jews and their Lies*, he called for the elimination of Judaism: 'Their synagogues should be set on fire ... they should be deprived of their prayer books and Talmuds in which such idolatry, lies, cursing and blasphemy are taught ... their rabbis must be forbidden under threat of death to teach any more.'[3]

Christianity thus stands accused. Despite Jesus' gentle words of compassion, Christians are guilty of the most callous, inhumane acts of violence against Jews. For two millennia the Church has continued and intensified the tradition of anti-Judaism which it inherited from the Graeco-Roman world. Today there are many Christians who are ashamed of this legacy of anti-Semitism and anxious for the Church to change its attitudes. Such a spirit of reconciliation has animated numerous official Church pronouncements which have sought to reverse its teachings.

Such efforts are to be welcomed. Yet, the wounds of the past are deep and the Jewish community is still traumatized by its ill-treatment at the hands of Christians over the centuries. This legacy of the past should not be forgotten in any discussion of the Holocaust. Within the Nazi party, there were many who sought to reconcile the policies of National Socialism with the Christian faith. Indeed, before the Nazi seizure of power, a number of Evangelical supporters of the NSDAP joined forces and demanded that the Evangelical Church and 28 *Land* churches be homogenized into one Reich church. These Nazi Protestants represented what they called 'Positive Christianity' – a form of racial ideology formulated in theological terms. In their view, God sanctified the Aryan lifestyle.

Is it surprising that many Jews continue to remain suspicious of Christian motives? As far as Catholics are concerned, the Vatican remained neutral during the Nazi period. Feeling itself vulnerable during the war, the Catholic Church remained silent in the face of Nazi monstrosities, and at times adopted an apparently pro-German position. The greatest charge against Pope Pious XII is that despite numerous appeals, he refused to speak out against the Nazi policy of extermination which in 1944 was described by Winston Churchill as 'probably the greatest and most horrible crime ever committed in the whole history of the world'.[4]

What is the Jewish community to make of such Christian failures? Given the long history of Christian persecution and the Church's ambivalent attitudes during the war, it is questionable whether positive Jewish-Christian dialogue is possible in a post-Holocaust world. Christians may wish to expunge their feelings of guilt for past atrocities, but it seems unlikely that on the deepest level the Jewish community will be able to forgive their Christian neighbours for centuries of hatred, persecution, torture and murder.

Another factor which has frequently evoked anti-Jewish feelings has been the economic success of Jewry. In seventeenth-century Poland, for example, Jews who served as administrators of noblemen's estates were slaughtered in peasant revolts – their role as middlemen for those who were perceived as oppressors of the masses led to this onslaught. Again, in the early modern period German merchants feared the economic influence of their Jewish rivals; in their view Jewish trade would undermine their economic position. In modern times, Jews were also perceived as the embodiment of corrupt capitalism. Such thinkers as Karl Marx, despite his Jewish origin, bitterly caricatured Jewish financiers, portraying them as exploiters of the suffering underclass. Conversely, the Nazis viewed Jews as the prime movers of Bolshevism. Repeatedly Hitler accused Jewry of engineering a world-wide Communist conspiracy.

Through the centuries such factors led to the elimination of the Jewish population in the countries where they lived as well as to the confiscation of their property. This was so in medieval Europe as well as in modern times. During the Third Reich, Nazis not only used Jewish slave labour in the war effort but also deliberately robbed the Jewish population of their property and money. Racial ideology served as the justification for outright theft. Typical of such callous intent was the comment of Christian Wirth, the commandant of Belzec, who ecstatically described to an onlooker the gold that had been taken from the teeth of those who died in the gas chamber:

He was in his element and showing me a big jam box filled with teeth, said, 'See the weight of the gold! Just from yesterday and the day before! You can imagine what we find every day, dollars, diamonds, gold!'[5]

Notes

1 Arthur Hertzberg (ed.), *The Zionist Idea: A Historical Analysis and Reader*, New York, 1959, p. 209.
2 Dan Cohn-Sherbok, *The Crucified Jew*, Eerdmans, Grand Rapids, Michigan, 1997, p. 33.
3 *Ibid.*, p. 73.
4 R. Landau, *The Nazi Holocaust*, London, 1992, p. 216.
5 Martin Gilbert, *Holocaust*, London, 1987, p. 428.

2. German hatred of the Jews

At the end of the eighteenth-century the spirit of the Enlightenment stimulated Christian Europe to seek to ameliorate Jewish life. With the establishment of the Napoleonic era, Jewish existence was transformed. Yet such improvements in Jewish existence were met by considerable resistance. Throughout Germany reactionaries continued to foster anti-Jewish sentiment, thereby generating considerable ill-will towards the Jewish populace.

German anti-Semitism in modern times

In response to steps towards Jewish emancipation in the late eighteenth-century, Christian anti-Jewish attitudes intensified throughout Europe. When Napoleon convened the Great Sanhedrin, it was feared that the Emperor had concluded a pact with the forces of evil. According to a number of German theosophists, Napoleon's efforts to enfranchize Jewry was a final struggle between Good and Evil. With the defeat of Napoleon, such propaganda ceased. Yet the fear that Jews were seeking world dominion through their emancipation continued to inspire fear and contempt.

As a result of such sentiment outbreaks against Jews began in August 1819 in Würzburg and spread throughout German towns and the countryside. Similar excesses took place in Bohemia, Alsace, the Netherlands and Denmark. The populace was aroused by travelling rioters whose cry was 'Hep! Hep!'. In response the Christian mob armed with axes and iron bars proceeded to the Jewish quarter and demolished the synagogue. In Berlin a contemporary account related:

The excesses which have been committed against the Jews in several towns in Germany have given rise to fear amongst the Israelites in this capital; there have even been some small scenes here already. A few of the Jews' enemies paid a fair number of ne'er-do-wells to cry 'Hep! Hep!' under the windows of the country house of a banker of that nation. An old Israelite pedlar of ribbons and pencils was chased by delinquents in the street which echoed with the ominous cry; he made the best of it like a man with a sense of humour and continued on his way laughing and even shouting 'Hep! Hep!' incessantly himself, but having taken it into his head to peer into a shop and shout inside, a woman who happened to be on the threshold dealt him a violent box on the ears, to which he immediately replied with another. A police employee, who was within call, took him under his protection and, to get him out of reach of the ill-treatment to which he was still exposed, conducted him to the police station. ... The famous 'Hep! Hep!' has already caused some tumultuous scenes in several public places.[1]

As the century progressed, the advocates of German racism as well as metaphysical writers critical of Jews and Judaism continued to foster anti-Jewish sentiment. In particular the writings of two major proponents of Germano-Christian racism, Ernst Moritz Arndt and Friedrich Ludwig Jahn, perpetrated the myth of the supremacy of the German people. According to Arndt, it is the Germans who possess the divine spark.

'I do not think,' he wrote, 'I am mistaken in stating that the powerful and ardent wild stock called German was the good species into which the divine seed could be implanted to produce the most noble fruits. The Germans, and the Latins impregnated and fertilized by them, are the only ones to have made the divine germ flower, thanks to philosophy and theology, and as rulers to animate and guide ... the surrounding peoples, belonging to foreign species'.[2]

Such Germanness must be protected from contamination, and it was Arndt's desire that the Jews disappear as a separate people; this, he believed, could occur through their conversion to Christianity. 'Experience shows,' he stated, 'that as soon as they abandon their disconcerting laws and become Christian, the peculiarities of the Jewish character and type rapidly grow indistinct and by the second generation it is difficult to recognize the seed of Abraham.'[3] Similarly, for Jahn the struggle against foreign blood is a battle of life and death for German society and culture:

Hybrid animals have no real capacity for reproduction; similarly, mongrel peoples have no national survival of their own ... he who strives to bring all the noble peoples of the world into one herd runs the risk of ruling over the most despicable outcast of the human race.[4]

In the midst of such racial and patriotic sentiment, the Warburg festival was held in 1817 to commemorate the tricentenary of the Reformation and the tenth anniversary of the Battle of Leipzig. Delegates from fourteen primarily Protestant universities gathered together at Jena to found the *Allgemeine deutsche Burschenschaft* (United German Student Society). A solemn procession took place, followed by a divine service and an auto-da-fé of books and other objects regarded as anti-German. A letter from a Heidelberg student, Richard Rothe, described the event:

> The people in Jena want a Christian-German Burschenschaft but we had always wanted till then a general one in the strictest sense of the word and we therefore decided to give entry to Jews and foreigners as to anyone else if they had acquired academic rights through matriculation. Thereupon the Germans – there were about twenty of them – flew into a terrible rage. Since then they form a sect in the Burschenschaft and at general meetings are mainly distinguished by forming a perpetual opposition. ... They keep strictly together and have a way of their own. ... They are not too keen on their studies and act as if they have found the philosopher's stone, and meditate on how they will one day become Germany's saviours and redeemers.[5]

Alongside such patriotic attitudes which fostered the disparagement of Jewry, German metaphysicians castigated Judaism and the Jewish nation in terms reminiscent of previous Christian centuries. The theologian Friedrich Wilhelm Ghillany attempted to expose what he believed to be Jewish cannibalism. According to Ghillany such cannibalism was evidenced by the ritual murder of Jesus as well as subsequent ritual murders in Jewish history. In the light of such barbarism, he believed that it would be misguided to grant rights such men

> who adhere so rigidly to old inhuman prejudices, who regard us as impure, like serfs and dogs, just as their ancestors did, even if they do not flaunt it to our face? It is men such as these who claim full civil rights, the right to exercise functions of government, to become the superiors of Christians, judicial and administrative officers![6]

With similar antipathy the philosopher Ludwig Feuerbach attacked the Jewish people:

> The Israelites only opened their gastric senses to nature. They only enjoyed nature through their palate. They only became aware of God through the enjoyment of manna. ... Eating is the most solemn act or even initiation of the Jewish religion. In the act of eating the Israelite celebrates and renews the act of creation. In eating, man declares nature to be a nullity in itself. When the seventy elders climbed the mountain with Moses, then 'they saw the God of Israel. ... They stayed there before God; they ate and they drank' (Exodus 24:10–11). The sight of the highest being therefore only amused their appetite.[7]

With similar contempt the Hegelian Arnold Ruge emphasized the pernicious influence of Jewry on German society: 'They are maggots in the cheese of Christianity who are so unutterably comfortable in their reflective and stock-jobbing skin that they believe in nothing and precisely for this reason remain Jews.'[8] Another Hegelian, Bruno Bauer, polemicized against Jewish emancipation. In his *Die Judenfrage*, he criticized the Jewish people 'for having made their nest in the powers and interstices of bourgeois society'. The Jews' crime resided in 'not recognizing the purely human development of history, the development of human conscience'.[9]

Again, Karl Marx in his writings criticized the Jewish influence on bourgeois society. Material concerns, he argued, form the basis of Jewish life.

'The bill of exchange is the real God of the Jew,' he declared. 'His God is only an illusory bill of exchange. That which is contained in an abstract in the Jewish religion – contempt for theory, for art, for history, and for man as an end in himself – is the real, conspicuous standpoint and the virtue of the man of money. ... The chimerical nationality of the Jew is the nationality of the trader, and above all the financier.'[10]

German hostility towards the Jewish people in the nineteenth century reached its culmination in the writings of the composer Richard Wagner. In exile in Switzerland from 1849 to 1851, he studied Germanic myths. In his first book he presented an Aryan theory of the origin of humanity based upon these studies: 'Upon this island, i.e. these mountains, we have to seek the cradle of the present Asiatic peoples, as also of those who wandered forth to Europe. Here is the ancestral seat of all religions, of every tongue, of all these

20

nations, Kinghood.'[11] Later, Wagner identified the God Wotan with the Christian conception of the Son of God.

Such convictions served as the general background of his *Das Judentum in der Musik*. In this work Wagner stated that the quest to emancipate the Jews was based on idealistic notions rather than on a personal familiarity with the Jewish population:

> Even when we strove for emancipation of the Jews, however, we were more the champions of an abstract principle than of a concrete case: just as all our liberalism was not very lucid mental sport – since we went for freedom of the Folk without knowledge of that Folk itself, nay, with a dislike of any genuine contact with it – so our eagerness to level up the rights of Jews was far rather stimulated by a general idea, than by any real sympathy.[12]

For Wagner, the Jew was a degenerate element in society; even those who had been emancipated were incapable of making a positive contribution.

The second half of the nineteenth century witnessed the manifestation of anti-Semitic agitation throughout Germany and Austria. In 1871 *The Jew of the Talmud* was published by Canon August Rohling, a professor at the Imperial University of Prague. This work, based on *Judaism Unmasked* by Johann Andreas Eisenmenger, revived the Christian myth of ritual murder. The twelve ritual murder trials of Jews in German regions held between 1867 and 1914 were largely due to Rohling's influence.

Another major figure of this period was Wilhelm Marr, who is credited with coining the term 'anti-Semitism'. In his *The Victory of Judaism over Germanism*, Marr argued that Judaism had been victorious in the modern world: 'We are the losers and it is natural that the winners should shout *Vae victis*. We are so Judaized that we are beyond salvation and a brutal anti-Semitic explosion can only postpone the collapse of our Judaized society, but not prevent it.'[13] On the basis of such views, Marr founded an Anti-Semitic League in 1871. Similar attitudes were expressed in a series of articles by the journalist Otto Glagau in the magazine *Die Gartenlaube*: 'The Jewish tribe does not work,' he stated. 'It exploits the manual or intellectual production of others. This foreign tribe has enslaved the German people. The social question is basically the Jewish question.'[14]

In 1878 the minister Adolf Stoecker, chaplain of the Imperial

Court, founded the Christian Socialist Workers' Party which promulgated anti-Semitism as a central policy. In consequence, violence erupted in Berlin in 1880 and 1881. Mobs assaulted Jews in the streets, drove them from cafes, and smashed their store windows; in the provinces synagogues were burned. At the same time, Bernard Forster, Nietzsche's brother-in-law, who visited Wagner's Bayreuth, organized a petition which called for a census of the Jews in Germany and their exclusion from the teaching profession.

Through the influence of the historian Heinrich Treitschke, anti-Semitism gained considerable respectability, and anti-Semitic movements and parties became increasingly common. International conferences were held, and various fraternities refused to admit Jewish students. In addition, the German custom of the student duel was denied to Jews. Numerous anti-Semitic treatises also began to circulate at the end of the century. All these works were eventually overshadowed by *The Foundations of the Nineteenth Century* by the Anglo-German writer, Houston Stewart Chamberlain. In his study Chamberlain maintained that the antiquity and mobility of the Jewish nation illustrates the confrontation between superior Aryans and parasitic Semites. On the political front Karl Lueger, the leader of the Austrian Christian party, publicly espoused anti-Semitic policies in 1887 with the encouragement of Pope Leo XIII and Cardinal Rampolla. Eventually he was elected mayor of Vienna. In Germany the *Antisemitische Volkspartei* won four seats in 1890. Three years later its numbers in the *Reichstag* increased to sixteen.

In the years leading up to World War I, the Jews became scapegoats for the problems afflicting German society. Objections were raised against the assimilation of German Jewry, and numerous Christian writers protested against the pernicious influence of Jewish attitudes. Such antipathy was symbolic of the age. Once the realities of World War I had become evident, Jews were blamed for all the ills afflicting German society. In this environment of Judaeophobia the philosopher Max Hildebert Boehm drafted a bill of indictment in the *Jahrbücher* (Yearbooks) protesting against Jewish assimilation. As the war progressed, anti-Semitism erupted despite the fact that Jews had been actively involved in the war effort. As events began to go badly, Jews were blamed for the lack of German success. Allegedly Jews were not fighting for their country – those in the army had relatively pleasant jobs behind the front; others were making money out of the war. Such attitudes served as the background for the rise of the Nazi party in the years following Germany's defeat.

Discussion: German Judaeophobia

From this survey it might appear that German attitudes towards the Jews were unique in the modern world. This, however, was not the case – throughout Europe similar attitudes prevailed. In France, for example, numerous books were published listing a wide range of grievances against the Jewish community. Repeatedly Jews were portrayed in demonic terms, and even advocates of emancipation agreed that the Jews constituted a fallen nation. Such disparagement continued into the next century. Despite the improvements in Jewish life that had taken place under Napoleon, the negative stereotype of the Jew continued to haunt French consciousness. According to the *Archives israélites*, the leading writers continued to perpetrate such myths:

> Every one of them at least once in his lifetime is determined to cut himself a doublet in Middle Ages style and, when their imagination runs dry, they knock up a history of the Jews. There is not a novelist, a would-be short story writer, not the most wretched manufacturer of feuilletons who has not got a fantastic picture of the Jews of yore in his bag.[15]

While literary figures were caricaturing the Jewish people, anti-Semitism was also being promoted by French Socialists. Hostile to the industrialization of the modern world, these propagandists castigated what they perceived to be the pernicious influence of Jewry. For these Socialist thinkers the Jew personified evil. Echoing the sentiments of previous centuries, such thinkers as Pierre Proudhon recommended a course of action similar to what was carried out by the Nazis:

> Jews. Make a provision against that race, which poisons everything, by butting in everywhere without ever merging with any people. – Demand its expulsion from France. ... The Jew is the enemy of mankind. That race must be sent back to Asia or exterminated.[16]

In England similar attitudes were widespread in the post-emancipation period. Despite the generally tolerant environment in the country, the presence of Jews continued to arouse public antipathy. The image of Shakespeare's Shylock in his *Merchant of Venice* and Fagin in Dickens' *Oliver Twist* reinforced stereotypes of Jewish behaviour and generated prejudice against the Jew. When the Tory Prime Minister Benjamin Disraeli attempted to improve the condition of English Jewry, a number of writers vehemently castigated the Jewish community. In his *Ages of Man*, for example, Robert Knox attacked Disraeli's analysis of the Jewish problem.

> 'A respect for scientific truth,' he wrote, 'forbids me refuting the romances of Disraeli; it is sufficient merely to observe here that, in a long list of names of distinguished persons who Mr Disraeli has described of Jewish descent, I have not met with a single Jewish trait in their countenance, in so far as I can discover; and therefore they are not Jews, nor of Jewish origin.'[17]

In Russia the emancipation of the Jew also provoked similar reactions. In 1844, for example, the Jewish folklorist Vladimir Dhal concluded that although ritual murder was not practised by the vast majority of Jews, it did occur among the Hasidim. Subsequently trials for ritual murder took place. The latter half of the nineteenth century also witnessed counter-emancipatory tendencies among Russian writers. Feodor Dostoevsky, for example, complained in a letter to the procurator of the Holy Synod about the number of Jews he encountered. Remarking on the Jews he observed in Berlin, he wrote: 'It's unbearable. ... Germany, or at least Berlin, has become Judaized.' In response the procurator asserted that Jews had become a threatening force in Russia as well.

> What you write about the Yids is perfectly correct. They have invaded everything. ... They are at the root of the Social Democratic movement and tsaricide. They control the press and the stock market. They reduce the masses to financial slavery. They formulate the principles of contemporary society, which tends to dissociate itself from Christianity. ... And nobody dares say that here the Jews control everything.[18]

Given the prevalence of such hostility throughout Europe, why was it in Germany that the Holocaust occurred? What led the German nation to seek to exterminate the Jewish people in the most horrific fashion? Arguably the onslaught against Jewry could have taken place anywhere, yet Nazi Germany was unique in embracing racial doctrine as a guiding ideology of the Third Reich. For the Nazis, the Jews were not simply a pernicious influence on society – they threatened to contaminate the purity of German blood. In their view, Germanness must be protected from any form of contamination.

Such racial theory evolved over several centuries and continued to dominate racist theory in the nineteenth century. Pre-eminent among such theoreticians, Richard Wagner's son-in-law Houston Stewart Chamberlain became one of the pioneers of the doctrine of Aryan supremacy. In his major work, *The Foundations of the Nineteenth Century*, Chamberlain argued that the Aryan race has always exerted a regenerative effect on societies threatened by disintegration, and that lesser blood types had always brought about cultural and social degeneration. According to Chamberlain, all great achievements are attributable to the Teutonic race whereas the Jewish people are cultural destroyers. Once the Jew has infiltrated any society, it becomes corrupt.

Such theories had a profound effect on Hitler whose own writings are infused with racial-anthropological ideas. Presupposing the existence of higher and lower races, Hitler declared that the Aryans alone were a culture-creating race. The Jewish race, however, is the embodiment of evil. On this basis, he condemned the inbreeding of races. In the quest to achieve a better and stronger society, he argued that only those who are healthy should produce children. What is required is a vigorous obstruction of reproductive capacities of those who would weaken the body politic. If the recovery of the social order is to occur, the Aryan race must predominate in all spheres of society. The Jewish nation as the enemy of humankind must be rooted out, and its destructive influence eliminated.

Inheriting anti-Semitic stereotypes passed on through centuries of persecution, the Nazis were convinced that the Jewish people were the perpetrators of a world conspiracy designed to undermine Western civilization. As a sub-human, evil and corrupting influence, Jewry became the central target of a genocidal policy of extermination; racially impure, they were to be eliminated for the sake of the *Volk*. Embracing social Darwinism, the Nazis believed they were acting heroically for the fatherland. Here then is an explanation for what has been perceived as a uniquely evil manifestation of human cruelty. The Holocaust should be seen as the consequence of the toxic mixture of anti-Semitism and racism. How else can one understand how one of the most civilized societies of the modern world engaged in one of the greatest crimes against humanity?

Notes

1 Leon Poliakov, *The History of Anti-Semitism*, Vol. III, London, 1975, p. 303.
2 *Ibid.*, p. 381.
3 *Ibid.*, pp. 382–3.
4 *Ibid.*, pp. 384–5.
5 *Ibid.*, pp. 389–91.
6 *Ibid.*, p. 414.
7 *Ibid.*, p. 415.
8 *Ibid.*, p. 417.
9 *Ibid.*, p. 420.
10 *Ibid.*, p. 423.
11 *Ibid.*, p. 434.
12 *Ibid.*, p. 436.
13 Dan Cohn-Sherbok, *The Crucified Jew*, Eerdmans, Grand Rapids, Michigan, 1997, p. 166.
14 *Ibid.*, p. 166.
15 Poliakov, *op. cit.*, p. 350.
16 *Ibid.*, p. 376.
17 *Ibid.*, p. 335.
18 Cohn-Sherbok, *op. cit.*, p. 174.

3. Hitler

The Holocaust is inexplicable without Hitler. The driving force behind the Nazi rise to power, Adolf Hitler was the architect of the Nazi quest for European supremacy. Born in humble circumstances, Hitler emerged as the leader of the National Socialist Party, and guided his party to victory in the troubled climate of the Third Reich. Once installed as Chancellor, he became a tyrannical dictator, leading his country to war in the vain attempt to create a German empire that would endure for a thousand years.

The making of the Führer

Born on 20 April 1889 in Braunau on the River Inn, Hitler's origins were complex. In 1837 a 41-year-old maid, Maria Anna Schickelgruber, returned to her native village of Strones pregnant and unmarried. Rejected by her family, she was housed by a neighbouring tenant farmer. On 7 June 1837 she gave birth to a baby boy who was baptized as Alois Schickelgruber. On his birth certificate the space for the father's name was left blank. This child was Hitler's father.

Several candidates have been suggested as Alois Schickelgruber's real father: a Graz Jew, Frankenberger; Johann Georg Hiedler, the person Maria Anna subsequently married; and Johann Nepomuk Hiedler, the brother of Johann Georg Hiedler. The first of these suggestions – that Hitler's grandfather was actually Jewish – was discussed by the former Reich minister, Hans Frank. In his autobiography, Frank disclosed that Hitler called him in 1930 to investigate the allegation that he was of Jewish origin. Frank disclosed that he discovered that Maria Anna Schickelgruber had been employed as a cook in a Jewish household at the time her baby was conceived. Further, Frank claimed that Frankenberger had paid maintenance to the mother from the time the child was born until the boy was fourteen. In addition, the Frankenbergers continued to correspond with Maria Anna for a subsequent number of years. When confronted with this account, Hitler denied the story and insisted that his grandmother had told him that she only took money from the Frankenbergers because she was poor. Yet this explanation is impossible because Hitler's grandmother had died more than forty years before he was born.

In any event, Johann Georg Hiedler who married Maria Anna was an unemployed journeyman-miller who appears never to have worked full-time. Because of her poverty, Maria Anna turned to her husband's brother for support; he took her son to his farm in Spital and raised him as his son. At the age of 13, Alois left home to become a shoemaker in Vienna. Subsequently he entered the Imperial Board of Revenue where he worked his way up to a senior position. At the urging of his foster father, Alois eventually changed his name to Hitler. On 6 June 1876 Johann Nepomuk Hiedler and three other relatives went to Weitra and swore before the local notary that Johann Nepomuk's brother, whose name they misspelled as Hitler, was the real father of Alois Schickelgruber. The next day they travelled to Döllersheim and persuaded the parish priest to alter the birth register. Not surprisingly Hitler left his origins vague. In *Mein Kampf* he simply states that his father was an imperial customs official while his mother is presented as a loving and devoted housewife.

On 20 April 1889 Adolf Hitler was born, the fourth child of his father's third marriage to Klara Pölzl, a domestic servant from Spital. Hitler appears to have been lovingly spoiled by his parents particularly after the death of two brothers, Gustav and Otto, and his sister Ida. However, when Hitler resisted his father's suggestions about a future career, there was considerable friction between father and son. In January 1903 Alois died of a heart attack. In September 1904, Hitler was transferred to another school in Steyr about 15 miles from his home, where he lived in a rented room. No longer under parental control, Hitler did badly. As one of his former teachers commented some years later:

He lacked self-discipline, being notoriously cantankerous, wilful, arrogant and irascible. He had obvious difficulty in fitting in at school.

Moreover he was lazy ... his enthusiasm for hard work evaporated all too quickly. He reacted with ill-concealed hostility to advice or reproof; at the same time, he demanded of his fellow pupils their unqualified subservience, fancying himself in the role of leader.[1]

After leaving school, Hitler lived in Linz where his mother had moved in 1905; there he fantasized about becoming a painter and architect. In 1907 Hitler went to Vienna where he hoped to enrol at the Academy of Fine Arts, but failed the entrance exam. During this period Hitler's mother was diagnosed as suffering from breast cancer and was treated by a Jewish physician, Dr Eduard Bloch, but died the same year. After his mother's funeral, Hitler returned to Vienna where he sat for the examination at the Academy a second time but failed.

Between 1908 and 1913 Hitler lived in men's hostels and cheap flats. During this period, he formulated a philosophy which was based on Social Darwinism, anti-Communism, and anti-Semitism. In his view, life is a struggle between the fittest. For Hitler, compassion is a weakness, a sign of decadence which must be overcome in the quest for survival. For this reason he regarded both Christianity and socialism as ideologically deficient. As far as the Jews were concerned, Hitler expressed deep loathing based on his early experiences. Growing up in Linz, he explained, he had given no thought to Jewry. But in Vienna he became aware of their presence:

Once, as I was strolling through the Inner City, I suddenly encountered an apparition in a black caftan and black hair locks. Is this a Jew was my first thought. For, to be sure, they had not looked like that in Linz. I observed this man furtively and cautiously, but the longer I stared at this foreign face, scrutinizing feature for feature, the more my first question assumed a new form: Is this a German?[2]

For Hitler the Jew could never become a German because he was racially and religiously distinct. The difference between Jews and Germans was so vast as to make them inherently aliens. Jews, he asserted, were

not Germans of a special religion, but a people in themselves; for since I had begun to concern myself with this question and to take cognizance of the Jews, Vienna appeared to me in a different light than before. Wherever I went, I began to see Jews, and the more I saw, the more

29

sharply they became distinguished in my eyes from the rest of humanity.[3]

Comparing Jews with vermin, he wrote:

Was there any form of filth or profligacy, particularly in cultural life, without at least one Jew involved in it? If you cut even cautiously into such an abscess you found, like a maggot in a rotting body, often dazzled by the sudden light – a kike![4]

The influence of the Jews was poisonous in the press, art, literature and the theatre:

It sufficed to look at a billboard, to study the names of men behind the horrible trash they advertised, to make you hard for a long time to come. This was pestilence, spiritual pestilence, worse than the Black Death of olden times, and the people was being infected with it.[5]

Turning to the press, Hitler made similar observations about the influence of Jews who, he believed, controlled what was published:

I now saw the liberal attitude of this press in a different light; the lofty tone in which it answered attacks and its method of killing them with silence now revealed itself to me as a trick as clever as it was treacherous; the transfigured raptures of their theatrical critics were always directed at Jewish writers, and their disapproval never struck anyone but Germans. The gentle pin-pricks against Wilhelm II revealed its methods by their persistency, and so did its condemnation of French culture. The trashy content of the short story now appeared to me as outright indecency, and in the language detected the accents of a foreign people.[6]

According to Hitler, Jews were also responsible for prostitution and the white slave traffic. This led to Hitler's recognition of 'the Jew as the cold-hearted, shameless, and calculating director of this revolting vice traffic in the scum of the big city'.[7]

In propounding his opinions, Hitler embraced the belief in a world conspiracy as depicted in *The Protocols of the Elders of Zion*. The Jews, he maintained, seek to dominate world events; in pursuit of this aim a small group of wealthy and influential Jewish figures meet secretly to devise their plans. By inciting social division, the Jew is able to burrow into a healthy society and thereby prepare for the domination of the world. Such logic led Hitler to conclude that the Jew is the personification of Satan who ravages his victims.

Convinced that a people's greatness depends upon the purity of its blood, he argued that the German people can only recover its strength by eliminating inferior types from its midst and preventing alien peoples from polluting its true nature. The German state must therefore breed only the most racially pure specimens to ensure a glorious future. Such a vision provided the basis for the Nazi policy of extermination of Jews as well as gypsies, cripples and the mentally retarded.

At the outbreak of World War I, Hitler volunteered for the German army and underwent basic training. After only ten weeks, his regiment, the Sixteenth Bavarian Infantry Regiment, was sent to the western front. Serving as a courier between regimental staff in the rear and fighting units in advanced positions, Hitler spent most of the war in the trenches. Eventually he was promoted to the rank of corporal and decorated for bravery in December 1914 and in August 1918 with the Iron Cross First and Second Class.

In October 1918 Hitler was caught in a poison gas attack south of Ypres and temporarily blinded. Shipped back home to Pasewalk hospital in Pomerania, he was informed by the hospital pastor that Germany had signed an armistice.

'I could stand it no more,' he later recorded. 'It was impossible to stay any longer. While everything went black before my eyes, stumbling, I groped my way back to the dormitory, threw myself on the cot and buried my burning head in the covers and the pillows. I had not wept since the day I had stood at the grave of my mother.'[8]

After Hitler recovered at the end of November 1918, he returned to Munich where he reported to the reserve battalions of his regiment. In February 1919 he volunteered for guard duty in a prisoner-of-war camp at Traunstein near the Austrian frontier, but returned a month later to Munich. In the same year Bavaria was controlled by left-wing radicals led by Kurt Eisner who was assassinated; in May Free Corps formations overthrew the government and took over power. In this milieu Hitler worked for a board of enquiry established to examine alleged traitors within the army, and became an instructional officer.

In September Hitler was instructed to investigate a new party, the

German Workers' Party, which espoused nationalistic, anti-Semitic and anti-democratic ideas. Attracted to its ideology, Hitler joined the party and eventually left the army. As board member number 7, Hitler was in charge of recruitment and propaganda, and within three months of joining he suggested sweeping changes in the party. Persuaded by Hitler, the executive committee agreed to stage mass rallies and scheduled a mass meeting in the banqueting hall of the *Hofbräuhaus* on 24 February 1920.

At this gathering Hitler read out 25 theses of the new party platform to a crowd of nearly 2000. Among these principles were the following which formed the basis for future policy:

1. We demand on the basis of the right of national self-determination, the union of all Germans in a Greater Germany.
2. We demand equality for the German nation among other nations and the revocation of the peace treaties of Versailles and Saint Germain.
4. Only a racial comrade can be a citizen. Only a person of German blood, irrespective of religious denomination, can be a racial comrade. No Jew, therefore, can be a racial comrade.
5. Non-citizens shall be able to live in Germany as guests only, and must be placed under alien legislation.
6. We therefore demand that every public office, no matter what kind, and no matter whether it is national, state, or local must be held only by citizens.
8. Any further immigration of non-Germans is to be prevented. We demand that all non-Germans who entered Germany after 2 August 1914 be forced to leave the Reich without delay.
10. It must be the first duty of every citizen to perform mental or physical work. Individual activity must not violate the general interest, but must be exercised within the framework of the community, and must be for the general good.
25. To implement all these points, we demand the creation of a strong central power in Germany. A central political parliament should possess unconditional authority over the entire Reich.[9]

A week after this meeting, the German Workers' Party changed its name to the National Socialist German Workers' Party. In April

1920 the first branch of the party was established outside Munich, and by the end of the year branches had been formed in ten provincial areas outside Munich and another outside Bavaria. Because of such growth, the party became incorporated under German law and established a series of by-laws. In December the party acquired an official newspaper, the *Völkischer Beobachter*, whose editorial policy was controlled by Hitler. On 22 January 1921 the party held its first national congress in Munich.

Due to tensions within the party, Hitler resigned on 12 July, 1921 and the old guard denounced him. However, he was restored to party membership and granted considerable power. One of Hitler's main aims at this time was to impose a tighter administrative structure on the party. In addition, he encouraged all branches of the party to acquire flags and insignia, report local developments, and submit lists of all new members. By the beginning of 1922 the NSDAP had 6000 registered voters and had staged 81 public meetings. Such growth was largely due to Hitler's oratorical and administrative skills.

Discussion: Hitler and the Jews

How is one to understand Hitler's intense Judaeophobia? As we have seen, in *Mein Kampf* he explained his formative encounters with Jewry in Vienna. But is this the true explanation for his vehemence? In the view of some scholars, Hitler's anti-Semitism was the result of a developing psychopathology. Initially, as Hitler himself pointed out, he encountered few Jews in Linz, and in Vienna one of his close acquaintances in the hostel for the homeless was the Jew, Josef Neumann. The origin of Hitler's antipathy appears to have been his exposure to anti-Semitic literature during his Vienna period. When Hitler lived on Felberstrasse in Vienna, he frequently purchased the anti-Semitic magazine *Ostara*. Further, he was an avid reader of tabloid newspapers such as the *Deutsches Volksblatt* which denigrated Jews. Further, Hitler came under the influence of such political anti-Semites as the Viennese mayor Karl Lueger and the pan-German nationalist Georg Ritter von Schönerer.

The negative stereotypes of the Jew as presented in such publications was reinforced by the increasing numbers of Jews in Vienna. This influx caused considerable alarm among the unem-

33

ployed who viewed these newcomers as a threat to their economic existence. For Hitler, what he perceived as foul-smelling aliens were leeches on German society. The Jews, he believed, were the source of Germany's problems, and in describing them he frequently used terms drawn from scatology or parasitology. Anything which came in contact with this putrid race, he believed, was poisoned.

Hitler's passionate hatred of Jews may well have been the product of a fundamental personality disorder, typical of those marginalized in society. It is not uncommon for such individuals to fantasize about their omnipotence and exhibit phobias about dirt and contamination. Typically they have divided personalities which can display admirable qualities while at the same time projecting despised characteristics onto various scapegoats. Further, these persons tend to see the world in terms of good and evil. There is no doubt that Hitler displayed these characteristics during his youth and later as an adult.

Another possible explanation of the origin of Hitler's Judaeo-phobia relates to the death of his mother. In 1907 Hitler's mother was diagnosed as dying of incurable cancer, and her doctor, Dr Eduard Bloch, a Jewish physician, recommended an iodoform treatment. This was a costly and painful procedure. As one expert observed, 'Iodoform absorbed into the system quickens the pulse and attacks the nerves and the brain, inducing restlessness, headaches, insomnia, fever, and – in severe cases – delirium with hallucinations'.[10] When his mother died after undergoing such treatment, Hitler was overcome with grief. It may be that this early event in Hitler's life set in motion his deep-seated animosity to Jews.

In this connection, some scholars have remarked that when Hitler was blinded by mustard gas in the autumn of 1918, this event may have reminded him of the iodoform administered to his mother ten years previously. Both mustard gas and iodoform are powerfully scented liquids which burn the skin and leave a foul-smelling odour. Possibly, Hitler relived his mother's treatment at the hands of Dr Bloch. Just as the Jewish doctor had been responsible for his mother's suffering and death, Hitler regarded Jews as culpable for the war. Germany, he was certain, had been sabotaged by a Jewish conspiracy. Possibly he believed that it was now necessary for Jews to be treated in the same way. The poisoners should be poisoned in order to avenge his mother and the fatherland.

Hitler's mother's death and his repeated failures to enter the art academy had a profound effect on his outlook. Bereft of parents, Hitler was alone in the world with few prospects. Supported only by the inheritance from his mother, he lived in men's hostels and cheap apartments; at times he slept in the open either on a park bench or under an archway. Mingling with desperate and hardened characters in Vienna, Hitler came to perceive life as a jungle in which only the ruthless could survive. Paradoxically, Hitler was not drawn to left-wing ideologies which promoted the interests of the underclass; instead, he admired the strength that had placed the dominant elite in positions of superiority. These formative experiences no doubt served as the background to Hitler's advocacy of a form of Social Darwinism.

For Hitler, the strength and weakness of man is determined by blood. According to Hitler, superior blood will inevitably overcome inferior blood. In his view, the best blood occurs when animals mate with their own species. Any crossing of blood produces inherently inferior types. Since human beings are part of nature, the same biological laws apply. Nature encourages separation between races, while promoting reproduction between members of the same racial groups. Hence the white, black, and yellow races seek their own kind. However, since human racial groups are fundamentally different, any cross-breeding undermines racial purity. In Hitler's view, the worst blood defilement occurs when a Jew mates with an Aryan.

On the basis of this philosophy of nature, Hitler divided the human race into three distinct groups: Aryan culture founders, culture bearers and culture destroyers. Only the Aryan, he maintained, is able to create culture. The Jew, however, is without genuine culture since he is unable to create one. Instead, the Jew exploits what others have created – he is a parasite feeding on the body of healthy cultures. Like a harmful bacillus, the Jew spreads out more and more only if a favourable medium exists for him to do so. In *Mein Kampf*, Hitler described Jews as personifications of the devil, defilers of Aryan blood, blood-suckers, vampires, purveyors of prostitution and syphilis, the ferment of decomposition, rapists of Aryan women, harmful bacillis, maggots, poisoners, pestilence, spongers, fungi and foul-smelling creatures. Yet, even though the Jew had seriously undermined German blood, Hitler was convinced that the German people could recover its racial purity by weeding out this pestilence from its midst. Such a vision of the future Nazi state was in all likelihood grounded in Hitler's early experiences among Vienna's destitute where he developed his ideology of life as a struggle.

Notes

1 F. Jetzinger, *Hitler's Youth*, London, 1958, pp. 68–9.
2 Adolf Hitler, *Mein Kampf*, London, 1992, p. 52.
3 *Ibid.*, p. 52.
4 *Ibid.*, p. 53.
5 *Ibid.*, p. 53.
6 *Ibid.*, pp. 54–5.
7 *Ibid.*, p. 55.
8 Adolf Hitler, *Mein Kampf*, New York, 1941, pp. 266–7.
9 Rita Steinhart Botwinick, *A History of the Holocaust*, New Jersey, 1996, p. 56.
10 Rudolph Binion, *Hitler Among the Germans*, New York, 1976, p. 17.

4. The Nazi party

Since its defeat in World War I, the German nation experienced humiliation, economic disruption and cultural disorder. Longing for a return to past glory, Conservatives sought to restructure society along traditional lines. In such a milieu the German Workers' Party advanced extreme nationalist policies. Under Hitler's influence, this party, renamed the National Socialist German Workers' Party or Nazi party, quickly became a major force in German life.

The rise of Nazism

The Nazi party emerged in the aftermath of World War I. After four years of conflict, the Allied armies conquered the German nation. Amid political instability, Kaiser Wilhelm fled to Holland. Intent on punishing Germany, the Allies formulated a peace treaty – the Treaty of Versailles – which stripped the German nation of all power. Germany was deprived of one-eighth of its lands along its eastern and western borders as well as her colonies and overseas investments. In addition, the German army was limited to 100,000 men, her navy drastically reduced, and the German people compelled to pay a large reparations bill. In a war-guilt clause of this treaty, Germans were blamed for the war. By signing this document, the German representatives were accused of betrayal, and many Germans never forgave them for their actions. Within only three years the leader of the delegation, Matthias Erzberger, was assassinated.

After the war the Weimar government consisted of an elected legislature (the *Reichstag*) along with a President who was in essence a figurehead who stood above daily affairs. Following national elections, the President appointed the leader of the majority party in the *Reichstag* as Chancellor; it was the responsibility of the Chancellor to form a cabinet from his colleagues. However, because political parties were often unable to form a majority, governments consisted of coalitions of various parties. In addition, the constitution provided for representatives from the eighteen states to sit in the *Reichstag*. An important clause of the constitution also gave power to the President to suspend the constitution during emergencies.

After the war the major parties ranged across the political spectrum with the Communists, Marxists and radical socialists on the left. Centrist parties embraced more moderate policies: the Catholic Party, for example, favoured constitutional change which aimed to create a more stable country. On the right, ultra-nationalists, Nazis and fascists pressed for the creation of a totalitarian dictatorship. In their view, it was necessary that a single political party ensure the maintenance of a strong and prosperous nation.

For the ultra-nationalists, the Communist Party represented the greatest threat to political stability. Influenced by Soviet Communism, the German Communist Party was supported by urban workers who pressed for revolutionary methods to bring down the Weimar regime. In order to prevent such an occurrence, the Social Democrats under Friedrich Ebert made a pact with the German army. When such a threat materialized, the army subdued the Communists. From this time, the military grew in strength, and the Weimar government was constantly pressurized by the military. In this milieu, regular soldiers returning from the war joined the *Freikorps*, a volunteer militia which engaged in street fighting. This group was part of the force which the government employed to crush the Communists.

On the right, ultra-nationalists extolled the fatherland. In 1920 a military-aristocratic alliance was joined by industrialists in an unsuccessful coup – when the military refused to respond to the call to defend the nation, the labour unions crushed the rebellion by refusing to provide Berlin with basic services. Yet this defeat did not spell the end of rightist politics. Even more extreme parties emerged in the wake of this setback including the National Socialist German Workers' Party.

In the 1920s the Social Democrats suffered during this period of unrest. In 1922 one of their most distinguished Jewish members, Walter Rathenau, was assassinated. Hated by the extreme right because of his view that the Treaty of Versailles should be respected, his murder was heralded as a victory by the nationalists even though

Rathenau had concluded the Treaty of Rapallo with the Soviet Union. During this period the death of the first President of the Republic, Friedrich Ebert, also contributed to the general instability of the country. Added to these political problems, the French sent troops to occupy the industrial German Ruhr for failing to pay reparations. In response, the German government encouraged workers to strike. As a result, miners and industrial workers were supported through the national treasury, a policy which led to a further decline in the economy. To meet this crisis, the government printed more money even though it was not backed by gold. This action led to rampant inflation.

Although this economic situation was disastrous for ordinary workers as well as those on pensions, some industrialists profited. To deal with the collapsing economy, the government put the Mark on a par with its pre-war currency. Such a readjustment, however, further weakened many businesses, and the standard of living deteriorated. Faced with this ongoing crisis, the international community sought to support Germany through various actions.

Such an initial recovery collapsed in the face of the world-wide Depression of the late 1920s. Following the destabilization of the American economy, the economies of the European countries crumbled as well. American financial institutions called in their loans, and importers who had bought German products ceased to function, In response to such deteriorating conditions, ultra-rightist groups promised not to place any restrictions on private property and maintained that they would be able to manage the economy without foreign intervention.

Exploiting such political and economic instability, the Nazis sought to bring order back to society. From 1919 to 1924 the party was situated in Munich and Bavaria where it attracted a variety of members from extreme right-wing groups of ex-soldiers, anti-Communists and tsarist émigrés. On 7 November 1923, the major leaders of Bavaria's right-wing organizations including Hitler formalized a coup d'état. The next evening a large gathering assembled at a large beer hall, the *Bürgerbräukeller* in Munich, to listen to a major address from the State Commissioner, Dr Gustav von Kahr. Just before 8 p.m., Hitler arrived at the *Bürgerbräukeller*. As Kahr was speaking, Göring accompanied by about 25 of his SA men with pistols and machine guns burst into the main hall while other SA troops cordoned off the building.

Hitler and his men then mounted the speaker's platform and announced that a national revolution had broken out all over Germany. He then pushed Kahr, General Otto von Lassow and General Hans von Seisser (the other two members of the Bavarian triumvirate) into a side room as he brandished his pistol and declared that the Bavarian government had been deposed and that they would now serve as part of the new government. Hitler then entered the main hall and encouraged the crowd to join the coup. While these events were taking place, SA members elsewhere in the city unleashed a wave of terror against Jews and political opponents.

However, once the triumvirate left the *Bürgerbräukeller*, the putsch unravelled. Military units were assembled to put down the revolt. The next day the marchers led by Hitler and General Ludendorff were fired upon and Hitler and his other conspirators were arrested. Taken to the fortress of Landsberg am Lech, Hitler was eventually tried and convicted of high treason. From 11 November 1923 to 20 December 1924 Hitler served time for this crime along with other Nazi conspirators and composed the first volume of *Mein Kampf*. During this period the Nazi Party began to disintegrate. However when Hitler returned to Munich he was determined to rebuild the party.

From 1924 to 1928 there was comparative political and economic stability in German society – this was reflected in the 1928 election results. The Nazi Party received only 2.6 per cent of the vote and appeared to be disappearing from the political scene. However, the Democrats and the German People's Party continued to lose support, thereby weakening the middle ground. Further, the conservative Nationalists were also in decline – their share of the vote was only 14 per cent. However, various independent splinter parties nearly doubled their vote. Hence in 1928 the political centre of the Weimar Republic was imploding, as were the conservative parties.

As one of the splinter groups struggling for support, the Nazi Party gained strength in the northern provincial farming communities. As a consequence, the Party abandoned its previous emphasis on urban development and sought to create new organizations. Such local organizations were designed to appeal to factional interests; networks were created designed to recruit key local individuals. Two years previously the Hitler Youth and the National Socialist German Students' Association had been established; in 1929 the NS Union of Socialist Pupils was established aimed at attracting upper-middle-class children. In 1928 the Association of National Socialist Jurists was founded; this was followed by the NS Association of German Physicians and the NS Teachers' Association. In addition, the League of Struggle for German Culture was founded to combat the powers of corruption within German society. Repeatedly the Nazis stressed that their party was concerned with the needs of the small person faced by large capitalist conglomerates.

A further strategy of the Party was to agitate in rural areas and penetrate existing agricultural communities and peasant organizations. After the 1928 election, the Nazis created a network of local advisers who spread propaganda in farming areas. Subsequently, the main farmers' body came under Nazi control. Because farm income had declined to a level 44 per cent below the national average, the farming community was anxious to improve the economic state of the country. Nazi policies which offered a solution to these problems were eagerly embraced by those who found themselves in a perilous state.

In March 1930 the government fell, and power passed from the *Reichstag* to the President of the Republic, Paul von Hindenburg. As a consequence, Hindenburg appointed a succession of presidential cabinets that ruled by use of Article 48 of the Weimar Constitution. Initially Heinrich Brüning was appointed Chancellor and imposed cuts in government expenditure and formulated a deflationary budget. When this budget was vetoed by the *Reichstag*, he passed his programme by presidential decree, and called for an election in which the Social Democrats gained 143 seats, the Nazi Party 107, and the Communist Party 77. The centre middle-class parties collapsed, and as a result no coalition was possible. Until 1932 Brüning continued to press forward with economic reform, yet his policy led to massive unemployment and polarized the electorate.

In May 1932, Hindenburg's term of office was to expire, and he was persuaded to run again for public office despite the fact that he was 84 and in failing health. After a bitter campaign against Hitler, Hindenburg won with a majority of 53 per cent. By the end of May Hindenburg dismissed Brüning who was succeeded by Franz von Papen, a Centre Party politician, who called an election for July 1932 in which the Nazi Party secured 13.8 million votes. As leader of the largest party, Hitler should have been appointed Chancellor. Hindenburg, however, refused, and Hitler would not join any government unless he became Chancellor. Meanwhile von Papen was working towards dismissing the *Reichstag* and abolishing elections, a policy which would have destroyed the Weimar Constitution. However, between July and November 1932 no action was taken.

In November a second election was held and the SPD, Centre Party, Democrats and Nazis all lost votes whereas the Nationalists, the People's Party and the Communists strengthened their positions. Intent on dismissing the *Reichstag*, von Papen sought to use the army to control civil insurrection and disband all political parties and organizations. On 3 December 1932, von Papen was dismissed and General von Schleicher, formerly Minister of Defence, became Chancellor. Von Papen then sought to replace von Schleicher with a von Papen-Hitler-Nationalist government. Faced with the alternative of the dissolution of the *Reichstag* and rule by state of emergency, Hindenburg complied and on 30 January 1933 Hitler was appointed Chancellor, von Papen became Vice-Chancellor, and eight other conservatives plus two Nazis joined the cabinet.

Discussion: The Nazi rise to power

How can one account for the incredible success of the Nazi Party? From its beginnings as a tiny splinter party, it rose to become the major force in German political life. There is no question that Hitler was the driving force behind its growth and ultimate victory. From the beginning of its development Hitler played a fundamental role. When he joined the party as a board member in September 1919, he became responsible for recruitment and propaganda. Disconcerted by the chaotic character of the party, Hitler was determined to institute discipline within the ranks. After only three months, Hitler recommended a series of changes aimed at broadening the base of the party.

Exhibiting enormous energy, Hitler established contact with like-minded party members, sent out invitations to meetings, and increased the membership list. In addition, he convinced the party to have its meetings in the cellar of the Sternecker Beer Hall rather than at the much more informal Café Gasteig. Although the old members regarded Hitler as having delusions of grandeur, he was convinced that the party image had to change. Hitler was also determined to recruit new blood into the party from recruits with a military background; in time, he believed, these individuals would become a new leadership corps within the party.

The mass meeting held on 20 February 1920 illustrated Hitler's growing importance. When Hitler addressed the gathered throng, they were energized. Speaking to a packed audience, Hitler sought to inflame his listeners with a passion for revolutionary change. Identifying with the suffering of ordinary citizens, Hitler inveighed against those who had sacrificed Germany. Such a performance was mesmerizing. The audience was spellbound by Hitler's message, gestures, voice and rhetoric.

With an uncanny sensitivity, Hitler was able to put into words the thoughts and feelings of the average German. On this occasion, and repeatedly throughout his political career, Hitler brought his listeners to a state of ecstatic enthusiasm. Audiences were transfixed by Hitler's delivery, and spontaneously burst into applause amid cheering and table-pounding. On some occasions there were wild cries and uncontrolled sobbing. Hitler's skill as a speaker thus had a crucially important impact on the Nazi rise to power.

Hitler's abilities as a propagandist also extended to his perception of the need for symbols and myths in the party organization. In August 1920 Hitler agreed that the swastika should become the party's prime symbol. Subsequently he explained its significance:

> in the red we see the social ideal of the movement, in the white the national idea, in the swastika the mission of the fight for the victory of Aryan man, and at the same time also the victory of the idea of creative work which in itself is and always will be anti-Semitic.[1]

Determined to inspire the ranks with loyalty and enthusiasm, Hitler insisted that all party members wear Nazi insignia during duty hours. Further, he designed the banners for the SA adorned with an eagle atop an encircled swastika. In all these endeavours, Hitler had a remarkable psychological grasp of the mystical imagery which would bind members of the party together and inspire them with dedication to party values. For many, the iconography of the party – swastika, party incantations, uniforms, standards, medals, badges and batons – became the equivalent of religious pageantry with the same emotional force.

Who were those who initially became the rank and file of the Nazi Party? From the beginning the party appealed to the socioeconomically disenfranchized classes of the post-war period consisting of demoralized members of the lower middle classes, demobilized and declassed soldiers, alienated students and intellectuals, upper-middle-class professionals and business owners frightened by the rise of Communism, and those on the margin of society with few employment prospects. Statistical evidence reveals that for the period 1919–23 the party drew its membership largely from the lower middle class[2], yet the party membership cut across both class lines and occupations and appealed to individuals for diverse reasons.

Otto and Gregor Strasser, for example, were attracted to the Nazi party because they believed that Nazism represented a German form of socialism. Ernst Röhm, Rudolf Hess and Hermann Göring, on the other hand, joined the party because they saw it as an extension of the German army as well as a means of realizing their own ambitions. Others such as Dietrich Eckart, Alfred Rosenberg, and Julius Streicher, as well as Heinrich Himmler and Joseph Goebbels, became party members for ideological reasons. Again, others joined the party because they had severe difficulties in adjusting to peacetime conditions and viewed Nazism as a mode of life suitable to their temperaments. Hitler's entourage consisted largely of such individuals, including Heinrich Hoffmann, Hitler's official photographer, Eva Braun, the Führer's mistress, Max Amann, the Führer's business manager, Ulrich Graf, one of Hitler's bodyguards, Emil Maurice, one of Hitler's most loyal confidants, Christian Weber, Hitler's errand boy, and Julius Schaub, one of Hitler's bodyguards and personal adjutant. Alongside such outsiders, respectable and well-placed Germans such as Ernst Hanfstaengl and Winifred Wagner were drawn into the Nazi circle out of admiration and fascination for Hitler. Representatives of big business were also attracted to Nazism because they perceived National Socialism as the only effective counterpoise to Marxist-based parties on the left.

Turning to the question of Nazi support in the elections, modern research has revealed that the Nazi constituency was broad-based, including a wide range of individuals. There were, however, three major groups that did not vote for Hitler. Firstly, politically organized Catholics appear to have been immune to Nazi propaganda. Secondly, the organized working class who had previously voted for socialist parties and worked in heavy and large-scale industries were similarly unmoved by Hitler's appeal. Thirdly, the Jewish population constituting less than 1 per cent of the population, were loyal supporters of liberal democratic politics. On the whole they retained their allegiance to the German Democrats and the Social Democrats. It was unthinkable that they would vote for the Nazis.

Nazi supporters, however, came from a wide range of groups. In the three post-1928 elections, the Nazi party recruited heavily from first-time voters; this was largely the effect of the Nazis' efforts at infiltrating student and youth organizations. Added to these voters, those engaged in farming were overwhelmingly attracted to the ideology of the Nazi party. So, too, were retailers, small businessmen and civil servants. In addition, traditional supporters of the middle-class parties – Nationalists, Democrats, and the People's Party – increasingly embraced Nazism. Similarly, the upper and upper-middle classes came to accept that the Nazi Party would be able to control political and economic life. Finally, the Nazis also gained considerable support from non-socialist working-class groups in small to middle-sized enterprises. Such individuals included farm labourers, home-workers, craftsmen, artisans, workers in small to medium-sized enterprises, and uniformed workers in municipal and service industries.[3]

In transforming the fortunes of the Nazi party in these crucial years, the master propagandist of the Nazi regime, Joseph Goebbels, played a crucial role. In 1929 Goebbels was appointed Reich Propaganda Leader of the NSDAP; subsequently he orchestrated a pseudo-religious cult of the Führer as the saviour of Germany. Once the Great Depression caused widespread confusion and despair, he managed to channel the fears and aggression of the unemployed masses, and in the election campaigns of 1932, he succeeded in focusing national attention on Hitler. During 1932 Hitler gave a total of 209 public speeches; 50,000 phonograph records of Hitler's speeches were distributed; and propaganda movies were disseminated throughout the country. Behind all these activities, which no doubt crucially influenced Hitler's success at the polls, was the hand of Goebbels, the cynical manipulator of public opinion. His mastery of the techniques of mass persuasion were profoundly to influence the course of events as the Nazis – now the most powerful political force in German life – were on the threshold of a new age.

Notes

1 Adolf Hitler, *Mein Kampf*, New York, 1941, p. 737.
2 Klaus P. Fischer, *Nazi Germany*, London, 1995, p. 33.
3 R. Landau, *The Nazi Holocaust*, London, 1980, pp. 102–3.

5. Nazi racism

In the development of Nazi ideology, racist doctrines were of fundamental importance and had a crucial impact on German society following Hitler's ascendancy to power. From 1933 to 1945 Germany became a racial state, enacting legislation designed to protect Aryan blood from contamination by undesirables within society.

The background to Nazi racism

Nazi racial theories were grounded in post-Enlightenment notions about the nature of human society. In 1775 the German philosopher Immanuel Kant argued that blacks and whites are racially distinct. In his view, there are different human races, even though they all belong to a single genus. Such differences, however, are no guide to their respective value. Subsequently racial theories disagreed with Kant, insisting that physical and psychological differences between races are an indication of their relative worth. On this basis they constructed racial hierarchies largely based on physical criteria.

The German theologian Johann Kaspar Lavater, for example, sought to deduce spiritual and psychological characteristics from physiognomy; similarly, the Dutch anatomist Pieter Camper measured the facial angles of different races, and categorized them in terms of physical beauty. The German physician Franz Joseph Gall used cranial measurement to differentiate races in terms of intelligence, moral disposition, and beauty. Using a similar method, the German philosopher Christoph Meiners ranked races in terms of beauty or ugliness. In his opinion, fair people were superior to all others whereas darker individuals were ugly and uncivilized. Arguing along the same lines, the philosopher Carl Gustav Carus argued that the universe is endowed with a soul which underwent various metamorphoses leading to the creation of human beings. The complexions of the human races, he maintained, reflect their degree of inner illumination.

Parallel with these views, racial-anthropological theorists sought to justify European domination of other peoples. Such a doctrine was based on earlier beliefs that ancient German tribesmen who were tall, blue-eyed and blond possessed honourable virtues. Such convictions served as the basis for the belief that Germans were the bearers of civilization to peoples of an inferior nature. In the *World Struggle of the Germans and Slavs* published in 1847, Moritz Wilhelm Heffter maintained that the German drive to the east was a necessary consequence of the superiority of the German nation. Arguing along similar lines, Heinrich von Treitschke eulogized the racial struggle against Prussians, Lithuanians and Poles. A form of magic, he believed, had emanated from eastern German soil which had been fertilized by German blood. Such a belief was designed to legitimize the Germanization of Prussia's Polish minority.

In addition to such racial doctrines, Nazism was buttressed by ideas drawn from various anthropological theories. In *Essai sur la noblesse de France*, published in 1735, Count Henri de Boulainvilliers stressed that the French nobility was descended from Frankish-Germanic invaders whereas townsmen and peasants were the descendants of the ancient Gauls. Such a notion was embraced by ideologists as well as historians of the Restoration. Among those who subscribed to this view was Count Joseph Arthur de Gobineau who asserted that his family was descended from ancient Frankish aristocracy. According to Gobineau, white, yellow and black races were not equal in value. In his opinion, the rise and fall of civilizations were racially determined. All high cultures were created by Aryans; cultures went into decline when the Aryan ruling class bred with members of inferior races. When such intermingling occurred, he maintained, rebellions ensued by the racially inferior groups against the Aryan ruling races. This took place in ancient Egypt, Greece and Rome. In modern times, the French *Ancien Régime* was destroyed by a similar revolt.

Nazi racism was also supported by a variety of notions derived from Darwinism. In *On the Origins of Species*, Charles Darwin attempted to demonstrate that natural selection was fundamental to the evolution of the species. According to Darwin, in nature there is a constant struggle for existence. Only those species which are capable of adaptation are able to survive. Hence, the process of natural selection results in the development of each species. In *The Descent of Man*, he discussed the effects of modern society on this process and argued that breeding is necessary to counterbalance the impact of the absence of natural selection.

The application of Darwin's theories to human society was undertaken by a number of writers who pressed for the creation of utopian communities. Francis Galton, for example, embraced the principle of natural selection. In his view, members of the professions as well as healthy members of the middle class should be encouraged to reproduce. However, those persons who were unable to pass a genetics test should be encouraged to emigrate. As the founder of hereditary health care which he referred to as eugenics, Galton formulated a programme for improving the human race through genetic regulation. Such ideas applied to mating, education, public health and welfare.

Subsequently Darwin and Galton's writings were disseminated in Europe and the United States. In Germany the zoologist Ernst Haeckel sought to promote Darwin's theories, and advanced a new philosophy of human life called 'Monism'. This ideology was based on comparative zoology, and was designed to lead to moral perfection. In the *History of Natural Creation*, Haeckel argued that the Central European races were the most highly developed. No other peoples could be compared to them physically or intellectually. By virtue of their abilities, they would triumph over all other races and dominate the entire world. However, in order to ensure their ascendancy, selective breeding would be required. In propounding this view, Haeckel cited the case of ancient Sparta:

All of the weak, sickly, or physically deficient children were slain. Only those children who were completely healthy and strong were allowed to live, and only they were later allowed to reproduce. Therewith the Spartan race was not merely maintained in selected strength and virtues, but rather with each generation their physical perfection was increased. Certainly, in large measure, the Spartan people owed their unique level of masculine strength and tough heroism to this artificial selection or breeding.[1]

In line with such a policy, Haeckel recommended in *The Riddle of Life* that the sick be eliminated:

What profit does humanity derive from the thousands of cripples who are born each year, from the deaf and dumb, from cretins, from those with incurable hereditary defects etc. who are kept alive artificially and then raised to adulthood? ... What an immense aggregate of suffering and pain these depressing figures represent for the unfortunate sick people themselves, what a fathomless sum of worry and grief for their families, what a loss in terms of private resources and costs to the state for the healthy! How much of this loss and suffering could be obviated, if one finally decided to liberate the totally incurable from their indescribable suffering with a dose of morphia.[2]

Similar ideas were found in the writing of the physician Wilhelm Schallmeyer. In his *Heredity and Selection in the Life of Nations: A Study in Political Science on the Basis of the New Biology*, he argued that the state has a responsibility to ensure the healthy character of its people – the birth rate and racial character of the nation must be protected from adverse influences. In his view, child marriages should be encouraged, and earnings-related allowances should be given to mothers. All such measures, he stressed, should be available to anyone examined by a qualified expert in socio-biological science. However, anyone who did not pass should be denied a certificate to marry, isolated and sterilized.

Later in the century Alfred Ploetz published *The Efficiency of Our Race and the Protection of the Weak*. In his view, the West Aryan or German race was the most civilized, but was being undermined by the increasing protection of the weak in society. In his view, the conception of children should not be haphazard, but instead regulated according to scientific principles. If a deformed child should appear, then a college of physicians should determine if it should be killed. Furthermore, Ploetz argued that only inferior persons should be sent to the front during wartime. Such measures were designed to improve the quality of the race.

Other pioneers of modern eugenics emphasized the decisive impact of genetics on human personality. In their view, it is not possible to improve the capabilities of successive generations through training. Rather, human life is predetermined by its essential make-up – persons are composed of positive or negative biological material. In this light, such scientists as Alfred Grotjahn, a professor of social hygiene at Berlin University, advocated sterilizing those who were not members of the respectable working classes. These individuals included the insane, the workshy, those with sexually-transmitted diseases and alcoholics.

These scientists and others were anxious to protect the civilized classes from those who could make little if any contribution to society. In their view, welfare programmes protected the unfit and undesirable. Such concerns emerged in Germany in the aftermath of World War I. In 1923 Gerhard Boeters, the Zwickau District Health Officer, disclosed that doctors in his district were sterilizing the mentally handicapped. With the onset of the Depression and mass unemployment, the use of scarce resources became a pressing question for the government. By July 1932 the Prussian government had formulated a Reich Sterilization Law which was later passed to the Reich Government.

Similar views about race were also voiced by a range of nineteenth-century thinkers. Although their opinions were not based on scientific evidence, they argued that human society must confront the problem of scarce resources. In 1880, for example, the philosopher Friedrich Nietzsche declared that those who were unfit should be eliminated from society:

> Satisfaction of desire should not be practised so that the race as a whole suffers, i.e. that choice no longer occurs, and that anyone can pair off and produce children. The extinction of many types of people is just as desirable as any form of reproduction. ... Much more so: marriage only 1) with the aim of higher development; 2) in order to leave behind the fruit of such persons. Concubinage is enough for all the rest, with measures to prevent conception. ... We must do away with all this crass lightheartedness.[3]

Other thinkers proposed various innovations based on social engineering. Willibald Hentschel, for example, pressed for the creation of stud villages in which suitable men would be encouraged to mate with up to ten women. Hentschel's ideas later had an important effect on the Artamanen League which included leading Nazis such as Heinrich Himmler and Rudolf Hoess. Another figure of this period, Jorg Lanz, argued for the breeding of blond Aryan supermen. Such a notion was promoted through *Ostara: Newspaper for Blond People*.

Turning from these early thinkers to Hitler's own views, it is not clear what racist material Hitler read. Nonetheless, his ideology is deeply influenced by previous racial theories: *Mein Kampf* is imbued with such doctrine. In his view, there are a number of universal truths about human nature:

Even the most superficial observation shows that Nature's restricted form of propagation and increase is an almost rigid basic law of all the innumerable forms of expression of her vital urge. Every animal mates only with a member of the same species. The titmouse seeks the titmouse, the finch the finch, the stork the stork, the field mouse the field mouse, the dormouse the dormouse.[4]

In his discussion of racism, Hitler emphasized the need for promoting racially selective breeding. Following the view of racial-hygienicists, he promoted the victory of the better and stronger. What is required above all is purity of the blood. Only the healthy should produce children, and steps should be taken to obstruct the reproductive capacities of those who will weaken the Aryan race. Repeatedly in *Mein Kampf* and in his speeches, Hitler recommended a variety of measures to promote the birth rate of desirable members of German society. Child allowances, public housing projects and educational opportunities were among a range of policies designed to encourage parents to have more children. As part of this racial plan, Hitler argued that outlying colonies should be settled by those of the highest racial purity. Such individuals were to be chosen by racial experts.

Conversely, Hitler insisted that the recovery of Germany would only be possible if the struggle against Jewry were won. In this combat against the forces of evil, Hitler perceived himself as fulfilling a divine directive: 'I believe today that I am acting in the sense of the Almighty Creator; by warding off the Jews, I am fighting for the Lord's work.'[5] For Hitler, the Jew represented the greatest threat to his utopian racial plan. Utilizing apocalyptic imagery, he believed that the Jew was the agent of the devil, and that in the battle between good and evil, the future of humanity was at stake.

Discussion: Racial theory

In a post-Holocaust world the racial theories of the eighteenth, nineteenth and early twentieth centuries appear preposterous. How could reputable philosophers and scientists have propounded notions with such disastrous consequences? Cloaked under a veneer of patriotism, the writers we have surveyed sought to provide a justification for European dominance and a policy for subjection and geographical expansion. In advancing doctrines about racial superiority and inferiority, these thinkers came to believe that their views were scientifically grounded and justified by empirical evidence.

Yet, racial-anthropology is nothing more than a pseudo-science with no basis in fact. According to these theorists, races can be classified according to strict physical criteria, yet such demarcation is exceedingly difficult, if not impossible, to stipulate. As we have seen, these theoreticians themselves held different and conflicting views. And certainly as far as Jewry is concerned, Jews do not constitute a particular racial group; rather, the Jewish community consists of a wide range of physical types with varying genetic backgrounds. There is no such thing as Jewish blood, even though through the centuries Jews have tended to intermarry. While in the past it has been possible to isolate stereotypic Jewish physiognomic characteristics, such features were by no means uniform or universal.

Regarding the systems outlined by racial theorists, there has been no generally accepted system of classification. Some like Immanuel Kant regarded different races as equal because they all belonged to the same genus. Later theorists disagreed: Christoph Meiner believed that it was possible to rank races on the basis of beauty or ugliness – fair people, he argued, were more beautiful than those who were of a darker complexion. Yet, it is obvious that such aesthetic judgements are purely subjective. Adopting a different approach, Carl Gustav Carus advanced metaphysical doctrines about a world soul which evolved into human beings; the complexions of the races, he contended, are reflections of inner illumination. Again, such a belief has no scientific foundation.

Similarly, anthropological theories proposing that Germans were the bearers of a superior culture lack any historical basis. Such figures as Moritz Wilhelm Heffter and Heinrich von Treitschke simply used such a doctrine to justify German expansionism eastward. Count Joseph Arthur de Gobineau's conviction that Aryans constituted a superior race and this justified inbreeding was also fuelled by the desire to legitimize discriminatory policies. Further, his racial analysis of rebellions which occurred in ancient civilizations lacks any historical foundation.

So, too, those writers who promoted social Darwinism were deluded in believing that their views were scientifically grounded. While Darwin's investigation of the natural world was in accord with scientific principles, the application of his studies to human society lacked the same rigour. Hence, Francis Galton's conclusions about natural selection were not based on empirical observation as he implied; his eugenic theories were nothing more than personal proposals for social engineering. Ernst Haeckel's monistic philosophy likewise lacked any scientific basis, and his advocacy of selective breeding was grounded in a particular form of social utilitarianism. The same criticism applies to Wilhelm Schallmeyer's recommendations for the improvement of human society, Alfred Ploetz's endorsement of breeding programmes, and Alfred Grotjahn's advocacy of sterilization.

The dangers of such pseudo-scientific ideas are now clear: Hitler's quest to rid society of what he believed to be undesirable elements led to mass murder. The inherent flaw in a programme of selective breeding, sterilization, euthanasia and extermination lies in its moral assumptions. In advocating such policies, racial theorists – including the Nazis – believed that the good of society was a supreme goal which took precedence over all other considerations. In *Mein Kampf* and in numerous speeches, Hitler expressed his belief that Germany had a special destiny in world history. This involved protecting Aryan blood from contamination at all costs. Any means would be justified in attaining this end, including murder.

In advocating such a policy, Hitler and his executioners were convinced that the ends justified the means, no matter how terrible. What can we make of such moral calculation? From an ethical point of view, Nazi utilitarianism appears monstrous and grotesque. The photographs and newsreels of German barbarism in the death camps is a permanent reminder of the consequences of such a policy. So, too, are the terrible accounts of the euthanasia programme in which innocent victims were gassed out of a desire to serve the state. Yet we should not turn a blind eye to the fact that despite our repulsion at scenes of wanton killing during the Third Reich, some of the principles lying behind Nazi policy have become a feature of contemporary society.

A central principle inherent in eugenic theory is that humanity benefits from the elimination of those who make no contribution to the community. In *Riddle of Life*, Haeckel stressed that cripples, the deaf and dumb, cretins, those with incurable hereditary defects and those kept alive artificially merely drain away resources which could be put to better effect for the healthy. In his view, such individuals suffer immeasurably and cause great grief for their families. It would be much better, he argued, if such pain could be eliminated through euthanasia.

Although modern societies have not instituted programmes of mercy killing as outlined by Haeckel and others, the underlying presupposition of various medical treatments is that some persons are dispensable. In cases of amniocentesis, for example, pregnant mothers are permitted to know in advance whether the child they are bearing suffers from serious physical or mental disabilities. Parents, we believe, should have the right to terminate a pregnancy in such cases. Contemporary society has thus provided the legal means whereby future members of the community can be eliminated before birth if parents wish to be spared the anguish as well as the financial consequences of looking after them. In principle, then, certain elements of Nazi eugenics have permeated contemporary attitudes concerning those who are perceived as disposable.

Thus, though we recoil in horror from the excesses of Nazism, we should not sweepingly condemn Nazi eugenics without recognizing that in modern society we embrace some of the underlying presuppositions of eugenic policy ourselves. Indeed, public attitudes regarding health, education and welfare are frequently shaped by a utilitarian calculus, not unlike that employed by Nazi thinkers. In a world of scarce resources, difficult decisions need to be made, and in evaluating issues such as abortion, genetic engineering, cloning, premature birth, organ transplants, embryonic research, voluntary and involuntary euthanasia, we face the same type of problems as those which German society sought to resolve during the Third Reich. In seeking to untangle the ethical and practical dilemmas that these topics raise, we will need to be clear about the basic assumptions we make about human life and the society we seek to create.

Notes

1 Michael Burleigh and Wolfgang Wippermann, *The Radical State: Germany 1933–45*, Cambridge, 1996, p. 30.
2 *Ibid.*, p. 31.
3 *Ibid.*, p. 170.
4 Adolf Hitler, *Mein Kampf*, London, 1992, p. 258.
5 *Ibid.*, p. 348.

6. Hitler's executioners

In the Nazi assault on the Jewish people, thousands of individuals were involved in the process of annihilation. From SS men who carried out orders to persecute and murder innocent victims in Germany to the *Einsatzgruppen* killing squads who executed men, women and children in Poland and Russia, German citizens were intimately engaged in this reign of terror. There were, however, a number of central figures who played a crucial role in the onslaught against those viewed as polluters of Aryan blood.

The inner circle

Pre-eminent among Hitler's executioners was Hermann Göring, Hitler's designated successor. Born in Rosenheim on 12 January 1893, Göring entered the army in 1914 as an Infantry Lieutenant. Subsequently he became a decorated combat pilot. In 1922 he was appointed to command the SA Brownshirts. The following year he was wounded in the Munich Beer Hall putsch, and was compelled to flee from Germany. Returning to Germany in 1927, he rejoined the NSDAP and became a deputy in the *Reichstag*. During the next five years he played a major role in Hitler's rise to power; in 1932 he became President of the *Reichstag*. When Hitler was appointed Chancellor on 30 January 1933, Göring became Prussian Minister of the Interior, Commander-in-Chief of the Prussian police and Gestapo and Commissioner for Aviation.

Together with Heinrich Himmler and Reinhard Heydrich, Göring established the early concentration camps for political prisoners. After the *Reichstag* fire in February 1933, he implemented a number of decrees that undermined civil rights in the country, and directed operations which eliminated Ernst Röhm and other SA leaders during the Blood Purge of 30 June 1934. The next year he became Commander-in-Chief of the Air Force. In 1936 he was appointed Plenipotentiary for the Implementation of the Four Year Plan – this position gave him virtual control over the German economy. In his position as head of the Four Year Plan, Göring was in charge of the Aryanization programme which resulted in the virtual confiscation of the wealth and property of the German Jewish community. Jewish-owned property was bought at only a percentage of its real value; the state then retained this small payment from the sellers who received only a small percentage in monthly instalments.

In 1938 Göring remarked that it might be necessary to place Jews in ghettos in the future. In less than two years he demanded the physical separation of the Jews from the Aryan German population. After the destruction of Jewish-owned buildings during *Kristallnacht* on 9 November 1938, Göring decreed that Jews should be eliminated from the German economy, as well as from schools, resorts, parks and forests. In addition, he decreed that insurance companies must pay for all damages to Jewish properties, but that these payments should be made to the state rather than to policy-holders. All buildings that had been devastated were to be repaired at the owners' cost. Further, he fined the German Jewish community a billion Marks. The rationalization for such action was that the Jews were ultimately responsible for the onset of this pogrom.

Although Göring sought to retain control over the Jewish population, this role was taken over by Himmler. In 1939 Göring instructed Reinhard Heydrich to carry out preparations with regard to a general solution of the Jewish question in those territories of Europe under German influence. It should be noted, however, that Göring – unlike Himmler and others – was not a racial fanatic. He never agreed with Hitler's assessment of Jewish influence nor their potential threat to the state. Nonetheless, even though he did not attend the Wannsee Conference on 20 January 1942, Göring was implicated in the eventual extermination of Jewry which took place in the last few years of the war.

Among those with whom Göring engineered the destruction of European Jewry, Reinhard Heydrich played a central role. Born in Halle on 7 March, 1904, Reinhard Heydrich joined the *Freikorps* in 1919. Three years later he entered the *Reichsmarine* (the navy). In 1931, however, he was compelled to resign from the navy for having sexual relations with the daughter of a shipyard owner. In July he joined the NSDAP and subsequently the SS. On 25 December 1931 he was appointed SS Major; in July 1932 he became SS Colonel and Chief of the Security Service (the SD). The next year he became SS-Brigadeführer, and as a reward for his involvement in the Röhm putsch he was appointed SS Lieutenant-General.

With typical Aryan features, Heydrich epitomized the type of individual the Nazis sought to create through their policy of racial selection. An athlete who was also a talented violinist, Heydrich impressed Heinrich Himmler who selected him to be his assistant. Heydrich soon became chief of the Berlin Gestapo; by 1936 he was appointed head of the Reich Main Security Office. As one of the instigators of *Kristallnacht*, he sent Adolf Eichmann to Vienna to organize a Centre for Jewish Emigration.

Despite his physical appearance, Heydrich was racked with uncertainty about his racial origins. The possibility that he was half-Jewish may well have been the cause of his virulent hatred of Jewry. With heartless cruelty, he was contemptuous of those he viewed as enemies of the state. In 1939 Heydrich was appointed head of the Reich Main Security Office (RSHA) which incorporated the Gestapo, the criminal police and the SD. This organization constituted a gigantic network which centralized and transmitted information to all parts of the Nazi empire.

Once Poland was conquered, Heydrich ordered the ghettoization of Polish Jews as well as the appointment of Jewish councils, the *Judenräte*, which were given the authority to regulate Jewish affairs. Such councils were tools created by the Nazis to maintain law and order. Cynically manipulating Jewry, the Nazis sought to redirect Jewish contempt, frustration and hostility against those Jews chosen to administer life in the ghettos. Together with Eichmann, Heydrich also organized the deportation of Jews from annexed parts of Poland, Germany and Austrian territories to the General Government, a Western Polish territory conquered by Germany. Ghettos, he believed, served only as a temporary solution to the Jewish question.

Following the invasion of Russia in 1941, Göring commissioned Heydrich to carry out a total solution of the Jewish question in those territories of Europe under German influence. Two terms were used to describe this operation, 'total solution' and 'final solution', and Heydrich was commanded to take responsibility for those measures. His *Einsatzgruppen*, which had been employed in killing thousands of Poles and Jews, were to be employed in this operation.

On 20 January 1942 Heydrich convened the Wannsee Conference to discuss the means of implementing the Final Solution. The language used at this meeting was designed deliberately to disguise the Nazis' policy of mass murder. During the conference Heydrich described how Jews who were capable of work would be brought to occupied areas in the east and employed in road building. Some, he noted, would not be able to survive such physical labour, but those who survived would be given appropriate treatment since they represented a germ cell of a new Jewish development.

A third major figure in the Nazi plan of extermination was Heinrich Himmler, head of the Gestapo and the *Waffen-SS*, Minister of the Interior, and the organizer of the mass murder of Jews living in the Third Reich. Born in Munich on 7 October 1900, Himmler served as an officer cadet at the end of World War I. He then worked as a salesman for fertilizer manufacturers. Later he joined a paramilitary organization and was actively involved in the Munich Beer Hall putsch. From 1925 to 1930 he was the acting propaganda leader of the NSDAP. In 1927 he married and became a chicken farmer. Two years later he became head of Hitler's personal bodyguard, the SS.

In 1930 Himmler was elected to the *Reichstag* and sought to expand membership of the SS. In addition, he organized the Security Service under Reinhard Heydrich. In March 1933 he was appointed Munich Police President, later becoming Commander of the political police throughout Bavaria. In the same year he was appointed Commander of all political police units outside Prussia. On 20 April 1934 he became head of the Prussian Police and Gestapo. In the same year he also masterminded the purge against the SA, thereby enabling the SS to gain ascendancy. By 17 June 1936 Himmler had become head of the Gestapo in addition to his position as *Reichsführer* of the SS. During this period he established a concentration camp in Dachau for political prisoners and extended the range of those who could be incarcerated.

According to Himmler, the aim of the German nation was to become racially pure – in the process, he believed, it would be necessary to eliminate those whom he viewed as sub-humans. In his quest to produce such a race of superior individuals, Himmler was intent on creating a new elite in line with the laws of selection. The SS man was to represent a new human type whose mission was to colonize the east.

In propounding this ideology, Himmler was intent on ensuring that the purity of the blood would be protected through the implementation of a broad policy embracing racial selection and special marriage laws. In this quest, Himmler created a state-registered stud farm where young girls were selected for their noble traits. These persons were to mate with SS men, and through this breeding programme a race of supermen was to be created. On 8 October he pronounced that 'it will be the sublime task of German women and girls of good blood acting not frivolously but from a profound moral seriousness to become mothers to children of soldiers setting off to battle'.[1]

Seeking to inspire the SS with this vision of a purified human race, Himmler sought to rationalize mass murder as an act of loyalty. 'One principle must be absolute for the SS man', he declared in a speech on 4 October 1943 to a group of SS leaders in Poznan:

> We must be honest, decent, loyal, and comradely to members of our own blood and to no one else. What happens to the Russians, what happens to the Czechs, is a matter of indifference to me. Such good blood of our own kind as there may be among the nations we shall acquire for ourselves, if necessary by taking away the children and bringing them up among us. Whether the other peoples live in comfort or perish of hunger interests me only in so far as we need them as slaves for our *Kultur*. ... We Germans, who are the only people in the world who have a decent attitude to animals, will also adopt a decent attitude to human animals, but it is a crime against our own blood to worry about them and to bring them ideals. I shall speak to you here with all frankness of a very grave matter ... yet we will never speak of it publicly. I mean the evacuation of the Jews, the extermination of the Jewish people. ... Most of you know what it means to see a hundred corpses lying together, five hundred, or a thousand. To have stuck it out and at the same time – apart from exceptions caused by human weakness – to have remained decent fellows, that is what has made us hard. This is a page of glory in our history which has never been written and shall never be written.[2]

Once Himmler was made Minister of the Interior in 1943, he gave orders to export eastern peoples for slave labour, gas millions of Jews, conduct mass abortions and sterilizations of ethnic groups, and conduct experiments on those in the camps.

In promoting this programme, Joseph Goebbels played a crucial role as propagandist of the Nazi regime. Born on 29 October 1897 he was a student at the University of Heidelberg. During World War I he was rejected for military service because of a crippled foot. In 1922 he joined the NSDAP; initially he was a business manager of the party in the Ruhr district and was a collaborator with Gregor Strasser, the leader of the social revolutionary North German wing of the party. In 1926 he became Nazi district leader for Berlin-Brandenburg; the following year he founded and edited his own weekly newspaper.

In 1929 Hitler appointed Goebbels as Reich Propaganda Leader of the NSDAP. In this capacity Goebbels created the Führer myth and helped in the election campaigns of 1932. The next year he was appointed Reich Minister for Public Enlightenment and Propaganda, a post which gave him complete control of the media. On 10 May 1933 he organized the ritual of book burning in Berlin, and in later years he advanced the theory of the international Jewish financier who was allied with the Communists. At the Party Day of Victory in 1933, Goebbels sought to expose the Jewish penetration of the professions and public life. In November 1938 he instigated the *Kristallnacht* onslaught against German Jewry. Later he promoted the Final Solution and supervised the deportation of Jews from Berlin in 1942.

Discussion: The murderers

Who were these men who surrounded Hitler? By any account they were unstable figures whose psychological make-up and early experiences led them into right-wing politics. Göring, for example, was an opportunist, overwhelmed by vanity and the quest for luxury. In the end, Hitler concluded that he was his greatest disappointment. Born into a wealthy Bavarian family, Göring was, as we have seen, a decorated fighter pilot in the Luftwaffe during World War I, yet at the end of the war he found it difficult to adjust to civilian life. As a result, he joined the Nazi party in 1922. Impressed by this new recruit, Hitler made him commander of the SA. When the Beer Hall putsch failed, Göring was wounded but escaped from the country.

On his return to Germany, Göring held a variety of positions and wielded enormous power once Hitler become Chancellor. Although he was popular with the German public, Göring was motivated by opportunism, greed and vanity. His life alternated between intensely dedicated work and gluttony. After a period of frenzied activity, he would lapse into idleness. Like Hitler, Göring was a sociopath, lacking conscience and rejecting normative authority. However, unlike Hitler, Göring was not driven by ideological commitment – rather he sought to gratify both material and personal needs. Arguably even his brutality, which Hitler admired, was the product of calculation rather than sadistic tendencies.

Living in palatial surroundings, Göring owned four mansions, a hunting lodge, two castles and a place in the Leipziger Platz in Berlin. In addition, he possessed hundreds of uniforms, extravagant jewellery, a yacht and various cars. Either personally or through his agents, Göring acquired priceless objects from museums, art dealers or wealthy owners in conquered territories. His vast collection, which was displayed in his villas and castles, included works by such masters as Hals, Van Dyck, Goya, Rembrandt, Velazquez, Rubens, Titian, Raphael, David, the Cranach School, Boucher and Vermeer. Such self-aggrandizement was accompanied by gross exhibitionism. Tailors created costumes to suit his whims and uniforms in every colour which he changed throughout the day along with jewellery and waistbands.

Eventually, however, Göring lapsed into lethargy and fantasy. By 1943 he had become a bloated, grotesque figure; he was discredited and isolated, hated by Hitler who blamed him for Germany's defeats. At the end of the war when Hitler declared that he would remain in the Berlin bunker, Göring misconstrued the Führer's words, assuming that he had abdicated. When he requested that he be allowed to take over the running of the country, he was dismissed from his posts, expelled from the party and arrested. On 9 May 1945 he was captured by the American Seventh Army and put on trial at Nuremberg the following year.

What is so striking about Heinrich Himmler was his ordinariness. Rat-like in appearance, he was born into a typical Bavarian middle-class family. In all likelihood his upbringing contributed to his unbending, ideologically committed outlook. His father was a rigid, pedantic and legalistic school teacher, and it was only through his influence that Himmler was accepted into an officers' training school. Unathletic and unassertive, his son was an unlikely candidate for military leadership despite his longing to be of service to the fatherland.

At the end of World War I, Himmler was only eighteen and without a career. Rootless and insecure, he became an agricultural student rather than enter a traditional profession. Studying at the Technical University of Munich, he followed a restricted pattern which he meticulously recorded in his diaries. Rarely venturing outside of this strict regime, he remained unattached but this did not prevent him from meddling in other people's affairs, including the choice of his brother's wife. During this period, Himmler was fascinated by racist literature and began to consort with right-wing movements in Munich.

Having obtained his agricultural diploma in 1922, he worked as a technical assistant doing work on manure. Adrift and with few job prospects, he joined the Nazi Party in 1923. After the failure of the Beer House putsch, he contemplated emigrating to Russia or Latin America and becoming a farmer. But after Hitler's return from prison, his fortunes began to improve and as the years passed he became a central figure in the party. His dedication to Hitler and the party was tantamount to a conversion: like many others, he found in Hitler a saviour to whom he could devote all his energies. In 1923 he married a divorced nurse of Polish origins who was eight years his senior. Although the two were similar in temperament, Himmler was unhappy in his marriage; in later years he kept a mistress and became the father of two illegitimate children. Paradoxically, Himmler was determined to create a master-race, even though he himself was the opposite of the racial ideal which he hoped to foster.

Unlike Himmler, Heydrich exemplified such a physical type. Fair-haired, blue-eyed and tall, he grew up in a strict Catholic family in which cleanliness, order, discipline and achievement were demanded. As an introspective and shy young man, Heydrich had few friends. Despite his arrogance, he had a deep secret which plagued him throughout his life. Plagued by a sense of racial inferiority caused by his suspected half-Jewish origins, Heydrich was driven by the quest for power as well as deep suspicion of those around him. At every turn he suspected others of treachery and intrigue. As a result, in his various positions of authority, he reacted heartlessly to anyone who was perceived as an enemy of the state. Known as the 'Blond Beast', he specialized in blackmail, terror and persecution.

Among the Nazi leadership, Goebbels too was an oddity. Although intelligent and well-educated, he in no way conformed to the ideal Aryan type. Puny in stature, he had a large head on a thin body, brown hair and a swarthy complexion. Most significantly, he walked with a limp and had to wear a special shoe and braces since his left leg was several inches shorter than his right. Known as the 'mouse general' and the 'malicious dwarf', he was despised and feared by his enemies. Ashamed of such physical defects, Goebbels claimed that his lameness was due to a war wound. No doubt such physical infirmity contributed to his own contempt for humanity, his desire to sow hatred in the masses, and his lust for power and mastery. Such were the figures who surrounded Hitler in his drive for world supremacy. Idealizing the Führer, they found in National Socialism a means of solving their psychological problems and fulfilling their deepest personal longings.

Notes

1 Robert Wistrich, *Who's Who in Nazi Germany*, London, 1995, p. 112.
2 *Ibid.*, p. 112.

7. The SS

In the creation of the Third Reich, the SS played an increasingly important role. In order to ensure the security of the state, Hitler needed an organization that would not feel constrained by bureaucratic entanglement. What was required was a separate body which could enforce the will of the Nazi regime. Such an organization would need to be independent of the state, and yet through its control of the police system, capable of operating either within the framework of law or outside of legal constraints. Initially the SS was subject to the SA. Eventually, however, it developed into a party police force, a regular army within the army. Infiltrating every aspect of German life, it spread its tentacles throughout the nation.

The origin and growth of the SS

Like the Nazi party itself, the SS began in Bavaria in the 1920s as a small bodyguard for the Führer. In January 1929 Himmler became *Reichsführer SS*. Even though this was a minor position within the party, Himmler was determined to create a black-shirted elite who would become the vanguard of a new racial state. Under the influence of racial theories promulgated by Walther Darré, Himmler sought to attract members to this new order. Recruits had to meet rigorous standards. They had to be at least 5'8" tall and of Aryan descent back to 1750 for officers and 1800 for enlisted men, and had to possess suitable health and hygienic characteristics.

Himmler found the model for this elite organization in the Jesuits, whom he saw as the spiritual police of the Roman Catholic Church. In his view, their members were totally dedicated to serving both the order and the Pope. In addition, Himmler modelled the SS on the Teutonic Order, those knights who as Christian missionaries had secured an empire in Eastern Europe. The SS, he believed, should resemble these bodies, but its members should be imbued with the ideals of National Socialism rather than Christian values. In 1937 he outlined his vision to an audience of SS Group leaders:

> We have set ourselves the goal not of creating an association of men which, like all men's associations, will sooner or later disintegrate, but rather of letting an order develop gradually. I hope than in ten years' time we will be an order and not only an order of men but an order of clans. An order to which the women are required to belong as much as the men. Let us be clear about this: it would be stupid to collect together good blood from the whole of Germany and to conceive this good blood in theoretical terms, while at the same time allowing it to marry and form families just as it wants. On the contrary, we want for Germany an upper stratum, a new nobility continually selected over the centuries.[1]

The principles of selection to the SS embodied the values espoused by the Nazi regime, as Himmler explained in a speech at the Reich Peasant Congress in November 1935:

> The first principle for us was and is the recognition of the values of blood and selection. . . . We went about it like a seedsman who, wanting to improve the strain of a good old variety which has become crossbred and lost its vigour, goes through the fields to pick the best plants. . . . The nature of the selection process was to concentrate on the choice of those who came physically closest to the ideal of the Nordic man. . . . The second principle and virtue which we tried to instil in the SS and to give it an indelible characteristic for the future is the will to freedom and a fighting spirit. . . . The third principle and virtue are the concepts of loyalty and honour. . . . The fourth principle and virtue that is valid for us is obedience, which does not hesitate for a moment but unconditionally follows every order which comes from the Führer or is legitimately given by a superior.[2]

Himmler's aim was to create a racial utopia. In a speech given to the leadership of the SS in June 1942, he described this vision:

> We must once again be rooted in our ancestors and grandchildren, in this eternal chain and eternal sequence. By rooting our people in a deep ideological awareness of ancestors and grandchildren we must once more persuade them that they must have sons. . . . Everything that we do must be justifiable vis-à-vis the clan, our ancestors. If we do not secure

this moral foundation which is the deepest and best because the most natural, we will not be able to overcome Christianity on this plane and create the Germanic Reich which will be a blessing for the earth. That is our mission as a nation on this earth. For thousands of years it has been the mission of this blond race to rule the earth and again and again to bring it happiness and culture.[3]

In line with this ideology every SS member was compelled to keep a genealogical clan book which listed family relationships. Drawing on his experience as a chicken farmer in Waldtrundering, Himmler believed that human breeding could follow the same patterns as found in animal husbandry. In his view, on the basis of Mendel's law of genetics, the German people could in 120 years' time become authentically German in appearance. What was necessary in this quest was to eliminate any undesirable elements in the gene pool through sterilization and racial laws restricting sexual intercourse.

Such a utopian vision was shared by Reinhard Heydrich who became Himmler's close ally. In June 1931 Heydrich came to Himmler's farm looking for work. This marked the beginning of an alliance which led to the mass murder of millions of Jews and others. As a 25-year-old ex-naval officer who was dismissed from the German navy because of an involvement with an unmarried woman, Heydrich impressed Himmler with his typical Aryan looks. Tall, slender, blond and attractive, Heydrich symbolized the highly intelligent and athletic type that Himmler envisaged as the future archetype of the German man.

In the spring of 1933, Himmler and Heydrich began their quest for power. On 9 March 1933 Himmler was appointed Police President of Munich; the next month he was promoted to Political Police Commander of Bavaria, a position which gave him virtual control of a wide-ranging network of police agencies as well as the concentration camp, Dachau. Assisting Himmler, Heydrich ensured that important positions were given to ruthless police officials, ideally members of the Nazi party. In addition, Heydrich aided Himmler in obtaining greater control over the police both in Bavaria and in Germany at large. Further, Heydrich consolidated the Security Service Branch (the SD) of the Nazi Party.

In the beginning the SD consisted of a group of idealists who had become isolated and rootless. Searching for some form of ideological commitment, they joined the NSDAP and its security forces. Initially the purpose of the SD was unclear, but it eventually served as an information service, a secret service, and a quasi-police unit. By 1937 it had 3000 members and an army of 50,000 informers. In its initial phase, the targets of the SD consisted of political opponents, Communists, trade unionists, as well as clergymen. Later, its operations were directed to racial enemies of the state including Jews and those deemed to be Asiatic inferiors. Under Adolf Eichmann, the SD department on Jewish Affairs drew up a list of Jewish groups throughout the world who were perceived as mounting a worldwide conspiracy. In pursuit of its anti-Jewish policy, the SD collaborated with other bodies in a quest to eliminate Jews from German public life through a policy of political and economic exclusion.

In creating an interlocking system of control, Himmler and Heydrich attempted to infiltrate the German police. Once the police forces in all German states (except Prussia) had been amalgamated, Himmler had nearly managed to consolidate his power over the police – only the Gestapo under Göring remained outside his authority. However, on 20 April 1934 Göring, who was embroiled in a feud with the SA about the direction of the Gestapo, allied himself with Himmler by appointing him inspector of the Gestapo. Although Himmler was technically subordinate to Göring as well as Frick as Minister of the Interior and Röhm as head of the SA and SS, he was able to act independently.

During the Night of the Long Knives Himmler's SS murdered Röhm, and thereby eliminated the SA. In recognition of his loyalty, Hitler recognized the SS as an autonomous unit, and Himmler was permitted to control the Gestapo. Following a prolonged conflict with Frick who sought to bring the Gestapo under the supervision of the Ministry of the Interior, a new law was passed in February 1936 which placed the Gestapo offices under the authority of the Minister of the Interior; however, this law also decreed that Gestapo regional offices came under the authority of the head of the Gestapo office in Berlin. Such ambiguity led to serious questions about whether the main Ministry of the Interior or the Gestapo in Berlin had final authority over this body. Several months later, Hitler gave Himmler complete control of the police. Although Frick was theoretically in charge, Himmler and Heydrich were able to exercise total control over the police. Later in the year, Himmler reorganized the police into a new security force.

Previously the term 'security police' had been applied to the entire police system: in the Weimar Republic, the police consisted of administrative and executive branches. The administrative branch dealt largely with personnel procedures and traffic problems; the executive was divided into four subdivisions: crime, urban constabulary, political police and gendarmerie. Under Himmler, the criminal and political police were separated from the other executive spheres and constituted the security police under Heydrich. The rest was put under a new ordinary police force directed by Kurt Daluege – this was merged into a new ordinary police. Thus, the security police now consisted of the Gestapo which had been taken over by Himmler from Göring, the criminal police (the *Kripo*) and the gendarmerie. Armed with these forces, Himmler's men infiltrated the entire German state, creating an interlocking assembly of the SS, police forces and the Gestapo.

In this reorganization, Heinrich Müller was transferred from Berlin and became head of the Gestapo. In addition to Müller, other important personnel included Bruno Streckenbach, the former chief of the Hamburg police who set up the first ghettos in Poland and formed *Einsatzgruppen* who rounded up and murdered Jews in Poland; Oswald Pohl who created a network of SS businesses based on slave labour and murder; Walter Stahlecker, who served as commander of *Einsatzgruppe A* which engaged in acts of mass murder in the Baltic states; Arthur Nebe who served as head of the *Kripo* and was the first to volunteer to exterminate Jews in Poland; Erich von dem Bach-Zelewski who liquidated numerous opponents; Otto Ohlendorf, the head of *Einsatzgruppe D*, who murdered at least 90,000 civilians in southern Russia; and Theodor Eicke, who was in charge of the concentration camp system. Among the ranks of the SS a number of lawyers provided a framework for mass extortion, torture and mass killing. In addition, various intellectual figures provided a rationalization for the SS programme.

Within Germany the SS was seen by most Germans as an exclusive elite. Increasingly a large number of individuals were drawn into the ranks of the SS who sought to defend the Führer as well as the institutions of the state. In the beginning, the SS was composed largely of ex-*Freikorps* members, however after Hitler's appointment as Chancellor in 1933 upper-class Germans from the old aristocratic elite joined as well. From the summer of 1933, Himmler began to restrict entry into the SS with the intention of excluding alcoholics, homosexuals and persons of dubious origins. The training programme for the SS was two years of rigorous instruction culminating in a ceremony in which they were permitted to swear the oath of loyalty:

> I swear to thee Adolf Hitler
> As Führer and Chancellor of the German Reich, Loyalty and Bravery.
> I vow to thee and to the superiors whom thou shalt appoint
> Obedience unto death
> So help me God.[4]

For the SS, belief in the Führer and the Nazi state was paramount as was the unquestioning acceptance of racial theory. The members of this new order were not subject to the judicial system; instead the SS had its own court of honour. Hardened through their training, the SS became the technicians of the concentration camp system. A special volunteer unit of SS men was recruited to serve in Death's Head Units whose members wore skull and crossbones on their black caps. The head of this system was Theodor Eicke, a sociopath who introduced a series of cruel and sadistic punishments in the camps. Prisoners were continually harassed, particularly while urinating and defecating. Some were thrown into cesspools if they were too slow. These enemies of the state were continually humiliated: they were urinated upon from head to foot, made to roll in the mud, hung from tree limbs and compelled to squat for hours with arms behind their heads while bending their knees, and forced to suffocate in torture chambers.

By the autumn of 1939 the SS was organized into four branches: (1) the General SS consisting of part-time workers; (2) the SD or Security Service; (3) the SS Military Formations which in 1939 were renamed the *Waffen-SS*; and (4) the Death's Head Units. Later in the year the state police and Gestapo agencies were merged into one body, the Reich Main Security Office, administered by Heydrich. This bureaucratic apparatus consisted of seven main departments: (1) Personnel; (2) Legal Affairs; (3) SD and subsequently Domestic Information Service; (4) Gestapo; (5) Criminal Police; (6) Foreign News Service; (7) Ideological Research and Evaluation. The number of overlapping SS institutions gave the SS enormous power and increased its sinister aura. Himmler's empire operated under a veil of secrecy, insinuating itself into every area of German life.

Discussion: The creation of the SS

The driving force behind the SS was Heinrich Himmler; as a committed racial ideologue, he was determined to reshape society through this elite body. What can be said about his aspirations? As we have seen, Himmler believed that the racial purity of Aryan blood must be preserved at all costs. In creating the SS, Himmler was convinced that a healthy peasantry was the key to the biological and moral health of the German nation. Drawing on previous racial theory, he was convinced that if Germany were to accomplish its historical objectives, the country needed to expand its agricultural area through a policy of resettlement. At an early age he stated: 'I am more convinced than ever that if there is a campaign in the East I will go with it. The East is the most important thing for us.'[5]

In seeking to realize this racial goal, the SS was to be the vanguard. SS men were to be racially pure as were those whom they married. On 31 December, 1931, Himmler outlined his plan:

1. The SS is a band of German men of strictly Nordic origin selected according to certain principles.
2. In accordance with the National Socialist ideology and with the realization that the future of our nation rests on the preservation of the race through selection and on the inheritance of good blood, I hereby institute from 1 January 1932 the 'Marriage Certificate' for all unmarried members of the SS.
3. The aim is to create a hereditarily healthy clan of a strictly Nordic German type.
4. The marriage certificate will be awarded or refused solely on the basis of racial health and heredity.
5. Every SS man intending to get married must procure for this purpose the marriage certificate of the *Reichsführer SS*.
6. SS members who marry despite having been denied marriage certificates will be removed from the SS; they will be given the chance of resignation.
7. It is the task of the SS 'Race Office' to work out the details of marriage petitions.
8. The SS Race Office is in charge of the 'Clan Book of the SS' in which the families of SS members will be entered after being awarded the marriage certificate or after acceptance of the petition to enter into marriage.

9. The *Reichsführer SS*, the director of the Race Office, and the specialists of this office are pledged to secrecy on their word of honour.
10. The SS is convinced that with this order it has taken a step of great significance. Derision, scorn, and incomprehension will not move us; the future is ours![6]

Such an elite was to be based on race as well as personal qualities rather than the traditional criteria of birth, property and education. Human beings were thus to be subject to selective breeding along the same lines as animal husbandry.

The inherent flaw with this vision is that it is based on a misapprehension of human reproduction. As we have noted, the hierarchical division of human beings into different races lacks any scientific justification. Despite the attempts of racial thinkers to produce a coherent theory of race as well as a set of principles for human breeding, their reflections are nothing more than speculative reflections about the creation of a utopian society. Hence, Himmler's quest to forge a new elite of the Aryan race was a misguided delusion lacking any sound basis in genetic theory.

Yet this was not the most serious defect of Himmler's racism. Much more significant were the moral consequences of this experiment in selective breeding. As we have seen, the SS were highly disciplined, loyal and obedient. As Himmler himself remarked in a speech emphasizing the virtues which the SS must foster: 'Obedience unconditionally follows every order which comes from the Führer or is legitimately given by a superior, obedience ... which obeys just as unconditionally and goes into the attack even when one might think in one's heart one could not bring oneself to do so.'[7]

Such obedience, however, led German men and women to engage in the most terrifying acts of human cruelty. In essence, any vestige of moral sensitivity was eradicated through SS training. This is the background to the types of horrific brutality inflicted by the SS on their victims. Jews and others were treated with complete callousness because in the Nazi vision of history, these individuals constituted a threat to Aryan superiority. As sub-human members of society, they could lay no claim to any form of human rights.

Here it is instructive to compare the treatment of animals in contemporary society with members of the Jewish population under the Nazis. In the modern world, we have largely adopted an instrumental view of the animal kingdom. Animals of all types are exploited in a variety of ways. Millions of hens, for example, which are kept in batteries suffer through cramped living conditions, unable to spread even one wing. In veal crates animals are unable to turn around and are fed a liquid, iron-deficient diet. Pigs are immobilized during pregnancy and birth, unable to tend properly to their young.

Such conditions in farming can be paralleled in many other areas of human interaction with animals. In scientific research, for example, animals are used in a wide variety of tests, many unconnected with the furtherance of medical advance. Animals are routinely used in the production of such cosmetics and toiletries as suntan lotion, eye make-up, bubble bath and nail polish. Non-medical uses extend to warfare experiments in which animals are subject to a range of modern weaponry including radiation, ballistic assault and biological warfare. Further, in product testing, a wide range of items such as paints, dyes, floor cleaners, chemical solvents, anti-freeze, brass polish and oven cleaners have first been used on animals.

How do we justify such wanton suffering? Humans, it is claimed, have been given dominion over animals. Further, it is widely believed that animals have been put on earth for human use. There is little doubt that the Nazis viewed the Jewish population in a similar light. Jews were not only less than human, they constituted a serious threat to the Nazi vision of a utopian society. For this reason, they could be treated brutally without any moral compunction. Indeed, it became a patriotic obligation to assist in their annihilation.

It was left to the SS to carry out this task: like animals led to the slaughter, Jews were rounded up, transported and massacred. Herded together in intolerable conditions, they were humiliated, starved and murdered. Surrounded by SS guards, they came to see themselves as nothing more than trapped creatures whose death meant nothing to their captors. As one of these victims recorded in his diaries: 'Truly we are cattle in the eyes of the Nazis. When they supervise Jewish workers they hold a whip in their hands. All beaten unmercifully'. Such acts, he continued, 'are enough to drive you crazy. Sometimes we are ashamed to look at one another. And worse than this, we have begun to look upon ourselves as "inferior beings", lacking God's image'.[8] Such was the moral consequence of the Nazi conviction that some members of society were sub-human parasites on the healthy body of the Aryan race.

Notes

1 B. F. Smith and A. E. Peterson, *Heinrich Himmler, Geheimreden 1933 bis 1945*, Frankfurt, 1974, p. 61.
2 W. Runge and W. Schumann (eds), *Dokumente zur Deutschen Geschichte 1936–39*, Frankfurt, 1973, pp. 124–5.
3 Smith and Peterson, *op. cit.*, pp. 160–1.
4 G. S. Graber, *History of the SS*, London, 1996, p. 82.
5 J. Ackerman, *Heinrich Himmler als Ideologe*, Göttingen, 1970, p. 198.
6 Nuremberg Document 2284–PS.
7 Runge and Schumann, *op. cit.*, 124–5.
8 Abraham Katsch (ed.). *The Warsaw Diary of Chaim A. Kaplan*, New York, 1973, p. 14.

8. German anti-Jewish legislation

On 30 January 1933 Hitler became Chancellor of the German Republic. Swearing the oath of office, he declared: 'I will employ my strength for the welfare of the German people, protect the Constitution and laws of the German people, conscientiously discharge the duties imposed on me and conduct my affairs and office impartially and with justice to everyone'. The ensuing events, however, illustrated that Hitler had no intention of governing democratically. Quickly he took steps to ensure that he would be able to rule without opposition, and that the Jewish population in Germany would be subject to an increasing series of restrictions which deprived them of fundamental rights.

Onslaught against enemies of the State

As Chancellor, Hitler's first act was to persuade Hindenburg and the Cabinet to dissolve the *Reichstag* and institute new elections in the hope that the Nazis would achieve a majority. Germany, he proclaimed, was on the verge of a new awakening. On 4 February Hindenburg signed a decree under Article 48 which enabled police to prohibit public meetings and suppress subversive literature – this law was directed primarily against Communists and Socialists as well as other opponents of the NSDAP.

On 27 February, the *Reichstag* was set on fire, and a Dutch Communist, Marinus van der Lubbe, was discovered in the building. The Communists were blamed for the burning of the *Reichstag*, and several days later Hindenburg signed a number of emergency decrees which inadvertently led to the dissolution of the Constitution.

Designed to prevent further Communist acts of subversion, these edicts suspended freedom of speech, press and assembly as well as the freedom from invasion of privacy and house search. In order to protect public order, the death penalty was imposed for various crimes including treason, arson and railway sabotage.

In the days before the election, the Nazi Party swamped voters with propaganda, alleging that only by voting for the Nazis would a Communist revolution be thwarted. Despite such efforts, the NSDAP failed to win a majority of votes. As a consequence, the NSDAP was compelled to enter into a nationalist coalition with the DNVP (German National People's Party). After the election, the Nazis increased attacks on their opponents. The SA (Storm Troopers) numbering 400,000 intensified its assault against Communists, Socialists, trade unionists and Jews.

Prior to the opening of the *Reichstag*, the Cabinet approved an Enabling Act which gave the government dictatorial powers. This bill, which included the right to pass laws required to consolidate the 'National Revolution', required a two-thirds majority because it entailed a change in the Constitution. With the support of the Centre and Liberal parties, the Act was passed despite the opposition of the Socialists and Communists. With the Enabling Act in place, the Nazis were able to pass laws without the consent of the Parliament, even though this constituted a violation of the Constitution. Hence, from the beginning of Hitler's Chancellorship, democratic procedures were overturned, and parliamentary authority was discarded in favour of dictatorial control.

With the power to act independently, the Nazis were now able to initiate a campaign of harassment against German Jewry. In its manifesto of 1920, the Party stated that:

> Only nationals can be citizens of the State. Only persons of German blood can be nationals, regardless of religious affiliation. No Jew can therefore be a German national. ... If it is not possible to maintain the entire population of the State, then foreign nationals (non-citizens) are to be expelled from the Reich.

In the past, attempts had been made to incite the German people to embrace such a policy. These early attempts had largely failed, but with the power of the Enabling Act, Hitler was able to initiate legislation which would isolate German Jewry from public life. The first phase of this onslaught, beginning in April 1933 and continuing until the middle of 1935, excluded Jews from taking part in German professional and cultural life.

On 1 April 1933 the Nazis proclaimed a boycott against Jewish shops, businesses and professional services. Several days previously Hitler met with Goebbels, who had become the Minister of Public Enlightenment and Propaganda. In a record of this meeting, Goebbels wrote:

> We shall only be able to combat the falsehoods abroad if we get at those who originated them or at those Jews living in Germany who have thus far remained unmolested. We must, therefore, proceed to a large-scale boycott of all Jewish business in Germany. Perhaps the foreign Jews will think better of the matter when their racial comrades in Germany begin to get it in the neck.[1]

Prior to the boycott, the NSDAP leaders issued instructions for the boycott: all party units were to form local boycott committees. At this Cabinet meeting Hitler explained that an organized boycott was necessary to control popular opposition to the Jewish populace; to calm those in the Cabinet who feared an adverse public reaction, he stated that the boycott would last only one day. The Party's instructions were to avoid violence. In the event the boycott lasted three days: Storm Troopers were stationed outside Jewish businesses with pickets which read: 'Don't buy from Jews!'. In addition, anti-Jewish slogans were written on the windows of stores, and customers were verbally and physically abused. Commenting on the scene, Goebbels wrote in his diary: 'I drive along the ... street in order to observe the situation. All Jews' businesses are closed. SA men are posted outside the entrances. The public has everywhere proclaimed its solidarity. Discipline is exemplary. An imposing performance!'[2]

Some Jews reacted to such acts of terror with a defiant pride. Robert Weltsch, for example, the editor of a Zionist publication, called on his coreligionists to remain loyal to their community and heritage. In an editorial, *Wear the Yellow Badge with Pride*, he wrote:

> The first of April 1933 can be a day of Jewish awakening and Jewish rebirth. If the Jews will it so! ... This is a sound reminder to all our traitors. He who slinks away from his community in order to improve his personal position shall not earn the reward of his treason. ... The Jew who denies his Judaism is no better a citizen that he who affirms it

uprightly. To be a renegade is shameful enough. So long as the world seemed to reward this shame it seemed profitable. The profit is swept away. The Jew is rendered recognizable as such. He wears the yellow badge.[3]

This assault against Jewry was followed on 7 April 1933 by the first anti-Jewish law: the Restoration of the Professional Civil Service Act. This decree eliminated Jews and political opponents of the Nazi regime from the civil service. Hindenburg's objections to this law were met in a paragraph which exempted officials who had already been employed as civil servants on or before 1 August 1914, or who had fought at the front for Germany or her allies during World War I, or whose fathers or sons had been killed in action. On the same day another law cancelled the admission of lawyers of non-Aryan descent to the bar and denied permission to those already admitted to practise law – this regulation was subject to the same exemption as the Professional Civil Service Act.

These laws were followed by similar laws which excluded Jews from the positions of lay assessors, jurors and commercial judges, patent lawyers, panel physicians in state social-insurance institutions, dentists, and dental technicians associated with these institutions. On 21 April a law was promulgated banning Jewish ritual slaughter (*shehitah*). Several days later the Law against the Overcrowding of German Schools and Institutions of Higher Learning limited the number of non-Aryan students. An accompanying edict fixed this limit at 1.5 per cent. This meant that the Jewish community would henceforth be responsible for the education of Jewish pupils in segregated schools.

On 6 May the Law for the Restoration of the Professional Civil Service was extended to honorary professors, university lecturers and notaries. On 10 May a campaign against disaffected writers, academics and intellectuals was initiated. A public burning of un-German literature was organized in Berlin – all books written or published by Jews or which dealt sympathetically with the Jewish tradition were consigned to the flames. On 14 July a law was passed which cancelled the citizenship of any German who had been naturalized after 1918. This was designed to disenfranchize the 100,000 Jews who had taken refuge in Germany from anti-Semitism in other lands.

This was followed on 28 September by a law which forbade the employment by government authorities of non-Aryans or of persons married to them. On 29 September the Hereditary Farm Act was passed which declared that only those farmers who could prove that their ancestors had no Jewish blood as far back as 1800 could inherit farm property. In addition, the Reich Chamber of Culture was established which aimed to bring all the country's cultural activities under control. The result of such legislation was the elimination of all non-Aryans from German cultural life. On 4 October, political papers came under state control. Hence within only six months the Nazis had restricted public life in Germany to Aryans: through a series of legal decrees, Jews had been removed from all positions in society.

Such segregation was facilitated through a decree promulgated on 11 April which defined a non-Aryan as anyone who was descended from non-Aryan, especially Jewish, parents or grandparents. Such descent was categorized as non-Aryan even if only one parent or grandparent was non-Aryan, especially if the person was of the Jewish faith. Thus, in cases of racial ambiguity, religious affiliation was crucial. In cases of uncertainty, it was necessary to obtain an opinion from the expert on racial research who was attached to the Reich Minister of the Interior.

Through such anti-Jewish legislation, Hitler had managed to consolidate his power within the state. Yet he was facing opposition from within the party itself. The SA under the leadership of Ernst Röhm constituted a major obstacle to Hitler's dictatorial control. Even though Röhm had been intimately involved in the rise of Nazism, he had grave doubts about the direction of the party. Fearing that Hitler was prepared to sell out to the conservatives, he was bitterly critical of the Führer:

Adolf is rotten. He's betraying all of us. He only goes around with reactionaries. His old comrades aren't good enough for him. So he brings in these East Prussian generals. They're the ones he pals around with now. ... But Adolf is and will always be a civilian, an 'artist', a dreamer. Just leave me be, he thinks. Right now all he wants to do is sit up in the mountains and play God. And guys like us have to cool our heels, when we're burning for action. ... The chance to do something really new and great, something that will turn the world upside down – it's a chance in a lifetime. But Hitler keeps putting me off. He wants to let things drift. Keeps counting on a miracle. That's Adolf for you. ... Where the hell is revolutionary spirit to come from afterwards? From a bunch of old fogies who certainly aren't going to win the new war.

Don't try to kid me, the whole lot of you. You're letting the whole heart and soul of our movement go to pot.[4]

Fearing the excesses of the SA, Hitler resolved on a course of action which eventually resulted in the elimination of the SA. Goaded by Röhm's opponents, Hitler became convinced that Röhm was plotting a coup and resolved to take action. On 1 July 1934 Hitler left Bonn for Munich where he was told that the SA had attempted an unsuccessful putsch. Hitler then drove to Bad Wiessee where Röhm and his men were staying at the Hotel Hanselbauer. Hitler and other Nazis stormed into the hotel and arrested Röhm. Meanwhile in Munich, SA men were rounded up. On Hitler's return to the city, a secret order was given to execute political opponents. Murder squads tortured and executed those whose names had been placed on death lists by Göring and Himmler. Röhm, too, was assassinated.

This event, the Night of the Long Knives, cleansed the party of potential opponents to Hitler's rule. The German people were informed that Röhm had been plotting against the party. Newspapers reported that Hitler had put an end to immoral homosexual activity within the ranks of the SA. The Führer declared that he had rescued the nation and prevented the loss of thousands of lives. In a speech in the *Reichstag* on 13 July, he justified his actions and the delegates applauded this bloodbath. To the army he proclaimed that from this time forward only the army would be the bearer of arms. The *Reichstag* then passed a decree that legalized this killing as an emergency measure necessary for state security. Joining in this rejoicing, Hindenburg sent Hitler a telegram congratulating him on this suppression of treason.

In the wake of these events, Hindenburg died. On 2 August, just an hour after his death, it was decreed that the office of President would be merged with that of Chancellor – this meant that Hitler was now established as head of state and commander of the armed forces. All German soldiers then swore a personal oath to the Führer in which they stated their obedience and loyalty to the new regime which had overcome its opponents and become the supreme power in the land:

I swear before God this sacred oath: I will render unconditional obedience to Adolf Hitler, the Führer of the German nation and people, Supreme Commander of the Armed Forces, and will be ready as a brave soldier to risk my life at any time for this oath.[5]

Discussion: Tightening of the noose

For Hitler, the NSDAP was more than a political party: it represented the hope for a new civilization based on race. Once Hitler was sworn in as Chancellor, it became possible for the Nazis to put their ideology into practice. At the core of Nazi social policy was the quest to rid Germany of a Jewish presence. As we have seen, the emergence of political anti-Semitism was a response to social and intellectual developments within Germany in the pre-war period. By the 1930s the Jewish community had become an easy target for the discontent and disorientation felt by many Germans in the wake of rapid industrialization and urbanization. Within German society Jews were easily identifiable, and much resented because of their relative success and affluence. By 1933, for example, Jews composed more than 16 per cent of lawyers, 10 per cent of doctors, and 5 per cent of editors and writers even though they constituted less than 1 per cent of the population.

From 1933 the assault against Jewry was gradual, and the early forms of persecution gave no indication of what was to follow. For many ordinary Germans, such agitation was no more than the Jews deserved. And, once the Nazis were firmly entrenched, any form of opposition – either from within the Jewish community or from sympathetic non-Jews – became totally impractical. Paradoxically, in such an environment of hatred and fear, it became possible for many Germans to harbour anti-Semitic sentiments while retaining positive relationships with individual Jews. As Melita Maschmann remarked in her memories of this period:

> I had learned from the example of my parents that one could have anti-Semitic opinions without this interfering in one's personal relations with individual Jews. There may be a vestige of tolerance in this attitude, but it is really just this confusion which I blame for the fact that I later contrived to dedicate body and soul to an inhuman political system, without this giving me doubts about my own individual decency. In preaching that all the misery of the nations was due to the Jews or that the Jewish spirit was seditious and Jewish blood corrupting, I was not compelled to think of you or old Herr Lewy or Rosel Cohn: I thought only of the bogey-man, 'The Jew'. And when I heard the Jews were being driven from their professions and homes and imprisoned in ghettos, the points switched automatically in my mind to steer me round the thought that such a fate could also overtake you or

old Lewy. It was only the Jew who was being persecuted and 'made harmless'.[6]

In 1933 it was impossible to predict the reign of terror that would be visited upon European Jewry during the Holocaust. In his autobiography completed before his execution after the end of the war, Rudolf Hoess, the commandant at Auschwitz, related events that no one could have anticipated during the early years of Nazi rule:

> I had to appear cold and indifferent to events which must have wrung the heart of anyone possessed of human feelings. ... I had to watch coldly while the mothers with laughing or crying children went to the gas chambers. ... I had to see everything. I had to watch hour by hour, by night and by day, the burning and the removal of bodies, the extraction of the teeth, the cutting of the hair, the whole grisly business. ... I had to do all this, because I was the one to whom everyone looked, because I had to show them all that I did not merely issue the orders and make the regulations but was also prepared to be present at whatever task I had assigned to my subordinates. ... In the face of such grim considerations, I would bury all human considerations as deeply as possible. ... I had to observe everything with a cold indifference. ... In Auschwitz, I truly had no reason to complain that I was bored. ... I had only one end in view, to drive everyone and everything forward, so that I could accomplish the measures laid down. ... Every German had to commit himself heart and soul, so that we might win the war. ... By the will of the *Reichsführer SS*, Auschwitz became the greatest human extermination centre of all time.[7]

At the beginning of Hitler's Chancellorship who could have predicted the tragedy that would unfold in the ensuing years?

One central question about this sequence of events continues to vex scholars of the Nazi period: what was the role of Hitler in the assault against European Jewry? According to historians of the 'intentionalist' school, Hitler was committed to the extermination of the Jewish people early in his political career. The Führer, they argue, willed their destruction. On the other hand, historians of the 'structuralist' school reject the view that Hitler had a long-term plan for the annihilation of Jewry. The Final Solution, they believe, was implemented as a consequence of the inner momentum of the Third Reich. According to this interpretation, responsibility for the Final Solution extends beyond Hitler to those who implemented this policy. In this regard, they stress that there is no concrete evidence that Hitler gave the order for mass murder.

Whatever the true interpretation of Hitler's role in the Final Solution, there is no question that the massacre against the SA was directly ordered by the Führer. While legislation aimed at depriving German Jews of their role in society was being promulgated, Hitler embarked on a murderous course of action against his own supporters. On 29 June 1934, while making a tour of labour camps in Westphalia, he made the final decision to act against the SA. At two o'clock the next morning, he took off from the Hangelar airfield near Bonn to fly to Munich. Before his departure, he telegraphed Röhm to expect to see him at Bad Wiessee the next day where he was enjoying his sick leave with SA companions.

The purge, however, had already begun. On 29 June various SA local leaders were arrested in Munich on the pretext that they were about to initiate a coup d'état. At the Ministry of the Interior, Hitler tore off the insignias of SA *Obergruppenführer* Schneidhuber and his deputy and cursed them for their deceit. The next day a column of cars sped from Munich to Bad Wiessee where Heines, the SA *Obergruppenführer* for Silesia was discovered sleeping with one of Röhm's men. According to accounts he was dragged out and shot on the road. In Munich itself, about 800 men of Sepp Dietrich's SS *Leibstandarte* Adolf Hitler were transported from their barracks and ordered to act as a shooting squad at the Stadelheim Prison.

Hitler ordered that a revolver be left in Röhm's cell, but Röhm refused to use it. According to an eye-witness, Röhm declared: 'If I am to be killed, let Adolf do it himself'. In the 1957 Munich trial of all those involved, it was revealed that he was shot by two SS officers. Röhm wanted to say something, but he was ordered to remain silent. Röhm then stripped to the waist and was killed. In Berlin, killings began on the night of 29–30 June, continuing throughout Saturday and Sunday. The main place of killing was the Lichterfelde Cadet School where leaders of the SA were executed. In addition, General von Schleicher and his wife were shot at their villa, as was General von Bredow. Gregor Strasser was arrested on Saturday and killed in the Prinz Albrechtstrasse Prison.

When Hitler returned to Munich on Saturday, Himmler gave him a list of those who had been killed; Hitler's finger moved down the list while Göring and Himmler spoke at his side. On Sunday the executions continued while Hitler gave a tea party in the Chancellery garden. During this period, as many as 54 men were shot in Breslau, and another 32 in Silesia. Here, there is no question that Hitler was the driving force behind this murderous activity. The Night of the Long Knives was a powerful illustration of the Nazi capacity for violence and bloodshed, a lesson learned too late by many Jews who continued to live in Germany and long for better days.

Notes

1 Lucy Dawidowicz, *The War Against the Jews*, London, 1990, p. 82.
2 R. Landau, *The Nazi Holocaust*, London, 1992, p. 25.
3 *Ibid.*, p. 124.
4 Klaus P. Fischer, *Nazi Germany*, London, 1995, p. 286.
5 *Ibid.*, p. 293.
6 Geoff Layton, *Germany and the Third Reich 1933–45*, London, 1998, p. 91.
7 *Ibid.*, p. 93.

9. The Nuremberg Laws

Legislation against the Jewish community culminated in the Nuremberg Laws which redefined German citizenship, prohibited the pollution of the race, and required couples to undergo medical examinations prior to marriage. These laws provided a legal justification for racial anti-Semitism and transformed the notion of German blood into an official government policy.

Legislating citizenship

Segregation between the races had been a feature of German anti-Semitism since the nineteenth century. Theodor Fritsch, for example, advocated the separation between Aryans and Jews in his *Antisemiten-Katechismus* which contained two commandments for maintaining racial purity:

> Thou shalt keep thy blood pure. Consider it a crime to soil the noble Aryan breed of thy people by mingling it with the Jewish breed. For thou must know that Jewish blood is everlasting, putting the Jewish stamp on body and soul unto the farthest generations.
> Thou shalt have no social intercourse with the Jew. Avoid all contact and community with the Jew and keep him away from thyself and thy family, especially thy daughters, lest they suffer injury of body and soul.[1]

In *Mein Kampf*, Hitler expressed similar racial ideas. 'Blood sin and desecration of the race are the original sin in this world and the end of a humanity which surrenders to it,' he wrote.[2] According to Hitler, marriage is not an end in itself – rather it should serve the higher goal of increasing and preserving species and race. 'A folkish state,' he insisted, 'must therefore begin by raising marriage from the

85

level of continuous defilement of the race, and give it the consecration of an institution which is called upon to produce images of the Lord and not monstrosities half-way between man and ape.'[3]

In line with this view, Göring stated in a campaign speech given in June 1932 that Jews would be removed from government offices and public life, and that the Nazis would prohibit marriages between Germans and Jews. The following year, a Law for the Reduction of Unemployment was issued which contained a section, Encouragement of Marriages, which offered financial aid to needy young couples who wished to marry. Candidates for such aid had to submit certificates which demonstrated their personal and racial health; in addition they had to pass a test which evaluated their loyalty to the state.

Embracing such a racial policy, the mayor of Mainz instructed the Mainz Registry Office in October 1933 to inform him of any impending marriage of a person of German origin with a Jew. This information was to be given to the regional office of the NSDAP so that the Party could suggest to the German partner that he or she should reconsider this decision. The Registry Office was to emphasize the problems that such a marriage could cause for both the individuals involved and their offspring. Such a policy became widespread throughout Germany once the Nazis had acceded to power.

In the same year Wilhelm Frick, Minister of the Interior, declared at the first meeting of the Council of Experts on Population and Race Policy:

> Only when the State and the public health authorities strive to make the core of their responsibilities the provision for the yet unborn, then we can speak of a new era and of a reconstructed population and race policy.[4]

For Frick, it was vital that those afflicted with serious hereditary diseases should be prevented from reproducing themselves. To ensure this would not occur, a law legalizing sterilization for nine categories of people afflicted with hereditary disease was promulgated on 14 July 1933. As a result, numerous institutions were established to ensure that racial breeding and purification would take place.

In line with such racial attitudes, Helmut Nicolai, President of Magdeburg, published his ideas of draft legislation for citizenship in the Third Reich. In his view, there were four types of individuals: full-blooded Aryan citizens, foreigners living in the country, Germans residing abroad, and Germans of alien blood such as Jews, Poles and gypsies. In his view, the fourth type should have state protection, but should not be allowed to hold public office, marry or have sexual relations with Aryans. On 27 July, 1935, Frick wrote to all states informing them that marriages between Aryans and non-Aryans would soon come under government legislation. On 13 September, Hitler stated that he wished such legislation for the ceremonial session of the *Reichstag* on 15 September.

Hans Pfundtner and Wilhelm Stuckart from the Ministry of the Interior were put in charge of this task, and they were joined by Bernhard Lösener, the expert on racial law in the Ministry. On 14–15 September, they drafted various bills which Frick took to Hitler for approval. Hitler then asked them to prepare a basic Reich citizenship law. At the Nuremberg Rally, these laws were adopted, radically affecting the status of German Jews. On the final day a session of the *Reichstag* took place which ratified new legislation concerning the new Reich Citizenship Law.

This Law for the Protection of German Blood and Honour was designed to protect the German nation from racial impurity:

> Entirely convinced that the purity of German blood is essential to the further existence of the German people, and inspired by the uncompromising determination to safeguard the future of the German nation, the *Reichstag* has unanimously adopted the following law, which is promulgated herewith:
>
> I. 1. A subject of the State is a person who belongs to the protective union of the German Reich, and who therefore has particular obligations towards the Reich.
>
> 2. The status of the subject is acquired in accordance with the provisions of the Reich and State Law of Citizenship.
>
> II. 1. A citizen of the Reich is that subject only who is of German or kindred blood and who, through his conduct, shows that he is both desirous and fit to serve the German people and Reich faithfully.
>
> 2. The right to citizenship is acquired by the granting of Reich citizenship papers.

3. Only the citizen of the Reich enjoys full political rights in accordance with the provision of the laws.

III. The Reich Minister of the Interior in conjunction with the Deputy Führer will issue the necessary legal and administrative decrees for carrying out and supplementing this law.[5]

In defence of the Nuremberg Laws, Dr Wilhelm Stuckart and Dr Hans Globke of the Reich Ministry of the Interior stated:

National Socialism opposes to the theories of the equality of all men and of the fundamentally unlimited freedom of the individual vis-à-vis the State, the harsh but necessary recognition of the inequality of men and of the differences between them based on the laws of nature. Inevitably, differences in the rights and duties of the individual derive from the differences in character between races, nations and peoples.[6]

The belief that Jews were at least marginally protected as second-class citizens under this new legislation proved to be an illusion. During this period Frick dismissed servants who were descended from three or four grandparents who were full Jews. In this way he removed the exclusion clauses which had been included in the Civil Service Law of 7 April 1933. In the weeks following Nuremberg, state officials discussed the question of how to define Jewishness. On 14 November 1935 the First Supplementary Decree of the Reich Citizenship Law listed a series of regulations:

I. 1. Until further regulations regarding citizenship papers are issued, all subjects of German or kindred blood who possessed the right to vote in the *Reichstag* elections at the time the Citizenship Law came into effect, shall for the time being possess the rights of Reich citizens. The same shall be true of those to whom the Reich Minister of the Interior, in conjunction with the Deputy of the Führer, has given provisional citizenship.

2. The Reich Minister of the Interior, in conjunction with the Deputy of the Führer, can withdraw the provisional citizenship.

II. 1. The regulations in Article I are also valid for Reich subjects of mixed Jewish blood (*Mischlinge*).

2. An individual of mixed Jewish blood is one who is descended from one or two grandparents who were

racially full Jews, in so far as he or she does not count as Jewish according to Article V, paragraph 2. A grandparent shall be considered as full-blooded if he or she belonged to the Jewish religious community.

III. 1. Only the Reich citizens, as bearers of full political rights, exercise the right to vote in political affairs or can hold public office. The Reich Minister of the Interior, or any agency empowered by him, can make exceptions during the transition period, with regard to occupation of public office. The affairs of religious organizations will not be affected.

IV. 1. A Jew cannot be a citizen of the Reich. He has no right to vote in political affairs, and he cannot occupy public office.

2. Jewish officials will retire as of 31 December 1935. If these officials served at the front in the world war, either for Germany or her allies, they will receive in full, until they reach the age limit, the pension to which they were entitled according to the salary they last received; they will, however, not advance in seniority. After reaching the age limit, their pensions will be calculated anew, according to the salary last received, on the basis of which their pension was computed.

3. The affairs of religious organizations will not be affected.

4. The conditions of service of teachers in Jewish public schools remain unchanged until the new regulations for the Jewish school systems are issued.

V. 1. A Jew is anyone who is descended from at least three grandparents who are racially full Jews. Article II, para. 2, second sentence will apply.

2. A Jew is one who is descended from two full Jewish grandparents, if (a) he belonged to the Jewish religious community at the time this law was issued, or joins the community later, (b) he was married to a Jewish person, at the time the law was issued, or marries one subsequently, (c) he is the offspring of a marriage with a Jew, in the sense of Section 1, which was contracted after the Law for the Protection of German Blood and Honour became effective, (d) he is the offspring of an extramarital relationship with a Jew, according to Section 1, and will be born out of wedlock after 31 July 1936.

VI. 1. Requirements for the pureness of blood as laid down in Reich Law or in orders of the NSDAP and its echelons – not covered in Article 5 – will not be affected.

2. Any other requirements for the pureness of blood not covered in Article V can be made only by permission of the Reich Minister of the Interior and the Deputy Führer. If any such demands have been made, they will be void as of 1 January 1936, if they have not been requested by the Reich Minister of the Interior in agreement with the Deputy Führer. These requests must be made by the Reich Minister of the Interior.

VII. 1. The Führer and Reich Chancellor can grant exemptions from the regulations laid down in the law.[7]

Discussion: Harassment and emigration

From 1933, culminating in the promulgation of the Nuremberg Laws, the Jewish population in Germany came under increasing assault. Year by year their civil rights were undermined, and German Jewry was compelled to create its own institutional structure. Under such circumstances, many Jews emigrated although a substantial number remained. Of the 525,000 Jews residing in Germany when Hitler became Chancellor, approximately a third left the country before *Kristallnacht*, and another third left during the following ten months. Compared with other Jewish communities, German Jewry was fortunate. Nearly 3 million Polish Jews were killed by German troops, and over 700,000 Russian Jews died in the Nazi onslaught. Some 400,000 Jews in Hungary were murdered, and in Austria, approximately half of the Jewish population of 200,000 perished.

Comparatively, then, German Jews did not suffer the same fate as other European communities. Yet why was there a reluctance to leave the country once the Nazis had attained power? Initially many Jews believed it would be possible to achieve some form of rapprochement with Hitler. In the first weeks of his chancellorship, Hitler sought to mollify non-Nazi conservatives and moderates while ridding the country of all left-wing opposition. As a group, German Jews desired peace and stability and Hitler's vision of a *Volksgemeinschaft* under Nazi leadership offered the possibilities of a strong and united Reich.

With the exception of Jewish Communists and socialists, German Jewry believed that it would be possible to continue to prosper under Nazism just as Italian Jews had survived Mussolini's rule. Various Jewish groups embraced the notion of national renewal; others found in the ascendancy of Nazism the framework for economic renewal. Those repelled by street fighting and sporadic violence looked to strong rule as necessary for social stability. Other assimilated and patriotic Jews looked to Hitler to restore Germany to its place among the nations. Liberals, on the other hand, believed that Nazis would eventually adopt a more reasonable political stance. The Zionists, too, believed that Nazism would encourage a return to the Holy Land. Such aspirations, however, were quickly undermined by anti-Jewish legislation. Yet, rather than encourage foreign protest against their plight, Jewish leaders feared Nazi reprisals.

For some Jews, the assault against German Jewry was not perceived as a calamity, but rather an opportunity for Jewish self-discovery and revival. As we have seen, for example, the Zionist journalist Robert Weltsch responded to the boycott against Jewish shops with the article *Wear the Yellow Badge With Pride* in which he encouraged Jews to affirm their Jewishness. Other Jews simply hoped that Hitler would adopt a more moderate course. The Jewish establishment, as represented by Leo Baeck, the head of the *Reichsvertretung*, called for community effort to help the unfortunate. In his view, educational and social facilities would enable the Jewish community to withstand this assault.

Initially adopting a policy of appeasement, Baeck and others engaged in dialogue with the government. In May 1933 Baeck declared that German Jews should join with the Nazis in rejecting Communism and accept that the renewal of Germany was a desirable goal. Such a strategy, however, failed to alter Nazi aspirations; in consequence, Jewish leaders sought to improve German Jewish life. What was needed, they believed, was a cohesive and self-supporting community which would encompass all Jews regardless of religious affiliation. Unity, they believed, was their only weapon against government directives.

For Baeck and others, emigration could only save a small segment of the Jewish population. Only very few Jews had the desire to leave Germany, and few could establish a new life abroad. Moreover, the practical difficulties of relocating half a million Jews was overwhelming. Leaving Germany was a solution only for younger Jews or those who were politically suspect. Hence, the only conceivable response to Nazi persecution was to find some form of accommodation with Nazism. In Baeck's view, Jewish unity was fundamental to ensure that members of the community would not engage in internal dispute. In the light of the public response to Weltsch's call for Jewish renewal, Jewish leaders advocated the creation of a central Jewish organization which would be composed of representatives of the various factions within German Jewry.

With the Nazi definition of Jewishness, it became clear that there was no way of escaping the Nazi onslaught. For Weltsch, there was now only one course of action. In an essay published on 16 May 1933, *Saying 'Yes' to Judaism*, he wrote:

> Nowadays the Jews' sense of belonging together is being strengthened. Jews who until recently passed by each other without a word of acknowledgement or mutual recognition have been drawn closer to each other. One thinks of another Jew as someone who shares the same fate, as a brother. Jews can speak to one another once again. .... A moment like this is a fruitful, holy moment, which can lift our hearts and create a community.[8]

For many Jews, ambivalence about emigrating became increased. The fear about loss of work or arrest gave way to consideration about ways to endure the Nazi regime. As the bonds of unity became greater, many Jews found it increasingly difficult to contemplate leaving Germany. Such feelings of uncertainty were aggravated by Hitler's apparent moderation during the period after the April 1933 boycott. In addition, the Law for the Restoration of the Professional Civil Service was not as devastating as had been feared. Only about 25,000 families were affected, leaving approximately 200,000 Jews who engaged in business unscathed. Moreover, the fact that this law stipulated that those who had begun their careers before 1918, who had fought in the army, or whose fathers or sons had been killed in battle, were exempt enabled many Jews to keep their jobs.

Some Jews came to the conclusion that Hitler might leave the community alone; indeed, he might even recognize that Germany needed its Jewish population. Possibly Nazism might not stay in power long. Speculation of this nature served as a deterrent to emigration. Leaving Germany was a final act – possibly it would not be necessary after all. At this stage it was not difficult to forsake

Germany, but there was a general reluctance to depart. Tragically, such hesitation was intensified by the fact that numerous Jewish émigrés who had fled abroad returned to Germany now that the Nazi revolution appeared to have ebbed.

During this confusing period the energies of the Jewish establishment were directed towards preserving and strengthening German Jewry. Figures like Baeck, who were privately convinced that Jews in Germany had no future, nonetheless sought to console the Jewish community. In a lecture given at a Munich synagogue in April 1934, he declared that Jews should not break the endless chain of generations any more than they could sever their links to God. Repeatedly Baeck called upon German Jewry to unite together to face the Nazi menace.

A year after Hitler's seizure of power, only one tenth of the Jewish population had departed. Most Jews were reluctant to leave, believing that the Nazi onslaught had reached its zenith. Even though they were hemmed in by over 300 laws and regulations restricting Jewish life, many continued to hope for better times. Although Jews ceased to have equal rights with German Aryan citizens, the majority retained their means of livelihood. In addition, the community under threat had drawn closer, and took comfort from such contact. What was required, many believed, was forbearance in the face of continuing hostility.

A sizeable number of Jews believed that by withdrawing from German public life, it would be possible to avoid further degradation. Yet such appeasement and retreat did not bear fruit. The vast majority clung to the belief that the law would restrain the Nazis. Urging restraint, Baeck continued to console the community for its loss and sought to persuade Jewry to engage in communal activities which would bind Jews closer to one another. Such advice was given in the expectation that despondent Jews would be able to find a common purpose. In the autumn of 1934, Baeck stated: 'We have passed a decisive test. ... We have been and remain loyal citizens of the state'.[9]

The Night of the Long Knives, however, brought about a crisis of confidence. The violence of this event coupled with Hindenburg's death led to despair. Appeasement of the Nazis no longer seemed a viable option. Nonetheless, many Jews believed that life could go on. Such optimism was shattered by the promulgation of the Nuremberg Laws. Through such legislation the Nazi Party had made its intention clear: Jews were to be denied their full political rights as citizens. The Nuremberg Laws meant in effect that Jews would no longer be able to look to German law or the courts for protection. To guard the purity of the blood, Jews were to be segregated from their neighbours.

Paradoxically, the reaction of the German Jewish community was divided. The Jewish establishment immediately issued a blueprint for planned Jewish life in the light of these new laws. It was now possible, they believed, for the Jewish community to develop along independent lines with its own institutions. Writing to Hitler, the *Reichsvertretung*'s leaders asked for their organization to be given official recognition. Other Jews, however, saw the Nuremberg Laws as the final nail in the coffin of Jewish life in Germany. There was no turning back, they believed; what was now required was emigration to Palestine before it was too late.

Notes

1 Lucy Dawidowicz, *The War Against the Jews*, London, 1990, p. 96.
2 *Ibid.*, p. 96.
3 *Ibid.*, p. 96.
4 *Ibid.*, p. 97.
5 RGB1. I (1935), pp. 1146ff in J. Noakes and G. Pridham (eds), *Nazism 1919–1945*, Exeter, 1995, pp. 536–7.
6 'Reichsbürgergesetz-Blutschutzgesetz-Ehegesundheitsgesetz' nebst allen Ausführungsvorschriften und den einschlägigen Gesetzen und Verordnungen. Erläutert von Staatssekretär Dr. Stuckart und Dr. Globke. *Kommentare zur deutschen Rassengesetzgebung Bd. I*, Munich-Berlin, 1936, p. 25.
7 RGB1. I (1935), p. 1333 in Noakes and Pridham, *op. cit.*, pp. 538–9.
8 John Dippel, *Bound Upon a Wheel of Fire*, New York, 1996, p. 109.
9 *Ibid.*, p. 147.

10. *Kristallnacht*

On 12 March 1938 Hitler triumphantly drove into Austria where he was greeted by cheering crowds – the multitude was ecstatic to see their country incorporated into the German Reich. Following this victory, Hitler turned his attention to Czechoslovakia. Throughout the summer Hitler demanded the cession of the Sudetenland to the German Reich. This German-speaking area of Czechoslovakia had never been included in Germany, but before 1914 it was part of the Austro-Hungarian empire. Once Austria was absorbed into the Reich, Hitler maintained that this area should be annexed as well. In September 1938 the British, French and Italians agreed to this demand – the Sudetenland was to become part of Greater Germany on 10 October. These events served as the background to the onslaught against German Jewry.

The Night of Broken Glass

On 27 October 1938, Hitler expelled 18,000 Jews living in Germany who had been born in the former Polish provinces of the Russian empire. One of these Jews was Zindel Grynszpan who had been born in Radomsko in Russian Poland in 1886. Since 1911 he had resided with his family in Hanover; his son Hirsch Grynszpan, however, had gone to study in Paris. Zindel later recalled these events:

> On the 27th October 1938 – it was Thursday night at eight o'clock – a policeman came and told us to come to Region II. He said, 'You are going to come back immediately; you shouldn't take anything with you. Take with you your passports.' When I reached the Region, I saw a large number of people; some people were sitting, some standing. People were crying; they were shouting, 'Sign, sign, sign.' I had to sign, as all of them

did. ... They took us to the concert hall on the banks of the Leine and there, there were people from all the areas, about 600 people. There we stayed until Friday night; about 24 hours; then they took us in police trucks, in prisoners' lorries, about twenty men in each truck, and they took us to the railway station. The streets were black with people shouting, 'The Jews out to Palestine.' After that, when we got to the train, they took us by train. ... Together we were about 12,000 people. When we reached the border, we were searched to see if anybody had any money, and anybody who had more than ten Marks, the balance was taken from him. ... The SS were giving us, as it were, protective custody, and we walked two kilometres on foot to the Polish border. They told us to go – the SS men were whipping us, those who lingered they hit, and blood was flowing on the road. ... When we got to the open border – we reached what was called the green border, the Polish border – first of all, the women went in. ... The rain was driving hard, people were fainting – some suffered heart attacks.[1]

When Zindel Grynszpan sent a postcard to his son in Paris, the young man went to the German Embassy in Paris and shot the first German official he encountered, Ernst vom Rath. Hitler and Nazi leaders denounced this act as part of a Jewish conspiracy; this led to a wave of violence against the entire German Jewish community. Fires were lit throughout the country, and Jewish buildings were set on fire and demolished. Subsequently the Nazi Party Supreme Court composed a secret report describing these incidents:

On the evening of 9 November 1938, Reich Propaganda Director and Party Member Dr Goebbels told the Party leaders assembled at a social evening in the old town hall in Munich that in the districts of Kurhessen and Magdeburg-Anhalt there had been anti-Jewish demonstrations, during which Jewish shops were demolished and synagogues were set on fire. The Führer at Goebbels' suggestion had decided that such demonstrations were not to be prepared or organized by the Party, but neither were they to be discouraged if they originated spontaneously. ... The oral instructions of the Reich Propaganda Director were probably understood by all the Party leaders present to mean that the Party should not appear outwardly as the originator of the demonstrations but that in reality it should organize them and carry them out. Instructions in this sense were telephoned immediately.[2]

One of those who witnessed such scenes of devastation was a young man from Holland, Wim van Leer, who was walking down the street in Leipzig and watched Storm Troopers besiege Jewish houses:

Suddenly third floor balcony window doors were flung open, and Storm Troopers appeared, shouting to their mates below. One yelled something about all blessings coming from above, and, in expectation, that part of the pavement beneath the balcony was cleared. Next they wheeled an upright piano on to the balcony and, smashing the balustrade with one mighty heave – there must have been eight of them – they pushed the piano over the edge. It nose-dived on to the street below with a sickening crash as the wooden casing broke away, leaving what looked like a harp standing in the middle of the debris.[3]

Another witness of *Kristallnacht* in Leipzig was the American Consul David Buffum. In his report on these events, he illustrated the savagery of this attack on the Jewish community:

The shattering of shop windows, looting of stores and dwellings of Jews which began in the early hours of 10 November 1938 was hailed subsequently in the Nazi press as a 'spontaneous wave of righteous indignation throughout German, as a result of the cowardly Jewish murder of Third Secretary vom Rath in the German Embassy at Paris'. ... At 3 a.m. on 10 November 1938 was unleashed a barrage of Nazi ferocity as had no equal hitherto in Germany, or very likely anywhere else in the world since savagery began. Jewish buildings were smashed into and contents demolished or looted. In one of the Jewish sections an 18-year-old boy was hurled from a third-storey window to land with both legs broken on a street littered with burning beds and other household furniture and effects from his family and apartments. This information was supplied by an attending physician. It is reported from another quarter that among domestic effects thrown out of a Jewish building a small dog descended four flights on to a cluttered street with a broken spine. ... One apartment of exceptionally refined occupants known to this office was violently ransacked, presumably in a search for valuables which was not in vain. ... Jewish shop windows by the hundreds were systematically and wantonly smashed throughout the entire city at a loss estimated at several millions of Marks. ... Three synagogues in Leipzig were fired simultaneously by incendiary bombs and all sacred objects and records desecrated or destroyed, in most cases hurled through the windows and burned in the streets. No attempts whatsoever were made to quench the fires, the activity of the fire brigade being confined to playing water on adjoining buildings. All of the synagogues were irreparably gutted by flames, and the walls of the two that are close to the consulate are now being razed. The blackened frames have been centres of attraction during the past week of terror for eloquently silent and bewildered crowds.[4]

Turning from these acts of violence, Buffum described the deportations to the concentration camps:

> The most hideous phase of the so-called 'spontaneous' action has been the wholesale arrest and transportation to concentration camps of male German Jews between the ages of 16 and 60, as well as Jewish men without citizenship. This has been taking place daily since the night of horror. This office has no way of accurately checking the numbers of such arrests, but there is very little question that they have run to several thousands in Leipzig alone. Having demolished dwellings and hurled most of the movable effects onto the streets, the insatiably sadistic perpetrators threw many of the trembling inmates into a small stream that flows through the Zoological Park, commanding horrified spectators to spit at them, defile them with mud and jeer at their plight.[5]

In towns and villages sacred objects, including Torah scrolls, prayerbooks and rabbinic texts, were thrown on to bonfires. In addition, synagogues were demolished – for this reason, this Nazi onslaught was called *Kristallnacht* (Night of Broken Glass). A typical example of such devastation took place in Höngen, a small village near Aachen. The nephew of the local butcher, Michael Lucas, recalled what had occurred:

> After a while, the Storm Troopers were joined by people who were not in uniform; and suddenly, with one loud cry of 'Down with the Jews', the gathering outside produced axes and heavy sledgehammers. They advanced towards the little synagogue which stood in Michael's own meadow, opposite his house. They burst the door open, and the whole crowd, by now shouting and laughing, stormed into the little House of God.
>
> Michael, standing behind the tightly drawn curtains, saw how the crowd tore the Holy Ark wide open; and three men who had smashed the ark threw the Scrolls of the Law of Moses out. He threw them – these Scrolls, which had stood in their quiet dignity, draped in blue or wine-red velvet, with their little crowns of silver covering the tops of the shafts by which the Scroll was held during the service – to the screaming and shouting mass of people which had filled the little synagogue. The people caught the Scrolls as if they were amusing themselves with a ball-game – tossing them up into the air again, while other people flung them further back until they reached the street outside. Women tore away the red and blue velvet and everybody tried to snatch some of the silver adorning the Scrolls.

Horrified by this scene, Michael Lucas was determined to rescue these sacred objects, but his wife pleaded with him to remain in the house. Remaining inside, he soon heard the sound of hammers:

Men had climbed on to the roof of the synagogue and were hurling the tiles down, others were cutting the cross-beams as soon as they were bare of cover. It did not take long before the first heavy grey stones came tumbling down, and the children of the village amused themselves as they flung stones into the many-coloured windows. When the first rays of a cold and pale November sun penetrated the heavy dark clouds, the little synagogue was but a heap of stone, broken glass and smashed-up woodwork.[6]

Among those Germans who reflected on these incidents was Melita Maschmann who was sympathetic to the animosity directed against German Jews:

Next morning ... I went into Berlin very early to go to the Reich Youth Leadership office. I noticed nothing unusual on the way. I alighted at the Alexanderplatz. In order to get to the Lothringerstrasse I had to go down a rather gloomy alley containing many small shops and inns. To my surprise almost all the shop windows here were smashed in. The pavement was covered with pieces of glass and fragments of broken furniture. I asked a patrolling policemen what on earth had been going on there. He replied: 'In this street they're almost all Jews'. 'Well?' 'You don't read the papers. Last night the National Soul boiled over.' I can remember only the sense but not the actual wording of this remark, which had an undertone of hidden anger. I went on my way shaking my head. ... I said to myself: 'The Jews are the enemies of the New Germany. Last night they had a taste of what this means. Let us hope that World Jewry, which has resolved to hinder Germany's "new steps towards greatness", will take the events of last night as a warning. If the Jews sow hatred against us all over the world, they must learn that we have hostages for them in our hands.'[7]

Not surprisingly *Kristallnacht* provoked vehement protests from abroad, and German goods were increasingly boycotted. The damage to property was approximately 25 million Marks. It appears that Hitler in collaboration with Goebbels decided to use this event as an opportunity to intensify action against the Jewish population. On 10 November 1938 Göring, Hitler and Goebbels discussed the technicalities of this new policy. Two days later Göring convened a conference to discuss this issue. Opening this meeting, Göring explained that he had received a letter written by Bormann, the chief of staff of the Führer's deputy on the order of the Führer requesting that the Jewish question be resolved. The problem, he emphasized, was economic in character.

If Jewish shops were destroyed, insurance companies would be compelled to cover the damage. At this point Goebbels intervened, urging that Jews should be eliminated from any positions in public life which might cause further provocations. What was necessary at this stage was for the Reich Ministry of Transport to decree that Jews and Germans must be separated from one another when travelling on trains. After debating the practicality of such legislation, Goebbels further recommended that there should be a law which barred Jews from German beaches, resorts and parks. In addition, he recommended that Jewish children should be removed from German schools.

The cost of *Kristallnacht* was borne partly by insurance companies and partly by the Jewish community. On 12 November Göring promulgated the Decree for the Restoration of the Street Scene in Relation to Jewish Business Premises:

> All damage which was inflicted on Jewish businesses and dwellings on 9 and 10 November 1938 as a result of the national indignation about the rabble-rousing propaganda of international Jewry against National Socialist Germany must at once be repaired by the Jewish proprietors of the Jewish businesses and dwellings affected. Insurance claims by Jews of German nationality will be confiscated for the benefit of the Reich.[8]

At the same time Göring sought to assist the rearmament programme by utilizing Jewish funds to increase the Reich's resources. On 12 November he issued a Decree Concerning Reparations from Jews of German Nationality:

> The hostile attitude of the Jews towards the German people and Reich which does not shrink even from cowardly murders, demands decisive resistance and heavy reparation. ... I therefore announce the following: (1) The Jews of German nationality are required to pay a contribution of RM 1 billion to the German Reich. A Jew can no longer be an employer within the meaning of the Law on the Organization of National Labour of 20 January 1934.

In addition, the law excluded Jews from German economic life:

I. 1. From 1 January 1939 the running of retail shops, mail-order houses and the practice of independent trades are forbidden to Jews.

2. Moreover, Jews are forbidden from the same date to offer goods and services in markets of all kinds, fairs or exhibitions or to advertise them or accept orders for them.

3. Jewish shops which operate in violation of this order will be closed down by the police.

II. 1. No Jew can any longer be manager of an establishment as defined by the Law on the Organization of National Labour of 20 January 1934.

2. If a Jew is a leading employee in a business concern he may be dismissed at six weeks' notice. After the expiration of this period, all claims of employees derived from the denounced contract become invalid, especially claims for retirement or redundancy pay.

III. 1. No Jew can be a member of a cooperative society.

2. Jewish members of cooperatives lose their membership from 21 December 1938. No special notice is necessary.[9]

Following such legislation, further steps were taken to exclude Jews from public life. On 28 December 1938 Göring issued a decree concerning the Führer's decisions about the Jewish problem:

Section A

1. Housing of Jews
1(a) The law for the protection of tenants is not, as a rule, to be abrogated for the Jews. On the contrary, it is desired, if possible, to proceed in particular cases in such a way that the Jews are quartered together in separate houses in so far as the housing conditions will allow.
2. Use of sleeping and dining cars is to be forbidden to the Jews.
3. Only the use of certain public establishments is to be prohibited to the Jews. In this category belong the hotels and restaurants visited especially by Party members. The use of bathing establishments, certain public places, bathing resorts, etc., can be prohibited to Jews.[10]

A further section of this law introduced new restrictions in the case of intermarriages based on the criteria of the children's religious affiliation and which spouse was the Jewish partner in the marriage.

Discussion: Exploiting *Kristallnacht*

For the German population, *Kristallnacht* symbolically represented the power of the state against the enemy within. But for the Nazis there were more sinister motives. The destruction of Jewish property during the Night of Broken Glass provided an opportunity to ensure that Jews would no longer participate in the economic life of the country. The aim of the meeting convened by Göring on 12 November was to take all necessary measures to eliminate Jews from the German economy. Göring insisted that what should be done must be profitable to the Reich. During the discussion Funk asked whether Jewish stores should be reopened. In reply, Göring stated that the decision would be up to the Party. Within the week Funk issued a letter stating that Jewish businesses should not be reopened unless they were managed by non-Jews.

During the meeting the question was also raised about enacting legislation barring Jews from public places including theatres, cinemas, beaches, resorts, and sleeping car compartments on trains as well as expelling Jewish children from German schools. Only a few days later, on 15 November, the Ministry of Education passed a bill barring Jewish children from schools, and on 28 November Heydrich issued a decree signed by the Minister of the Interior allowing district authorities to impose a curfew on Jews. Several weeks later the Führer approved a proposal to ban Jews from most public places.

The meeting then turned to the question of compensation for damage done to Jewish property. A representative of German insurance companies reported on compensation for damages brought about by the demonstrations. It was decided that insurance companies must pay the damages, however the German government would confiscate these payments. In addition, German Jewry would be made liable for the damage caused. Heydrich then pointed out that even if Jews were eliminated from the economy, the Nazis were determined to rid Germany of the Jewish populace. In his view, forced emigration should take place, and they should wear some form of identification. Göring asked whether ghettos should be instituted, but Heydrich rejected this suggestion. A ghetto, he stressed, would serve as a permanent hideout for criminals. Göring, however, believed that ghettos would serve a useful purpose.

The meeting concluded with a discussion about appropriate

remuneration. Göring asked whether Jewry should have to contribute one billion Marks in compensation. No objections were raised to this proposal. Göring then remarked that he would not want to be a Jew in Germany, and stated: 'If in the near future the German Reich should come into conflict with foreign powers, it goes without saying that we in Germany should first of all let it come to a showdown with the Jews.'[11] The same afternoon, Göring took steps to remove Jews from various economic spheres of activity. The Decree on Eliminating Jews from German Economic Life eliminated Jews from working in retail stores or export mail-order firms, acting as craftsmen, selling goods and services, working as executives and managers in any firm, and being a member of a cooperative. Simultaneously Göring issued the Decree on the Penalty Payment by Jews Who Are German Subjects which imposed a one billion Mark fine because the 'hostile attitude of Jewry towards the German *Volk* and Reich, which does not shrink even from committing cowardly murder, necessitates determined resistance and harsh penalty'.[12]

Allegedly such legislation was designed to punish German Jews, but the clear aim was to confiscate money from the community. In his testimony at Nuremberg after the war, Göring stated that the fine was designed to relieve Germany of its financial difficulties, particularly in anticipation of war. This explanation is confirmed by the discussion that took place at a meeting of the Reich Defence Council six days later. During the meeting Göring stressed the critical situation of the Reich Exchequer, and explained that relief had initially been attained through the billion Marks imposed on Jewry and through profits which had accrued to the Reich through the Aryanization of Jewish enterprises.[13]

The law of 12 November had disastrous results for the Jewish community. Jews were compelled to sell their enterprises and valuables including jewellery and works of art. Such robbery which had already taken place in Austria now became commonplace in Germany. Jewish children were expelled from German schools because of their noxious presence. As the Secretary of State explained in a letter of 15 November addressed to all state and party agencies:

After the heinous murder in Paris one cannot demand of any German teacher to continue to teach Jewish children. It is also self-evident that it is unbearable for German schoolchildren to sit in the same classroom with Jewish children. Racial separation in schooling has already been accomplished in general over the last few years, but a remnant of Jewish children has stayed in German schools, for whom school attendance together with German boys and girls cannot be permitted any more. . . . I therefore order, effective immediately: Attendance at German schools is no longer permitted to Jews. They are allowed to attend only Jewish schools.[14]

Several days later Jews were excluded from the general welfare system, and on 28 November the Minister of the Interior instructed all federal state presidents that some areas could be forbidden to Jews. On 6 December all of Berlin's Jews were banned from theatres, cinemas, cabarets, concert and conference halls, museums, fairs, exhibition halls and bathing places. In addition, Jews living in Berlin were banned from the city districts where government offices and cultural institutions were located. During this time Jews were also deprived of their driving licences, and admission to university libraries was rescinded. Later in the month access was prohibited to dining and sleeping cars on trains and to public swimming pools and hotels that catered to party officials.

Kristallnacht thus marked a major transformation of Jewish existence in Germany. No longer was it possible for Jews to believe that Hitler would modify his previous anti-Semitic attitudes in the light of political considerations. On the contrary, the Nazi seizure of power enabled the Party to bring to fruition policies which had earlier been an essential ingredient of its programme. The role of German Jewry in the life of the nation had been dealt with through a series of restrictive legislation. What was now required was the emigration of Jewry itself. To this end, on 24 January 1939 Göring gave Heydrich the power to implement the type of forced emigration pioneered by Adolf Eichmann in Austria. A Reich Central Office for Jewish Emigration was established to promote the emigration of Jews from Germany by every possible means. However, the outbreak of war curtailed this process – as time passed it became clear that another solution to the Jewish problem would be needed in the future.

Notes

1   Testimony of Zindel Grynszpan, Eichmann Trial, 25 April 1961, session 14 in Martin Gilbert, *Holocaust*, London, 1987, pp. 67–8.

2   Nuremberg Document PS-3063.
3   Wim van Leer, *Time of My Life*, Jerusalem, 1984, pp. 166–8.
4   Nuremberg Document L-202.
5   *Ibid.*, p. 556.
6   Eric Lucas, *The Sovereigns*, Kibbutz Kfar Blum, Palestine, 1945, pp. 169–71.
7   M. Maschmann, *Account Settled*, London, 1964, pp. 56–7.
8   W. Hofer (ed.) *Der Natinalsozialismus: Dokumente 1933–45*, Frankfurt, 1957, p. 295.
9   RGB1. I (1930), p. 1580 in J. Noakes and G. Pridham (eds), *Nazism 1919–1945*, Exeter, 1995, p. 561.
10 Nuremberg Document PS-841.
11 Lucy Dawidowicz, *The War Against the Jews*, London, 1990, p. 139.
12 *Ibid.*, p. 140.
13 *Ibid.*, p. 140.
14 Saul Friedländer, *Nazi Germany and the Jews*, London, 1997, pp. 284–5.

11. The onslaught against Poland

In the decades following World War I, the United States adopted an isolationist policy and France and England came to play a dominant role in world affairs. Traditionally France had relied on Russia to curtail German expansion, but the Communist revolution undermined such determination. As a result, France established alliances with various newly created eastern nations. The British, on the other hand, were preoccupied with controlling their empire. In 1934 Hitler signed a treaty with Poland, promising to maintain peace for ten years, however only a few years later Germany broke this pledge and pushed forward into eastern territory as the first step in the quest for *Lebensraum*, living space for Germans in underpopulated areas of Eastern Europe.

Massacre of Polish Jewry

According to the Treaty of Versailles, East Prussia was to be separated from the rest of Germany. For many Germans the loss of this territory was a disaster. Hitler's non-aggression pact with Poland was therefore welcomed by the Poles as a sign that Germany had officially accepted the terms of the Treaty. The Nazis, however, had no intention of honouring this agreement. On 2 September 1939 they invaded Poland and approximately 2 million Jews came under German domination. In this attack Polish Jews suffered like their fellow compatriots. Yet the conquest of Poland resulted in the massacre of Polish Jewry and the eventual extermination of Eastern European Jewry in the Nazi drive for land in the east.

Aware of the dangers of invasion, Polish Jews sought to flee from the German onslaught. Thousands of Jews set out on foot, in carts and in waggons for safety. Those in small towns went to major cities; Jews in the cities fled to the country. All moved eastward towards Russia and Russian-held territory. These refugees were joined by thousands of ordinary Poles who also sought to find refuge. On 7 September, for example, during the siege of Warsaw the military issued an order for all able-bodied men to leave the city – about 100,000 men set out towards the east, believing Hitler's promise that he would not wage war against women and children.

Once the Germans occupied Poland, Jews were deported from hundreds of localities in the Warthegau, and expelled from thousands of towns and villages throughout the country to large cities. Within a few months of occupation, thousands of Jewish settlements disappeared, and their inhabitants were compelled to leave their homes with only the bare necessities. By the end of 1940, for example, Warsaw had absorbed 78,000 refugees from Lodz and Kalisz, and about 7,000 other localities in the Warthegau. Approximately 330,000 Jews had become refugees.

Once German troops entered a town or city, they confiscated Jewish property and businesses. Jewish shops were ordered to be opened so that looting could take place. In large manufacturing centres, goods were confiscated. In small communities Jews were compelled to hand over valuables at the threat of death. Hostages were also taken to ensure the extortion of vast sums of money from Jewish communities. Throughout the country, the Nazis burned down synagogues, and pogroms became commonplace. Violence and massacres occurred everywhere.

In this onslaught German troops employed *Blitzkrieg* tactics on the Polish population. By using swiftly moving spearheads, assault teams of infantry, and a system of air-to-ground coordination of fighter planes, the Nazis engaged in a lightning war involving 1 million infantry, 1500 fighter planes, and about 1000 tanks. In the early hours of 1 September the German forces penetrated into Polish territory. At nightfall thousands of Jews in Warsaw gathered together to celebrate the Sabbath. As one of those present remarked:

The Jews of Warsaw prayed as never before. The synagogue at Tlomackie Street was full to overflowing and large crowds stood and prayed outside. People cried to the Almighty to have pity on them and their children. They begged for mercy for themselves and all those who might die on the battlefield.[1]

On Sunday 3 September 1939, Britain and France declared war against Germany, but this did not slow down the German advance. As Germans occupied Polish towns and villages, Jews were murdered by SS operational groups. In the frontier town of Wieruszow, the SS seized twenty Jews, took them to the market place, and executed them. The following day more than 1000 Jews who had fled from Piotrkow to the neighbouring village of Sulejow were massacred as German bombers attacked the village. On 5 September the Germans entered Piotrkow, set fire to Jewish property, and shot Jews who sought to escape from the burning buildings.

In the first few days of the German advance, such attacks occurred throughout the country. At the village of Widawa, for example, the Germans ordered Rabbi Abraham Mordecai Morocco to burn sacred books; when he refused to comply, he was burned holding the Torah Scrolls. On 8 September Jews living in Bedzin were forced into the synagogue which was locked and set on fire. Several days later 35 Jews were arrested in communal baths, taken to the slaughterhouse, and burned to death. Repeatedly Nazi troops forced Jews to clear rubble, carry heavy loads, hand over jewellery and gold, and scrub lavatories with prayer shawls. Further, pious Jews had their beards and sidelocks cut off.

During the first two months of the German conquest of Poland 5000 Jews were murdered behind the lines. During the occupation of Pilica, for example, the Germans forced Jews, especially men, to work – they were to clean and collect dust with their hands. They were compelled to undress, and behind each Jewish man stood a soldier with a fixed bayonet who ordered him to run. If he stopped he would be hit. Almost all the men returned bleeding. A few days later large trucks appeared; soldiers jumped off, went from house to house, and seized men regardless of their age. They were then photographed and their names recorded. Then they were marched into the market place and forced to cry out in German 'We are traitors of the people'. Subsequently they were taken to the forest and shot.

While these events were taking place, a conference was held in Berlin to consider the fate of Polish Jewry. Hosting this gathering, Reinhard Heydrich explained that Polish Jews were to be concentrated in major urban locations, and removed from large areas of western Poland. Following this conference, Heydrich issued a directive concerning the Jewish question in the occupied territory which established the basis for the organization of Jews in the following years:

> I refer to the conference held in Berlin today, and again point out that the planned total measures are to be kept strictly secret.
> A distinction must be made between:
> 1. The final aim (which will require extended periods of time) and
> 2. the stages leading to the fulfilment of this final aim. ... The planned measures require the most thorough preparation with regard to technical as well as economic aspects.
> It is obvious that the tasks ahead ... cannot be laid down in full detail.
> . . .
> For the time being, the first prerequisite for the final aim is the concentration of the Jews from the countryside to the larger cities. This is to be carried out speedily. ... In this connection, it should be borne in mind that only cities which are rail junctions, or are at least located on railway lines, should be selected as concentration points.
> On principle, Jewish communities of less than 500 persons are to be dissolved and transferred to the nearest concentration centre.

The memorandum then goes on to describe the organization of the Jewish communities:

1. In each Jewish community a Council of Jewish Elders is to be set up which, as far as possible, is to be composed of the remaining authoritative personalities and rabbis. ... The Council is to be made fully responsible, in the literal sense of the word, for the exact and prompt implementation of directives already issued or to be issued in the future.
2. In case of sabotage of such instructions, the Councils are to be warned that the most severe measures will be taken.
3. The Jewish Councils are to carry out an approximate census of the Jews in their areas.
4. The reason to be given for the concentration in the cities is that the Jews have taken a decisive part in sniper attacks and plundering.
5. ... the concentration of the Jews in the cities will probably call for regulations in these cities which will forbid their entry to certain quarters completely and that ... they may, for instance, not leave the ghetto, nor leave their homes after a certain hour in the evening, etc.[2]

Soon after this conference, pogroms against Polish Jewry became a common occurrence. At Siemiatycze, for example, SS men stormed the synagogue during the Day of Atonement service and sang a hymn of their own. As a historian of the period related, 'a great panic broke out among the worshipping Jews. Many jumped out of the windows. In the synagogue on Drogoczyner Street, Yosl the turner was shot while trying to escape, and remained hanging on the window sill'.[3] At Kielce hundreds of Jews were taken to the market place, and their beards were cut off. At Raciaz, Jews were compelled to cut off their beards and pull dustcarts. As an eye-witness stated: 'Since the Nazis were drunk with spirits and liquor, they cruelly thrashed old men, while some stood photographing these scenes of horror and hell. Between the beating and the photographing, they made us dance and jump, and hit us with sticks and mistreated us.'[4]

In Piotrkow, thousands of prisoners were taken into the hall of the Jewish religious school and forced to defecate. Then they were given prayer shawls, prayer books, curtains of the Ark and Torah covers and compelled to clean up the excrement with these objects. Elsewhere Jewish prisoners were treated with similar hostility. As one of these individuals later related, he and other prisoners of war were forced to clean lavatories with their bare hands. Another prisoner described the pain he endured on a march:

> The transport leader noticed this and told me to sit on one of the carts which accompanied us. I mounted the waggon, sat down and took off my shoes to ease the pain in my feet, which were covered with blood. Unfortunately, the German who had given out the bread saw this. He made me get off the cart, aimed his rifle at me and bellowed: 'Du kannst laufen, Jude.' 'You can run, Jew.' He began pushing me towards those at the front, who were about 500 metres ahead. By making a supreme effort I managed to avoid his bayonet and, given no alternative, began to run. For more than ten kilometres my 'guard' gave me no peace, constantly threatening to shoot me, cutting my coat with his bayonet. When the German cavalry passed us he pushed me among the horses so that they should trample me.[5]

When the Polish army was near defeat, Soviet and German forces reached the pre-arranged line east of Warsaw and the country was partitioned. Thousands of Polish soldiers surrendered to the Russian army. In certain areas German troops withdrew so that the transference of territory could take place. Just before the border was closed, Polish Jews fled eastward to the Soviet zone. Although some Jews were killed in the process, others were ordered by the Nazis to flee. As an eye-witness to these events described the scene on the bank of the San river:

> We arrived at the river San on the third day of our exile. What happened there is difficult to describe. On the bank of the river Gestapo-men were waiting and driving people into a boat, or rather raft of two balanced boards, from which women and children fell into the river. We saw floating corpses everywhere; near the bank women stood in the water, holding their children above their heads and crying for help, to which the Gestapo-men answered by shooting. Blood, masses of floating corpses. It is impossible to describe the despair, shouts and helplessness of people in such a situation.[6]

Once the expulsion of Jews eastward was completed, thousands of Jews were forced to live in German-occupied Poland. On 17 October 1939, more than a thousand Jews were transported from Moravska Ostrava to the Lublin region of Poland. Herded into railway coaches, they were compelled to endure a long journey without water. When they reached the station at Nisko, all engineers, builders and doctors were told to leave the train. However, because the doors were sealed, they had to climb out through the windows. These Jews were then addressed by Adolf Eichman who had been put in charge of Jewish resettlement:

> About seven or eight kilometres from here, across the river San, the Führer of the Jews has promised you a new homeland. There are no apartments and no houses – if you will build your homes you will have a roof over your head.

Explaining that there was no water, he continued, 'The wells are full of epidemics, there's cholera, dysentery, and typhus. If you dig for water, you'll have water'.[7]

Discussion: Jewish collaborators

Following Heydrich's directive, Jewish Councils (*Judenräte*) were created to deal with Jewish affairs throughout Poland. In each ghetto these individuals were compelled to perform administrative tasks dealing with daily affairs. Yet at the same time these bodies served German interests. By assuming responsibility for all aspects of Jewish life, including the deployment of workers, the distribution of food and clothing, the creation of educational facilities, the maintenance of a police force and law court, and deportation to the camps, these functionaries ensured that Jewish existence was regulated in accordance with Nazi policy.

Were these individuals culpable for the crimes inflicted by the Nazis against the Jewish people? According to a number of writers, such collaboration symbolized the moral collapse of even those individuals who had become the target of the Nazi onslaught. In *The Destruction of the European Jews*, Raul Hilberg portrayed the activities of the *Judenräte* as emblematic of Jewish passivity under German occupation. These administrative bodies became implements of the German will, guiding Jews through various stages of the process of destruction involving 'registrations for housing or ghettoization, statistical and other informational reports, taxation or sequestration for German uses, wall building, notification of victims to report for labour or "evacuation", even the compiling of transport lists, as well as round-ups conducted by the German police'.[8]

Arguing along similar lines, the German Jewish philosopher Hannah Arendt who reported on the Eichmann trial maintained that the Jewish leadership during the Holocaust was one of the darkest chapters in this tragedy. According to Arendt, Jewish leaders directly facilitated the murder of millions by performing crucially important tasks for the Nazis:

> In Amsterdam as in Warsaw, in Berlin as in Budapest, Jewish officials could be trusted to compile the lists of persons and of their property, to secure money from the deportees to defray the expenses of their deportation and extermination, to keep track of vacated apartments, to supply police forces to help seize Jews and get them on trains, until, as a last gesture, they handed over the assets of the Jewish community in good order for the final confiscation.[9]

In Arendt's opinion, if the Jewish people had been leaderless, chaos would have ensued and millions of lives would have been saved. It was, she believed, a major failure for the Israeli court not to make such an indictment. For Arendt, the Jewish reaction offers a striking picture of the moral collapse even among victims that took place in the face of the Nazi onslaught against Jewry.

In response to such charges, other scholars have sought to defend the Jewish councils established by the Nazis. In *Judenräte*, for example, Isaiah Trunk argued that there was no single response to Nazi terror. Rather, Jewry was divided in its reaction to Nazism. In addition, Trunk emphasized that Jews did not willingly comply with Nazi demands. Rather, Jews were forced to create local councils, serve as members, and provide services for the Nazis. Such individuals were not free to act; rather they were blackmailed through threats to their families. Members of the *Judenräte* therefore had no choice but to comply.

Such arguments, however, did not silence those who pressed their case. Hilberg, for example, found confirmation of his view in the diary of the head of the Warsaw *Judenrat*. As an assimilated Jew active in communal affairs, Adam Czerniaków became the leader of Jews in Warsaw. When the Nazis arrived, Czerniaków was ordered to appoint a Jewish council. According to Hilberg, Czerniaków became a caretaker of the Jewish people, intervening with the authorities to obtain concessions. Nonetheless he was repeatedly thwarted, though unable to escape from this task. Eventually he committed suicide. For Hilberg, Czerniaków was a psychological captive of the oppressor in a constant state of subservience as the Jewish people were led to their deaths.

Other members of the *Judenräte* have been criticized on other grounds. Chaim Rumkowski in Lodz and Jacob Gens in Vilnius, for example, were authoritative figures, believing that they alone could save their communities. Both negotiated with the Nazis to save lives in exchange for Jewish labour, and were deluded by their sense of self-importance. Rumkowski, for example, was known as King Chaim and rode about the ghetto in a horse-drawn carriage. Gens, too, acted like a dictator as Jacob the first. In both cases, the lives of innocent victims depended on their words and actions.

In defence, however, *Judenrat* leaders were not free agents in the ghettos they administered. They were beaten, intimidated, threatened, and in some cases murdered. None appear to have accepted Nazi ideology. Invariably, they were forced to engage in this work, fearful of reprisals to themselves or their communities if they failed to comply. As the historian Michael Marrus noted: 'It is hardly surprising then that those leaders who remained at their posts demonstrated "compliance" with Nazi orders and called for "order" within the ghetto. Beneath the surface, at times, there was other activity'.[10]

113

As Trunk noted, they were frequently deeply ambivalent:

They were afraid that resistance activities might hinder their carefully contrived strategies to gain time and postpone the liquidation of their ghettos for as long as possible. On the other hand, they favoured the idea of physical resistance when the end came.[11]

In the light of further investigations of life in the ghettos, it has become clear that the strategies used by Jews to survive were a function of the condition under which Jewry was compelled to live. It has become increasingly apparent that at the beginning of Nazi rule, Jewish councils believed that their intervention was crucial. In some cases, individuals did make a difference. In Minsk, for example, the *Judenrat* under the leadership of Ilya Moshkin helped coordinate resistance to the Nazis which continued after his death.

Furthermore in several cases the attempt of the *Judenräte* to protect Jews proved largely successful. In Vilnius, for example, the Jewish population engaged in productive activities after the German authorities in Lithuania decided to suspend the massacres that commenced with the attack on the Soviet Union. In consequence, the Jews of Vilnius were permitted to engage in labour. As the head of the *Judenrat* remarked:

Both in the maintenance of industry, and in our work in individual units, we must prove that, contrary to the accepted assumption that we are not fit for any kind of work, we have been very useful, and under present wartime conditions, there is no viable substitute for us.[12]

Similarly, Efriam Barash in Bialystok was convinced that the *Wehrmacht*'s order to produce boots saved the community from extinction. Again, 70,000 Jews of Lodz survived until August 1944 working for the Reich, although they were eventually killed by the Red Army. Hence, there is considerable uncertainty about the role of the *Judenräte* in the Nazi onslaught and the culpability of their leaders, despite the criticisms of Arendt and Hilberg of their lack of moral responsibility.

Notes

1   Alexander Zvielli, 'The Day the Nazis Went to War', *Jerusalem Post*, 31 August 1979.
2   R. Landau, *The Nazi Holocaust*, London, 1992, pp. 152–3.
3   Eliezer Tash, *The Community of Semiatych*, Tel Aviv, 1965, in Gilbert, *op. cit.*, pp. 89–90.
4   Abraham Isaiah Altus, 'The Nazi Invasion of Raciaz' in *Gal-Ed Memorial Book to the Community of Raciaz*, Tel Aviv, 1965, in Gilbert, *op. cit.*, 90.
5   Ringelblum Archive, quoted in Shmuel Krakowski, 'The Fate of Jewish Prisoners of War in the September 1939 Campaign', *Yad Vashem Studies XII*, Jerusalem, 1977, p. 303, in Gilbert, *op. cit.*, 90–91.
6   Jacob Apenszlak (ed.), *The Black Book of Polish Jewry*, New York, 1943, p. 143 in Gilbert, *op. cit.*, 93.
7   Testimony of Max Burger, Eichmann Trial, 27 April 1961, session 19.
8   Raul Hilberg, *Destruction of European Jews*, New York, 1979, p. 33.
9   Hannah Arendt, *Eichmann in Jerusalem*, New York, 1963, pp. 117–18.
10 Michael Marrus, *The Holocaust in History*, London, 1993, p. 116.
11 Marrus, *op. cit.*, p. 116.
12 Marrus, *op. cit.*, p. 118.

12. Massacre in Poland

The massacre of Jews in Poland following the Nazi conquest resulted in the deaths of thousands of innocent victims. With the consolidation of German control of the General Government, both Jews and non-Jews were murdered without compunction. Following Heydrich's decree that all Jews be removed from the Warthegau province (which was now incorporated into Greater Germany), areas south of Warsaw and Lublin became major centres for Jewish resettlement. It was here that the lives of Jewry became intolerable.

Harassment and murder

From mid-November 1939 Jews in Poland were prevented from working in governmental offices, travelling by train, buying or selling to Aryans, going to an Aryan doctor or having an Aryan patient. In these conditions, life became intolerable. Wherever Jews lived, they were subject to continual harassment. David Wdowinski, for example, the head of the psychiatric department of the Czyste Street hospital in Warsaw, recalled that a truck with German officers and civilians entered one of the apartments where Jews were living:

> There they demanded money, jewels, goods and food. They shut the women up in one room and the men in another. They stole everything they could lay their hands on and ordered the men to load it on to the trucks, to the accompaniment of kicks and beatings. The women were searched individually for anything that they might have hidden. But they were still unsatisfied with their loot. At the point of guns they forced the women and young girls to undress and they performed gynaecological examinations on each of them. And even this was not enough. They forced the women and girls to get up on the tables and jump to the floor

with legs straddled. 'Maybe something will fall out. One never knows how deep the Jewish swindlers can hide their jewels.'[1]

In another incident, a Jewish family from Silesia was humiliated by three German officers:

They demanded money and jewellery and threatened the woman at the point of a gun that she give them everything. She gave them all she had. Suddenly one of the officers noticed a small medallion hanging from around the neck of the little boy. This child had been ill from birth. He had petit-mal, a form of epilepsy, which forced on as many as 40 and 60 seizures a day, lasting one or two seconds. The child was mentally retarded. ... The only thing which gave this child any comfort was this very medallion. In the presence of the officers the child was taken with a seizure and the mother pleaded that the medallion be left for her child. One of the officers watching the child said: 'I see that the child is ill. I am a doctor, but a Jew-kid is not a human being', and he tore the medallion off the neck of the little boy.[2]

During this period hundreds of Polish synagogues were demolished and sacred texts violated. As an eye-witness to the destruction of books in the Talmudic Academy of Lublin recalled:

We threw the huge Talmudic library out of the building and carried the books to the market place, where we set fire to them. The fire lasted twenty hours. The Lublin Jews assembled around and wept bitterly, almost silencing us with their cries. We summoned the military band, and with joyful shouts the soldiers drowned out the sounds of the Jewish cries.[3]

Throughout the month of November, Germans demanded Jewish labour for work brigades. Treating Jewry like cattle, the Germans regarded these individuals as less than human. As one of the victims remarked: 'Truly we are cattle in the eyes of the Nazis. When they supervise Jewish workers they hold a whip in their hands. All are beaten unmercifully.' Such acts, he continued, 'are enough to drive you crazy. Sometimes we are ashamed to look at one another. And worse than this, we have begun to look upon ourselves as "inferior beings", lacking God's image.'[4]

Later in the month Hans Frank ordered the creation of Jewish councils in every Jewish community located in the General Government; these bodies were to consist of 24 members where there was a population of over 10,000 Jews, and twelve members in smaller communities. As Heydrich instructed, these bodies were to assume responsibility for the internal organization of Jewry within the General Government. One of the central aims of the Nazi plan was to impoverish Polish Jewry: repeatedly the Jewish community was ordered to pay large sums to the occupying forces.

On 29 November, for example, Hans Drexel, the German Civil Commissar in Piotrkow, presented the Jewish Council with a decree for the delivery of 350,000 zlotys. Unless this sum was paid, punitive measures would be taken against the community. While the Council attempted to raise this money, three hostages were held and beaten. Once the ransom was secured, it was delivered to the German Commissar, but further demands were made for more money as well as 12,000 eggs, 500 sacks of flour, 300 kilogrammes of butter and 100 sacks of sugar. Such extortion was typical of the way in which Polish Jewry was treated in the wake of the German conquest.

Once the German-Soviet demarcation line was established, the border was closed, preventing escape to the east. However, one last deportation was announced on 1 December in Hrubieszow where all men between the ages of 50 and 60 together with men from Chelm were gathered together in the city square. Wives and children attempted to join this throng, but were ordered home. As one of the marchers recalled: 'We started marching. One girl succeeded in following the marchers, shouting 'Father' all the way. At the first village, they took this girl away. We do not know what happened to her, but we heard a shot.'[5]

At the end of the day, 20 Jews were selected from this group including two rabbis, two synagogue officials, and others with long beards, and were never seen again.

As the march continued, one of the men was led away. His son jumped up and said, 'Leave my father alone, I will take his place. Take me.' They let him go too, and then they were shot in the back of the head so that the bullets came out of their foreheads. On the next day further killing took place:

> They would lay a hand on a man. He would lie down – whoever did not want to lie down would be hit on the head with a rifle butt and the blood ran. But most people were so tired that they could not resist. We were only shadows after all this marching. The slaughter on that day was horrible.[6]

Of the 1800 men who had set off from Hrubieszow about 1400 were murdered on the fourth day of the march. Eventually about 200 Jews reached the Soviet border on 9 December: 'The sun was rising. We were told to sing. Whoever would not sit down and sing would be shot. We started singing Jewish melodies.'[7]

On 11 December Jews living within the General Government were made liable to two years' forced labour with a possible extension. In consequence, numerous tasks were created for Jews deported to labour camps including clearing swamps, paving roads and constructing buildings. On 13 December the SS headquarters in Poznan decreed that all Jews still living in the western regions of Poland which had been annexed to Germany were to be shot. Those expelled from these lands generally went to Warsaw and Lodz, whose Jewish population had swelled to over 1 million.

There the assault against Jewry continued without restraint. In his diary for 16 December 1939, Chaim Kaplan noted that Jewish girls were forced to

clean a latrine – to remove excrement and clean it. But they received no utensils. To their question 'With what?' the Nazis replied 'With your blouses'. The girls removed their blouses and cleaned the excrement with them. When the job was done they received the reward: the Nazis wrapped their faces in the blouses, filthy with the remains of excrement, and laughed uproariously.[8]

A further indignity was recorded by Kaplan concerning a rabbi in Lodz who was compelled to spit on a Torah Scroll:

In fear of his life, he complied and desecrated that which is holy to him and to his people. After a short while he had no more saliva, his mouth was dry. To the Nazi's question, why did he stop spitting, the rabbi replied that his mouth was dry. Then the son of the 'superior race' began to spit into the rabbi's open mouth, and the rabbi continued to spit on the Torah.[9]

In her diaries Mary Berg, another witness of such atrocities, described an assault against Jewish families:

Several Nazis entered the apartment and, after a thorough search of all the rooms, forced the girls into the parlour, where there was a piano. When their parents tried to accompany them, the Nazis struck them over the head with clubs. Then the Nazis locked the parlour door and ordered the girls to strip. They ordered the older one to play a Viennese waltz and the younger one to dance. But the sounds of the piano merged with the cries of the parents in the adjoining room.[10]

By mid-December, the Jewish population in the General Government numbered between 2,500,000 and 3,500,000 Jews. In the view of Frank, there appeared to be no solution to the Jewish problem. 'We cannot shoot 2,500,000 Jews,' he wrote, 'neither can we poison them. We shall have to take steps, however, designed to extirpate them in some way – and this will be done.'[11] In line with this policy, Jews were forced to work in labour camps throughout Poland. Depicting the plight of one Jew who had been forced in the most appalling fashion, Chaim Kaplan wrote:

The work consisted of transferring cakes of ice from one place to another. The terrible cold pierces the flesh. Who could endure the icy chill? But there was no choice. It was the Nazis' order and, as such, could not be avoided. The Jew did his job with gloves, but the Nazi overseer forced him to do the work barehanded. The Jew was forced to fulfil the wishes of the oppressor, and with terrible suffering he moved the ice cakes barehanded, in below-zero cold. The Jew fell under the agony of this torture. His palms were so frozen that they are beyond help and his hands will have to be amputated.[12]

Although the aim of such camps was to force Jews to engage in physical labour, they also served as means of humiliating and torturing Jewish victims. As a Polish socialist leader who was imprisoned in a forced labour camp in the village of Stutthof later reported:

All the Jews were assembled in the courtyard; they were ordered to run, to drop down and stand up again. Anybody who was slow in obeying the order was beaten to death by the overseer with the butt of his rifle. Afterwards Jews were ordered to jump right into the cesspit of the latrines, which were being built; this was full of urine. The taller Jews got out again since the level reached their chin, but the shorter ones went down. The young ones tried to help the old folk, and as a punishment the overseers ordered the latter to beat the young. When they refused to obey they were cruelly beaten themselves. Two or three died on the spot and the survivors were ordered to bury them.[13]

In committing such crimes the Nazis believed they were acting in accordance with the principles of *Lebensraum*. Jews in Poland, they maintained, constituted a biologically undesirable population. Terror, torture and slaughter were acceptable given the quest to rid Europe of parasites which threatened the purity of the race. Such a policy was implicit in Hitler's speech to the *Reichstag* on 30 January 1939, the anniversary of his appointment as Reich Chancellor when he prophesied the extermination of European Jewry:

> Europe cannot find peace until the Jewish question has been solved. It may well be that sooner or later an agreement may be reached in Europe itself between nations who otherwise would not find it so easy to arrive at an understanding. ... One thing I should like to say on this day which may be memorable for others as well as for us Germans. In the course of my life I have very often been a prophet, and have usually been ridiculed for it. During the time of my struggle for power it was in the first instance only the Jewish race that received my prophecies with laughter when I said that I would one day take over the leadership of the State, and with it that of the whole nation, and that I would then among other things settle the Jewish problem. ... Today I will once more be a prophet: if the international Jewish financiers in and outside Europe should succeed in plunging the nations once more into a world war, then the result will not be the Bolshevizing of the earth, and thus the victory of Jewry, but the annihilation of the Jewish race in Europe.[14]

Discussion: The invasion of Poland

The onslaught on Poland resulted in the death of 6 million Poles, approximately 18 per cent of the population. This massacre was a calculated offensive, yet at the Nuremberg Trials Nazi leaders maintained that they were blameless for this reign of terror. Together with Hans Frank, the ruler of the General Government, and Albert Forster, the overlord of Danzig/West Prussia, Albert Greiser was instrumental in this mass murder. Nonetheless, he claimed during the war crimes trial that he was actually a friend of the Polish people and that Hitler was to blame for their deaths. In his view, he was simply a victim of Hitler's policies and a scapegoat for these crimes against humanity.

Such a defence, however, is without foundation. Those who were responsible for the eastern territories were simply under orders to bring about the Germanization of their provinces; no questions were to be asked about the methods they employed. As Greiser himself noted in a letter to the Führer that was read at Nuremberg:

> I, for my part, do not believe that the Führer needs to be consulted yet again about this matter, particularly in view of the fact that it was only recently during our last discussion concerning the Jews that he told me I could proceed with them according to my own discretion.[15]

From the beginning, the German invasion of Poland was not an ordinary conquest. Rather, soldiers displayed utterly callous disregard for the lives of those whom they encountered. In the view of those who lived through this period, the brutality of the Nazis was overwhelming. Wilhelm Moses, for example, who served in a regular army transport during the invasion, recalled that as he drove through a Polish village, an SS German regimental brass band played as seven or eight victims hung from the gallows. The tongues of these victims were hanging out, and the faces were blue and green. Subsequently, Moses and his truck were confiscated by the SS, and he was commanded to transport Polish Jews from one SS unit to another. When he was told by the Jews that they would be killed, he asked:

> 'Well, who said that they are going to kill you?'
> 'But of course they will kill us, they killed the others too, my mother, my father, my children have all been killed. They will kill us, too!'
> 'Well, are you Jews?,' asked Herr Moses.
> 'Yes, we are Jews,' they replied.
> 'What could I do?,' says Herr Moses. 'I am a tortured person. As a German, I can only tell you that I was ashamed of everything that had happened. And I no longer felt German. ... I had already got to the point where I said, 'If a bullet were to hit me, I would no longer have to be ashamed to say that I'm German, later, once the war is over.'[16]

Not only were Jews victimized, the Polish intelligentsia were also systematically killed. According to Nazi policy, Poland was to become a nation of slaves; therefore intelligent members of society were to be eliminated, and thereby prevented from reproducing. A typical incident exemplifying such a racial programme took place in November 1939 at the Jagellonian University in Cracow. As

Mieczyslaw Brozek, an assistant professor of philology, recalled, a meeting of staff was called and elderly professors were beaten by German soldiers with their rifle butts.

In concentration camps where professors were imprisoned, the conditions were overwhelming as Professor Stanislaw Urbanczyk remarked:

> What was really difficult to survive was the hunger and the cold. It was a particularly cold winter and in the space of one month over a dozen professors died. . . . One of my colleagues had a letter from his mother in his pocket, and when they found it during a search he was strung up on a post and had to hang there with his arms tied tight behind him for an hour or more.[17]

The intensity of the Nazi assault provoked some German soldiers to protest about such excesses. Colonel-General Johannes Blaskowitz, commander of the Ober-Ost region, for example, complained in a series of memoranda during the early months of the invasion:

> It is misguided to slaughter tens of thousands of Jews and Poles as is happening at present. . . . The acts of violence against the Jews which occur in full view of the public inspire among the religious Poles not only deep disgust but also great pity. . . . The attitude of the troops to the SS and police alternates between abhorrence and hatred. Every soldier feels repelled and revolted by these crimes which are being perpetrated in Poland by nationals of the Reich and representatives of State authority.[18]

As a result of the German onslaught, Poland was divided between Germany and the Soviet Union. On 23 August 1939 a Nazi-Soviet pact was signed by Molotov and Ribbentrop. The treaty contained an undertaking that neither Germany nor Russia would attack one another. In a Secret Additional Protocol, the treaty laid down their spheres of interest in Eastern Europe:

> 1. In the event of a territorial and political transformation in the territories belonging to the Baltic States (Finland, Estonia, Latvia, Lithuania), the northern frontier of Lithuania shall represent the frontier of the spheres of interest both of Germany and the USSR.
> 2. In the event of a territorial and political transformation of the territories belonging to the Polish State, the spheres of interest of both

123

Germany and the USSR shall be bounded approximately by the line of the rivers Narew, Vistula and San.

The question whether the interests of both Parties make the maintenance of an independent Polish State appear desirable and how the frontiers of this State should be drawn can be definitely determined only in the course of further political developments.[19]

In the partition of Poland, the German section contained 188,000 square kilometres of Polish territory containing a population of 20.2 million Poles – this was to become part of the Reich territory or formed into three divisions under Nazi control – West Prussia was under the authority of Albert Forster; Arthur Greiser was in charge of the Warthegau; and Hans Frank was put in charge of the General Government. As a consequence, Jews were deported from their homes throughout the country, as were ethnic Germans living in areas due to come under Soviet control. Such a restructuring of Polish territory led to incredible suffering for both Jews and Poles. Typical was the reaction of Franz Jagemann, an interpreter for the Nazis, who witnessed this human tragedy. Describing an action which took place in a village in the Gnesen district of Poland which was evacuated for incoming ethnic Germans:

> People were beaten ... people were kicked, there was blood. The worst thing about it for me was to see an elderly couple, they were over 70 and clearly didn't understand what was going on, they were beaten up and thrown on to a truck. One SS man, who was born in Upper Silesia, carried on as if he was berserk, screaming at the villagers and driving them together with violence. People were kicked, punched, pistols waved in their faces. It was like a proper hold-up.[20]

Notes

1 David Wdowinski, *We Are Not Saved*, London, 1964, p. 24.
2 *Ibid.*, pp. 24–5.
3 *Frankfurter Zeitung*, 28 March 1941 in Gilbert, *op. cit.*, 101.
4 Kaplan Diary, 18 November 1939, in Abraham Katsch (ed.), *The Warsaw Diary of Chaim A. Kaplan*, New York, 1973, p. 74.
5 Testimony of Hirsch Pachter, Eichmann Trial, 1 May 1961, session 2.
6 *Ibid* in Gilbert, *op. cit.*, 104.
7 *Ibid.*
8 Kaplan Diary, 16 December 1939, in Katsch, *op. cit.*, p. 87.

9 *Ibid.*, p. 87.
10 Mary Berg Diary, 18 December 1939, in S. L. Schneiderman (ed.), *Warsaw Ghetto: A Diary by Mary Berg*, New York, 1945, p. 24.
11 Hans Frank, diary entry for 19 December 1939, *Hans Frank Diary*, Warsaw, 1961, in Gilbert, *op. cit.*, 106.
12 Chaim Kaplan Diary, 5 February 1940, in Katsch, *op. cit.*, p. 116.
13 'The Sufferings of Jews in the Concentration Camp at Stutthof', *Bulletin of the Rescue Committee of the Jewish Agency for Palestine*, March 1945 in Gilbert, *op. cit.*, 115.
14 M. Domarus, *Hitler, Reden, 1932 bis 1945*, Wiesbaden, 1973, pp. 1057–8.
15 Lawrence Rees, *The Nazis*, London, 1997, p. 126.
16 *Ibid.*, p. 129.
17 *Ibid.*, p. 130.
18 *Ibid.*, p. 131.
19 William Shirer, *The Rise and Fall of the Third Reich*, London, 1996, p. 541.
20 Rees, *op. cit.*, p. 140.

13. The ghetto

Following the conquest of Poland, Jews were compelled to engage in compulsory labour. On 26 October 1939, Governor Frank decreed that all Jews living in the General Government should engage in physical work. On 11 December, the first supplementary regulation was issued which prevented Jews from changing their residence without permission. In addition, a curfew was imposed from 9 p.m. to 5 a.m. The following day the second supplementary regulation laid down that all Jewish inhabitants of the General Government from the ages of 14 to 60 would be subject to compulsory labour for a period of at least two years. These were the first steps leading to the creation of Jewish ghettos within this newly acquired territory.

Ghetto life

Once the deportations to the General Government ceased, there was uncertainty what to do with the massive Jewish population. On 21 September 1939 Reinhard Heydrich issued a directive to the *Einsatzgruppen* in Poland to put Jews into ghettos. In 1940 this plan was implemented, and the first ghetto was established in April 1940 in Lodz.

Ghettos were usually enclosed by walls or high fences, and gates were locked and guarded at night. The SS controlled all aspects of ghetto life, and the size of the ghettos was determined by the SS. Nonetheless, the management of the ghetto was under the direction of the Jewish council of elders, the *Judenrat*. The leadership of the ghetto varied considerably: at one extreme Jewish autocrats ruled over the community; at the opposite extreme ghettos were organized in a democratic fashion. Yet despite these differences, the most common criticism of the *Judenräte* was that favouritism was rampant. Leaders were in a position to protect their families and friends at the expense of other Jews.

Within the ghetto, Jewish elders were responsible for all institutions including schools, hospitals and orphanages. Those in charge of sanitation faced impossible difficulties, as did fire brigades. To carry on their work, the *Judenräte* were compelled to impose numerous taxes. The Jewish police force, the *Kapos*, attempted to keep order and count the columns selected for work outside the ghetto. On street corners personal belongings were sold for food, clothing and heating material. Continually the number of ghetto dwellers changed due to the deaths of the inhabitants as well as the influx of non-Polish Jews. To feed this changing population, the Jewish councils doled out food in soup kitchens; however, when the Nazis sought to reduce the number of Jews in the ghetto through starvation, only those families who had been able to hide something of value were able to sustain themselves through the black market.

The largest ghetto created by the Nazis was in Warsaw: inhabitants there had to survive on a food allocation of 300 calories a day. Heating materials were limited, and those who did not have access to the black market were unable to survive long under these terrible conditions. One of those who visited the Warsaw ghetto was Stanislav Rozycki who provided a chilling description of figures he encountered in the ghetto:

> The majority are nightmare figures, ghosts of former human beings, miserable destitutes, pathetic remnants of former humanity. One is most affected by the characteristic change which one sees in their faces: as a result of misery, poor nourishment, the lack of vitamins, fresh air and exercise, the numerous cares, worries, anticipated misfortunes, suffering and sickness, their faces have taken on a skeletal appearance. The prominent bones around their eye sockets, the yellow facial colour, the slack pendulous skin, the alarming emaciation and sickliness. And, in addition, this miserable, frightened, restless, apathetic and resigned expression, like that of a hunted animal. I pass my closest friends without recognizing them and guessing their fate. Many of them recognize me, come up to me and ask curiously how things are 'over there' behind the walls – there where there is enough fresh air, freedom to move around, and above all freedom.[1]

Shocked by what he experienced, Rozycki described in detail the suffering of Warsaw Jewry:

On the streets children are crying in vain, children who are dying of hunger. They howl, beg, sing, moan, shiver with cold, without underwear, without clothing, without shoes, in rags, sacks, flannel which are bound in strips round the emaciated skeletons, children swollen with hunger, disfigured, half conscious, already completely grown-up at the age of five, gloomy and weary of life. They are like old people and are only conscious of one thing: 'I'm cold', 'I'm hungry'. They have become aware of the most important things in life that quickly. Through their innocent sacrifice and their frightening help-lessness the thousands upon thousands of these little beggars level the main accusation against the proud civilization of today. Ten per cent of the new generation have already perished: every day and every night hundreds of these children die and there is no hope that anybody will put a stop to it.[2]

Yet it was not just the children who perished in this way; all those confined to the ghetto faced misery and death:

There are not only children. Young and old people, men and women, bourgeois and proletarians, intelligentsia and business people, all are being declassed and degraded. ... They are being gobbled up by the streets on to which they are brutally and ruthlessly thrown. They beg for one month, for two months, for three months – but they all go downhill and die on the street or in hospitals from cold, or hunger, or sickness, or depression. Former human beings whom no one needs fall by the wayside; former citizens, former 'useful members of human society'.[3]

In his diary, Rozycki went on to describe the severe overcrowding of the ghetto and its consequences:

For various reasons standards of hygiene are terribly poor. Above all, the fearful population density in the streets with which nowhere in Europe can be remotely compared. The fatal over-population is particularly apparent in the streets: people literally rub against each other, it is impossible to pass unhindered through the streets. And then the lack of light, gas and heating materials. Water consumption is also much reduced; people wash themselves much less and do not have baths or hot water. There are no green spaces, gardens, parks: no clumps of trees and no lawns to be seen. For a year no one has seen a village, a wood, a field, a river, or a mountain: no one has breathed slightly better air for even a few days this year. Bedding and clothing are changed very rarely because of the lack of soap.[4]

Such conditions inevitably caused a variety of physical ailments:

> One can easily draw one's own conclusions as to the consequences: stomach typhus and typhus, dysentery, tuberculosis, pneumonia, influenza, metabolic disturbances, the most common digestive illnesses, lack of vitamins and all other illnesses associated with the lack of bread, fresh air, clothing, and heating materials. Typhus is systematically and continually destroying the population. There are victims in every family. On average up to a thousand people are dying each month. In the early morning the corpses of beggars, children, old people and women are lying in every street – the victims of hunger and cold.[5]

Faced with such demoralizing and degrading conditions, inhabitants of the ghetto engaged in a struggle for food and living space. In the ghetto no one had the strength to engage in intellectual dispute or cultural activities, and the German overseers prohibited religious instruction as well as the publication of devotional material. As Rozycki recorded:

> Nothing can be printed, taught or learnt. People are not allowed to organize themselves or exchange cultural possessions. We are cut off from the world and from books. It is not permitted to open libraries and sort out books from other printed materials. We are not allowed to print anything, neither books nor newspapers; schools, academic institutions, etc. are not permitted to open.[6]

A Nazi organization, Strength by Joy, organized coach tours to observe the inhabitants of the Warsaw ghetto. In May 1942 the Polish government in exile issued a report containing a description of those confined in this way:

> Every day large coaches come to the ghetto; they take soldiers through as if it was a zoo. It is the thing to do to provoke the wild animals. Often soldiers strike out at passers-by with long whips as they drive through. They go to the cemetery where they take pictures. They compel the families of the dead and the rabbis to interrupt the funeral and to pose in front of their lenses.[7]

For propaganda purposes the Nazis made official films of the ghetto which emphasized the degradation of Jewish life. Reporting to the press about his visit, Alfred Rosenberg claimed:

Large ghettos have been established in the cities which function reasonably well but cannot represent the final solution of the Jewish question. I had the opportunity to get to know the ghetto in Lublin and the one in Warsaw. The sights are so appalling and probably also so well-known to the editorial staffs that a description is presumably superfluous. If there are any people left who still somehow have sympathy with the Jews then they ought to be recommended to have a look at such a ghetto. Seeing this race en masse, which is decaying, decomposing, and rotten to the core will banish any sentimental humanitarianism.[8]

Such suffering was intensified by the constant threat of violence. On the evening of 9 January 1941, for example, Mary Berg recalled a meeting of her house committee when Nazi police forced their way into the room; they searched the men and took whatever money they could. Then they ordered the women to undress:

Our subtenant, Mrs R, who happened to be there, courageously protested, declaring that she would not undress in the presence of men. For this she received a resounding slap on the face and was searched even more harshly than the other two women. The women were kept naked for more than two hours while the Nazis put their revolvers to their breasts and private parts and threatened to shoot them all if they did not disgorge dollars or diamonds.[9]

Once the Warsaw ghetto was created, Jews were deported from towns and villages west of the city. In a depiction of 3000 such deportees, Chaim Kaplan described their confusion and despair:

The exiles were driven out of their beds before dawn, and the Führer's minions did not let them take money, belongings or food, threatening all the while to shoot them. Before they left on their exile, a search was made of their pockets and of all the hidden places in their clothes and bodies. Without a penny in their pockets, or a covering for the women, children, old people, and invalids – sometimes without shoes on their feet or staffs in their hands – they were forced to leave their homes and possessions and the graves of their ancestors, and go – whither? And in terrible, fierce, unbearable cold![10]

As time passed, thousands of Jews were transported to Warsaw swelling the ghetto to over half a million residents. Refugees were sent to houses that had been evacuated; these dwellings were the worst living conditions in the ghetto. Twelve or fifteen people lived in a single room in the most terrible conditions. As Zivia Lubetkin recalled:

> When I came to look for this family, I found them on the floor, one on top of the other. They were in a corner of the room. I could not come up to them because there was no room to put my foot to cross the room. In this house, there was no lavatory in the whole house and they had a lavatory in the yard and they were on the fourth floor. There was no water in the house. And people lived in this way. They degenerated because there was no possibility of getting work, no employment. There was hunger. Sanitary conditions were below description, and of course, the typhoid epidemic began in those houses.[11]

At this time similar deportations of innocent victims were carried out to ghettos throughout the country. Moshe Shklarek described the horrors of such a deportation from Plock to Czestochowa:

> In the early hours of that morning the house shuddered from violent knocks on the door and from the savage cries of the Germans. 'Filthy Jews, outside!' Within a few moments we found ourselves huddled together in a crowd of the town's Jews on Sheroka Street.
>
> With the help of the *Volksdeutsche* [ethnic Germans] and with cruel blows and many murders, they loaded the assembled ones on to trucks, crowding them tightly, and the long convoy drove us out of town. We were not permitted to take anything with us, not even something else to wear other than what we had put on in our terrified haste.
>
> On the same day, after hours of difficult travelling, the trucks came to a stop in the midst of Dzialdowo camp, at the entrance to the town of Mlawa. Two rows of Germans, equipped with clubs and whips, stood in a line several tens of metres long, extending from the trucks to the camp gate.
>
> We were ordered to jump out of the trucks and run the gauntlet towards the gate. Before the first ones to jump had managed to set foot on the torture-pass, the clubs and whips flew and a torrent of blows rained down on the runners' heads. With difficulty and desperate haste, each one hurried to reach the camp gate, people falling and being trampled under their brothers' feet in their frantic race.
>
> Only an isolated few managed to get through the gate without being wounded by the blows and lashes of the Germans. In the aftermath of this act of terror, scores of slain bodies were left lying and were buried next to the single privy which was provided for the men and women who lived in the camp. The hundreds of wounded and injured lay without

131

any medical care in the stables that were full of mud and dung, and into which we had been squeezed and packed without room enough to free our aching limbs. In this camp we endured days of torment and distress, thirst and hunger.[12]

Discussion: Life and death in the ghetto

Once a ghetto was established, it became a crime to step outside its walls. On 10 November 1941, the governor for the district of Warsaw issued a decree instituting the death penalty for Jews illegally leaving the ghetto as well as for anyone aiding Jews or harbouring them. Similar decrees were issued throughout the General Government. As during the Middle Ages, Jews once again were separated from the rest of society. Yet, unlike the ghettos of the Middle Ages, the ghettos created by the Third Reich did not offer any form of protection to their residents. Instead, death haunted the inhabitants.

As we have seen, the appalling conditions of the ghettos reinforced the Jewish sense of isolation and hopelessness. In Warsaw the park which previously existed in the Jewish area of the city had been eliminated and only a few trees remained; in Vilnius there was only one tree. Invariably ghettos were located in the worst parts of the town, at times in outlying areas lacking basic facilities. Ghetto buildings were dilapidated, often in ruined condition due to bombings, looting and vandalism. The overcrowding was so great that there was no possibility of privacy. As one girl living in Warsaw remarked:

> My ears are filled with the deafening clamour of crowded streets and cries of people dying on the sidewalks. Even the quiet hours of the night are filled with the snoring and coughing of those who share the same apartment or, only too often, with the shots and screams from the streets.[13]

Such overcrowding created the most unsanitary conditions. Toilets, running water and sewage facilities were beyond repair. The air was contaminated by the smell from latrines and toilets. In the bitter Polish winter, staying warm became a ceaseless struggle. Everywhere inhabitants of the ghetto searched for fuel. As one observer noted, ghetto dwellers were 'like crows on a cadaver, like jackals on a carcass. They demolished, they axed, they sawed, walls collapsed,

1. Hitler at the *Reichstag* Fire Trial. (IWM HU 1781)

2. Nazi boycott of Jewish businesses in 1933. (IWM HU 68048)

3. Nazi burning of non-Aryan books in Berlin in May 1933.
(IWM NYP 68048)

4. SS stand
around a
collection of
Communist
placards and
standards in 1934.
(IWM MH 13442)

5. Anti-Semitic cartoon comparing the immorality of the Jews with the purity of the Aryan race. (IWM GER 305)

6. Nazi Party rally in Nuremberg in 1936. (IWM NYP 68056)

7. Banner declaring 'Jews are not wanted here' over the entrance to Rosenheim in Bavaria. (IWM MH 13348)

8. Medical register of the Hadamar sanatorium in Austria where handicapped and insane inmates were murdered in the euthanasia programme. (IWM EA 62182)

9. Jew in Warsaw in 1940 (IWM IA 37590)

10. A column of Jews guarded by German soldiers in Warsaw. (IWM IA 37578)

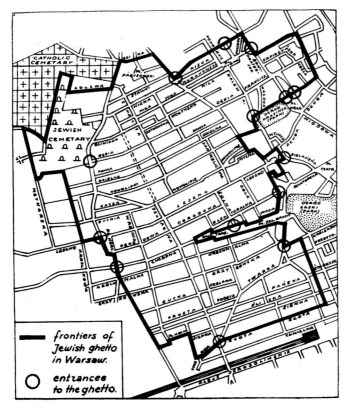

11. Warsaw ghetto. (IWM MH 6286)

12. Flossenburg concentration camp with barrack blocks and electrified fences. (IWM EA 64429)

left: 13. Cell at Breedonck with chain shackles fixed to the wall.
(IWM B 10081)

centre: 14. Operating table used for the dissection of dead prisoners at Vught concentration camp.
(IWM BU 3783)

bottom: 15. Gas chamber at Majdanek concentration camp.
(IWM BU 3783)

16. Former SS guards loading the bodies of dead prisoners onto a lorry for burial. (IWM BU 3783)

17. Hermann Göring at the Nuremberg Trial. (IWM HU 54863)

beams flew, plaster buried people alive, but no one yielded his position'.[14]

In such conditions, starvation became a normal occurrence. The official policy was to deprive the Jewish population of food. Hence on 4 November 1941 the German occupation authorities prescribed that Jews were to receive half of the weekly maximum consisting of no meat or meat products, 2½ oz fat, 3.3 lbs bread, and 4.4 lbs potatoes. The average food ration provided 1100 calories per person, however even this small portion was often spoiled or stolen. In her diary, Mary Berg wrote that the bread provided was black and tasted like sawdust. According to Chaim Kaplan, potatoes were 'our whole life. When I am alone in my room for a few moments of quiet, the echo of that word continues in my ears. Even in my dreams it visits me.'[15]

Within the ghetto beggars lined the streets singing doleful songs and laments. Entire families begged, huddled in rags. Unable to survive in any other way, smugglers were ubiquitous. Thousands of Jews engaged in smuggling food, including big operators who made enormous profits as well as small peddlers who obtained small supplies from middlemen. Despite the German insistence that no food should be imported into the ghetto, buildings bordering the ghetto became operational headquarters for illegal trade. Paradoxically, the smuggler played a heroic role in ghetto life – without the black market, many more Jews would have died as a consequence of Nazi policy.

How was it possible to maintain one's sanity in such horrendous conditions? Despite the constant threat of death, many Jews drew sustenance from the Jewish tradition. The folk wisdom of the ghetto was infused with religious maxims from the past: 'A Jew lives with hope'; 'While there's life, there's hope'. In Vilnius, a popular ghetto song exhorted Jews to remain confident in the future:

Moshe, hold on
Keep hold of yourself,
Remember we must get out ...
Moshe hold on; hold on Moshe –
It isn't very long,
The hour soon will toll.[16]

The rabbi of Zelechów was alleged to have told his followers: 'Every

Jew who survives openly sanctifies God.' In his view, all Jewish survivors were heroes in their resistance to the Nazis.[17] According to legend, Rabbi Isaac Nissenbaum in the Warsaw ghetto declared:

> Now is the time for the sanctification of life and not for the Sanctification of the Name through death. Once when our enemies demanded our soul, the Jew martyred his body for *Kiddush ha-Shem* [Sanctification of the Name]. Today when the enemy demands the body, it is the Jew's obligation to defend himself, to preserve his life.[18]

In the Chelm ghetto, Jews sang a Yiddish song based on the Psalms:

> O look from heaven and behold,
> Look down from the skies and see!
> For we have become as a derision,
> A derision among the nations.
>
> Therefore we plead with You ever:
> Now help us, Guardian of Israel,
> Now take notice of our tears,
> For still do we cry aloud, 'Hear O Israel'.
> O, take notice, Guardian of this nation.
> Show all the peoples that You are our God,
> We have indeed none other, just You alone,
> Whose Name is One.[19]

Coupled with such pious hope, secularists in the ghetto based their optimism on other grounds. In Bialystok, for example, inmates hoped for deliverance through the Red Army:

> Alas, how bitter are the times,
> But deliverance is on its way;
> It's not so far away.
> The Red Army will come to free us,
> It's not so far away.[20]

In Warsaw, political prophecy was another source of consolation, as new words were put to an old tune:

> Listen here, Haman you,
> Jews will live to settle scores.
> You will get your come-uppance.

134

Jews have lived and will endure.
But Haman, you will go to hell.[21]

In Vilnius, a popular song declared:

Let's be joyous and tell our jokes,
We'll hold a wake when Hitler chokes.[22]

Humour, too, became a source of encouragement in the ghetto.
When the German army came under attack on the Russian front,
anti-German jokes were frequently told:

What's the difference between the sun and Hitler?
The sun goes down in the West and Hitler in the East.'

What's new?
Didn't you hear? They are confiscating chairs from the Jews.
What happened?
Hitler got tired of standing outside Moscow and Leningrad.

Driven together in the ghetto, Jews turned to one another for solace. In
the Lodz ghetto, German children produced a Hanukkah programme
which symbolized the importance of such communal bonds:

Hunger, cold and conflicts were forgotten. Shoemakers and tailors,
physicians, lawyers, and pharmacists, all at once, we were one big
family. That could not have happened in Berlin … but here, behind the
barbed wire, something existed that united us all – our Jewishness.
When they sang together, they forgot their suffering and misery; they
were still alive and in song they praised God, who many times before
had performed miracles. When they sang about the little lamp whose oil
for one day lasted eight, the singers regained their courage and hope.[23]

Notes

1 T. Berenstein *et al.* (eds), *Faschimus-Getto-Massenmord. Dokumentation über Austrottung und Widerstand der Juden in Polen während des
zweiten Weltkrieges*, Frankfurt, ?1960, pp. 152–3 in J. Noakes and G.
Pridham, *op. cit.*, p. 1067.
2 *Ibid.*, pp. 1067–8.
3 *Ibid.*, p. 1068.

4   *Ibid.*, p. 1068.
5   *Ibid.*, p. 1068.
6   *Ibid.*, p. 1068–9.
7   T. Szarota, *Warschau unter dem Hakenkreuz*, Paderborn, 1985, p. 46 in J. Noakes and G. Pridham, *op. cit.*, p. 1069.
8   BA Z. Slg. 101 Nr. 41, pp. 55–7 in J. Noakes and G. Pridham (eds), *Nazism 1919–1945*, Exeter, 1995, p. 1069.
9   Mary Berg diary, 10 January 1941, in S. L. Schneiderman (ed.), *Warsaw Ghetto: A Diary by Mary Berg*, New York, 1945, p. 46.
10 Kaplan diary, 31 January 1941, in Abraham Katsch (ed.), *The Warsaw Diary of Chaim A. Kaplan*, New York, 1973, p. 239.
11 Testimony of Zivia Lubetkin, Eichmann Trial, 3 May 1961, session 25.
12 Recollections of Moshe Shklarek, 'The Revolt', in Mariam Novitch, *Sobibor, Martyrdom and Revolt, Documents and Testimonies*, New York, 1980, pp. 140–1.
13 Lucy Dawidowicz, *The War Against the Jews*, London, 1990, p. 260.
14 *Ibid.*, p. 260.
15 *Ibid.*, p. 260.
16 *Ibid.*, p. 269.
17 *Ibid.*, p. 269.
18 *Ibid.*, p. 269.
19 *Ibid.*, p. 270.
20 *Ibid.*, p. 270.
21 *Ibid.*, p. 270.
22 *Ibid.*, p. 270.
23 *Ibid.*, p. 274.

14. The war against Russia

Despite Nazi opposition to Communism, Hitler had concluded an agreement between Germany and the Soviet Union on 23 August 1939. At a meeting between the two Foreign Ministers, von Ribbentrop and Molotov, it was agreed that for ten years neither country would interfere with the other in the case of war. In addition, a secret protocol provided for the division of Poland. Hitler's aim in making such an agreement was to avoid a war on two fronts. By neutralizing Russia, he was able to conquer Poland and then turn his attention to the western front. Nonetheless, two years later Germany launched an offensive against the Soviet Union.

The Russian assault

Convinced that German *Lebensraum* required more land in the east, Hitler launched an offensive against Russia on 22 June 1941. In an announcement over the radio, Joseph Goebbels read a proclamation from the Führer:

> Weighed down by heavy cares, condemned to months of silence, I can at last speak freely – German people! At this moment a march is taking place that, for its extent, compares with the greatest the world has ever seen. I have decided again today to place the fate and future of the Reich and our people in the hands of our soldiers. May God aid us, especially in this fight.[1]

Prior to this announcement, Hitler had amassed 153 divisions, 600,000 motorized vehicles, 3580 tanks, 7184 artillery pieces and 2740 aeroplanes on the Russian frontier. In addition, the German army was supported by 12 Romanian divisions, 18 Finnish divisions,

3 Hungarian divisions, and 2 ½ Slovak divisions. Later these forces were joined by 3 Italian divisions, and a Spanish division. Adopting the pattern of earlier *Blitzkrieg* campaigns, Hitler launched a surprise assault of the Luftwaffe. This military attack was followed by a second attack on civilians by special extermination squads, the *Einsatzgruppen*.

From the beginning, it was recognized that this attack would be different from other invasions. In a conference held several months before this invasion, Hitler warned his senior commanders who were responsible for the campaign against the Soviet Union:

> The war against Russia will be such that it cannot be conducted in a chivalrous fashion. This struggle is one of ideologies and racial differences and will have to be conducted with unprecedented, merciless and unrelenting harshness. All officers will have to rid themselves of obsolete ideologies. I know that the necessity for such means of waging war is beyond the comprehension of you generals but I ... insist absolutely that my orders be executed without contradiction. The commissars are the bearers of ideology directly opposed to National Socialism. Therefore the commissars will be liquidated.[2]

According to Hitler, the Russian people were sub-human and their country was a Bolshevized wasteland. In his view, Russians were destined to become slaves to a superior people. The subjection of the Russian people was allocated to Himmler and four *Einsatzgruppen* (killing battalions). In pursuing this aim, Himmler and Heydrich had given orders that all Jews, Asiatic inferiors, Communist function-aries and gypsies should be murdered. In a series of decrees, Hitler ensured that this policy should be undertaken without any possibility of prosecution for those who complied. A guideline issued by the German High Command before the attack stated that ruthless and energetic measures should be taken against Bolshevistic agitators, guerrillas, saboteurs and Jews.

In this attack the SS *Einsatzgruppen* acted in close association with the army. Each *Einsatzgruppe* was composed of between 600 and 1000 men: the lower ranks contained Gestapo, criminal police, order police, *Waffen-SS* and various specialists. The leaders, however, were carefully selected largely from the SD. These forces followed directly behind the invading troops. On 2 July 1941 Heydrich issued written instructions to the four Higher SS and Police Leaders who had been appointed concerning the operations of the *Einsatzgruppen*:

The following will be executed:
All officials of the Comintern (most of these will certainly be career politicians); Officials of senior and middle rank and 'extremists' in the Party, the Central Committee, and the provincial and district committees;
The People's Commissars;
Jews in the service of the Party or the State;
Other extremist elements (saboteurs, propagandists, assassins, agitators, etc.); in so far as in individual cases they are not required, or are no longer required, for political intelligence of special importance, for future security police measures, or for the economic rehabilitation of the occupied territories. ... No steps will be taken to interfere with any purges that may be initiated by anti-Communists or anti-Jewish elements in the newly occupied territories. On the contrary, these are to be secretly encouraged. At the same time every precaution must be taken to ensure that those who engage in 'self-defence' actions are not subsequently able to plead that they were acting under orders or had been promised political protection. Special care must be taken in regard to the shooting of doctors or others engaged in medical practice.[3]

Although Heydrich refers here only to the execution of Jews in the service of the Party or the State, it appears that he was intent on the extermination of all Russian Jews when he addressed the *Einsatzgruppen* commanders on 17 June 1941. In any event, in the course of the war the *Einsatzgruppen* came to interpret their task as the extermination of the entire Jewish population. In this onslaught, an attempt was made to encourage Russian non-Jews to initiate pogroms against the local Jews, as is evidenced by an account of the operations of the *Einsatzgruppe A* dated 15 October 1941:

Native anti-Semitic forces were induced to start pogroms against Jews during the first hours of the invasion, though this proved to be very difficult. Carrying out orders, the Security Police were determined to solve the Jewish question with all possible means and most decisively. But it was desirable that the Security Police should not put in an immediate appearance, at least in the beginning, since the extraordinarily harsh measures were apt to cause a stir even in German circles. It had to be shown to the world that the inhabitants themselves took the first measures by way of natural reaction against the repression by the Jews over several decades and against the terror exercised by the Communists during the preceding period ... in accordance with basic orders, the cleansing of the Security Police had the goal of the most comprehensive elimination possible of the Jews. Extensive executions were thus carried out by special units in the cities and the plains.[4]

Typical of actions taken by the *Einsatzgruppen* was the operation in Lithuania, as described by Karl Jäger, the head of *Einsatzkommando 3* in a memo dated 1 December 1941:

> The carrying out of such actions is first and foremost a matter of organization. The decision to clear each district systematically of Jews required a thorough preparation of every single action and the investigation of the conditions in the particular district. The Jews had to be concentrated in one place or in several places. The place for the pits which were required had to be found and dug out to suit the numbers involved. The distance from the place where the Jews were concentrated to the pits was on average 4–5 km. The Jews were transported to the place of execution in groups of up to 500 with gaps of at least 2 km.[5]

A typical example of the horror that took place throughout Russia occurred in the city of Lvov shortly after the German invasion. At the beginning of the German occupation, Ukrainian mobs murdered Jews wherever they were found. A witness to this slaughter recalled the scene in the yard of a police station where more than 5000 Jews had been gathered:

> Thousands of men were lying here in rows. They lay on their bellies, their faces buried in the sand. Around the perimeter of the field searchlights and machine guns had been set up. Among them I caught sight of German officers standing about. We were ordered to lie flat like the others. We were pushed and shoved brutally, this way and that. My father was separated from me, and I heard him calling out in despair: 'Let me stay with my son! I want to die with my son!' Nobody took any notice of him.
>
> Now that we were all lying still, there was a hush that lasted for a moment or two. Then the 'game' started. We could hear the sound of a man, clearly one of us, stumbling awkwardly around, chased and beaten by another as he went. At last the pursued collapsed out of sheer exhaustion. He was told to rise. Blows were rained down upon him until he dragged himself to his feet again and tried to run forward. He fell to the ground again and tried to run forward. He fell to the ground again and hadn't the strength to get up. When the pursuers were at last satisfied that the incessant blows had rendered him unable to stir, let

alone run, they called a halt and left him there. Now it was the turn of the second victim. He received the same treatment. . . .

Thoughts raced in disorder and confusion through my mind. I was so exhausted that I fell asleep. Not even the agonizing screams, the sound of savage blows, or the continual trampling on our bodies could prevent me any longer from sinking into oblivion. . . .

The welcome state of unconsciousness passed all too quickly. I came to, and was startled by a painful stab of dazzling light. Powerful searchlights were focused on us. We sat up, one beside the other, so close that we could not stir. Directly in front of me sat two men with shattered skulls. Through the mess of bone and hair I could see the very brains. We whispered to them. We nudged them. But they did not stir. They just sat there, propped up, bulging eyes staring ahead. They were quite dead.[6]

In the assault against the Jewish population in the Soviet Union, the Nazis liquidated ghettos in which thousands of Jews had been gathered. The ghetto of Borissov in Byelorussia, for example, was besieged by German troops in October 1941. In his account the organizer of this onslaught, David Ehof, stated:

I sealed off the ghetto during the night . . . with additional guards. By this time, three graves had been dug near the airfield about 2km from Borissov by prisoners of war under the direction of the Secret Field Police. They were about 400 metres long, 3 metres wide and up to 2 metres deep and were intended for burying the corpses.

Early in the morning . . . we assembled the police, who were not yet sober, in front of the security administration building and explained to them that we were now going to begin shooting all the Jews in the ghetto. I also announced that I had been put in charge of shooting the Jews. I then once again called for a merciless reckoning with the Jews.

I then ordered my deputy Kowalski and the police platoon leader, Pipin, to organize the transport of the Jews to the place of execution and ensure that they were guarded. After the number of guards round the ghetto had been increased we sent the police in groups into the ghetto and sent in lorries to carry away the Jewish population which had been condemned to be shot. The police broke into the Jewish houses, chased the people to the square in the centre of the ghetto, drove them into the vehicles by force and transported them to the place of execution. There was no mercy shown either to old people, children, pregnant women or the sick. Anyone who offered resistance was shot on the spot by my orders – in the square, in the houses, on the trip to the place of execution – or they were beaten half to death. The condemned people were not only brought in lorries but also on foot in groups of 70 to 80 persons and were mercilessly beaten in the process.

The people who had been brought to the place of execution were placed about 50 metres from the graves and guarded until it was their turn to be shot. 20 or 25 people at a time were led to the place of execution, to the graves. At the graves they were undressed; they even had their good quality underclothes torn from their bodies. Having been completely undressed they were driven to the graves and were forced to lie down. The police and the Germans shot them with rifles and automatic weapons. ...

I arrived at the place of execution at about 11 o'clock in the morning and saw an indescribably horrific sight – the place of execution was filled with groans and cries and the continual shrieks of horror of the women and the children.[7]

Throughout the Soviet Union mass executions of Jews became commonplace. A harrowing account of such atrocities was given at the Nuremberg Trials by a German builder Hermann Grabe:

The people who had got off the lorries – men, women and children of all ages – had to undress on the orders of an SS man who was carrying a riding or dog whip in his hand. They had to place their clothing on separate piles for shoes, clothing and underwear. I saw a pile of shoes containing approximately 800–1000 pairs, and great heaps of underwear and clothing. Without weeping or crying out these people undressed and stood together in family groups, embracing each other and saying goodbye while waiting for a sign from another SS man who stood on the edge of the ditch and also had a whip. During the quarter of an hour in which I stood near the ditch, I did not hear a single complaint or a plea for mercy. I watched a family of about eight, a man and a woman, both about 50 years old, with their children of about 1, 8 and 10, as well as two grown-up daughters of about 20 and 24. An old woman with snow-white hair held a 1-year-old child in her arms, singing to it and tickling it. The child squeaked with delight. The married couple looked on with tears in their eyes. The father held the 10-year-old boy by the hand speaking softly to him. The boy was struggling to hold back his tears. ...

I walked around the mound and stood in front of the huge grave. The bodies were lying so tightly packed together that only their heads showed, from almost all of which blood ran down over their shoulders. Some were still moving. Others raised their hands and turned their heads to show that they were still alive. The ditch was already three-quarters full. I estimate that it already held about a thousand bodies. I turned my eyes towards the man doing the shooting. He was an SS man; he sat, legs swinging, on the edge of the ditch. He had an automatic rifle resting on his knees. ... The people, completely naked, climbed down steps which had been cut into the clay wall of the ditch, stumbled over the heads of those lying there and stopped at the spot indicated by the SS man. They lay down on top of the dead or wounded; some stroked those still living and spoke quietly to them. Then I heard a series of rifle shots. I looked into the ditch and saw the bodies contorting or, the heads already inert, sinking on the corpses beneath. Blood flowed from the nape of their necks.[8]

Discussion: Mass murder

The activities of the *Einsatzgruppen* in Russia marked a new stage in the onslaught against the Jewish community. Previously Jews had been persecuted, deported, ghettoized, and worked to death. However, there had been no policy of mass murder. The killing squads had, however, set the scene for a new approach to the Jewish problem. No doubt the decision to exterminate Jewry emerged gradually as the Nazis came to realize that they had no coherent plan what to do with the millions of Jews living in the east.

From 1940–1 Hitler had encouraged his *Gauleiter* to rid their territories of the Jewish population, expressing no interest in how this was to be accomplished. Yet the question remained: what should be done with the masses of Jews given that deportation to Madagascar, as had been proposed, was not a realistic option. Three million Jews were now amassed in ghettos, compelled to live in the most appalling conditions. These individuals constituted a threat to the racial health of Aryan civilization. On 31 July 1941 Göring, who was responsible for the Jewish question, signed the following document in response to a query from Heydrich's office:

To supplement the task that was assigned to you on 24 January 1939, which dealt with the solution of the Jewish problem by emigration and evacuation in the most suitable way, I hereby charge you with making all necessary preparations with regard to the organizational, technical and material matters for bringing about a complete solution of the Jewish question within the German sphere of influence in Europe.

Wherever other governmental agencies are involved, these are to cooperate with you.

I request you further to send me, in the near future, an overall plan covering the organizational, technical and material measures necessary for the accomplishment of the final solution of the Jewish question which we desire.[9]

Although this statement mentions a complete solution, it is not clear whether Göring was referring to a policy of complete extermination. It may be that this note simply referred to an extension of Himmler's responsibility for the Jewish question beyond Germany and an authorization to prepare the next steps in this overall programme. Yet it may well be that this document refers implicitly to a more wide-ranging solution to the Jewish problem involving extermination. Arguably, given the victories in Russia in 1941 and the killing of Jews by the *Einsatzgruppen*, Hitler may have authorized Himmler to provide a total solution to the Jewish question without inquiring how this would be done. The SS would then have been left to devise its own solution. No doubt such a plan would have required authority from a very high level within the Nazi party possibly including Hitler, but given the reaction to the euthanasia programme, Hitler may have decided that he should not be associated with any controversial policies.

There is nonetheless some evidence that Hitler approved of the decision to eliminate Jewry. In a statement by Adolf Eichmann to an Israeli interrogator in 1960, he stated:

> I think the war against the Soviet Union started in June 1941. And I think it must have been two months later, it could have been three months later, that Heydrich ordered me to come and see him. I went and he said to me: 'The Führer has ordered the physical extermination of the Jews'. He said this sentence to me and then, quite contrary to his habit, paused for a long time as if he wanted to test the effect of his words on me. At first I could not grasp the implications because he chose his words carefully. But then I understood and said nothing further because there was nothing more I could say.[10]

Further evidence in support of the claim that Hitler sought to exterminate the Jews is provided by an affidavit by Rudolf Hoess, the first commandant of Auschwitz, which he wrote after the war:

> In the summer of 1941, I cannot remember the exact date, I was suddenly summoned to the *Reichsführer SS*, directly by his adjutant's office. Contrary to his usual custom, Himmler received me without his adjutant being present and said to me in effect: 'The Führer has ordered that the Jewish question be solved once and for all and we, the SS, are to implement that order. The existing extermination centres in the East are not in a position to carry out the larger actions which are anticipated. I have therefore earmarked Auschwitz for this purpose'.[11]

Whatever the case, it is clear that the Nazi authorities did not know how to undertake such a major operation. There had been no previous example of the annihilation of millions of people consisting of men, women and children. Hence confusion ensued in 1941, and various methods were used to rid Europe of an unwanted population. From 1941–2 several methods of liquidation were employed. First, the *Einsatzgruppen* engaged in mass shooting of German, Austrian and Czech Jews who had been deported to Poland – this was an extension of the action against Russian Jewry. Another method was to use gassing vans like those which had been used in the campaign in East Prussia and Poland. Eventually gassing became the most suitable solution; this method had been employed in the euthanasia programme and the Führer's Chancellery was anxious to redeploy the personnel who had been involved in this work.

Notes

1   Alan Clark, *Barbarossa: The Russian-German Conflict, 1941–5*, New York, 1966, p. 65.
2   Alan Bullock, *Hitler: A Study in Tyranny*, New York, 1962, pp. 640–1.
3   H. Buchheim, M. Broszat, H. Krausnick and H. A. Jacobsen, *Anatomy of the SS State*, London, 1968, pp. 62–3.
4   Nuremberg Document 180-L.
5   H. Krausnick and H. H. Wilhelm, *Die Truppe des Weltanschauungskrieges. Die Einsatzgruppen der Sicherheitspolizei und des SD 1938–1942*, Stuttgart, 1981, pp. 536–7 in J. Noakes and G. Pridham, *op. cit.*, p. 1094.
6   Testimony of Leon Weliczker Wells, Eichmann Trial, 1 May 1961, session 22 in Gilbert, *op. cit.*, p. 164.
7   Krausnick and Wilhelm, *op. cit.*, pp. 578–9 in J. Noakes and G. Pridham, *op. cit.*, p. 1099.
8   Nuremberg Document PS-2992.
9   K. Pätzold (ed.), *Verfolgung, Vertreibung, Vernichtung Dokumente des faschistischen Antisemitismus, 1933 bis 1942*, Leipzig, 1984, p. 298 in J. Noakes and G. Pridham, *op. cit.*, p. 1104.
10 J. von Lang (ed.), *Das Eichmann-Protokoll, Tonbandaufzeichnungen der israelischen Verhöre*, Berlin, 1982, p. 69 in J. Noakes and G. Pridham, *op. cit.*, p. 1105.
11 T. Berenstein *et al.* (eds), *Faschimus-Getto-Massenmord. Dokumentation über Austrottung und Widerstand der Juden in Polen während des zweiten Weltkrieges*, Frankfurt, ?1960, p. 374 in J. Noakes and G. Pridham, *op. cit.*, pp. 1105–6.

15. The Wannsee Conference and aftermath

The Nazi onslaught against the Jewish people proceeded in stages, from prejudice and discrimination to annihilation. In this sequence of events, the Wannsee Conference of 20 January 1942 in a villa outside Berlin marked the final stage of this process. The result of the conference was the official adoption of the Final Solution to the Jewish problem. In the war against the Soviet Union, the *Einsatzgruppen* had systematically murdered Jews wherever they were found. Following Wannsee, the decision to exterminate Jews became a central feature of Nazi policy.

The beginning of the end

Having embarked on the task of deporting Jews to their destination in the east, Germany was confronted with the practical problem of defining criteria for those who were to be transported. In addition, the process of uprooting thousands of people from their homes, transporting them during wartime, and relocating them in new dwellings became a major logistical problem. What was required was a coordinated system. To resolve these dilemmas, Heydrich invited a group of senior officials to a conference to discuss this issue. An invitation addressed to *SS Gruppenführer* Hoffmann of the SS Race and Settlement Office in Berlin read:

> On 31.7.1941, the Reich Marshal of the Greater German Reich charged me, in cooperation with all the other relevant central agencies, to make all the necessary preparations with regard to organizational, technical and material measures for a complete solution of the Jewish question in

Europe and to present him shortly with a complete draft proposal on this matter. .... In view of the extraordinary importance which must be accorded to these questions, and in the interest of securing a uniform view among the relevant central agencies of the further tasks concerned with the remaining work on this final solution, I propose to make these problems the subject of a general discussion. This is particularly necessary since from 10 October onwards the Jews have been being evacuated from Reich territory, including the Protectorate, to the East in a continuous series of transports.[1]

Anxious to know what was envisaged, Hans Frank sent his State Secretary Dr Buhler to see Heydrich. In a meeting with the senior officials of the General Government, Frank explained what was to be done with the Jewish populace:

As for the Jews – I will be quite open with you – they will have to be finished off one way or the other. The Führer said once: if the whole of Jewry once again succeeds in unleashing a world war, then peoples who have been hounded into this war will not be the only ones to shed their blood because the Jews in Europe will meet their end. I know that many of the measures now being taken against the Jews in the Reich are criticized. It is clear from the reports on popular opinion that there are accusations of cruelty and harshness. Before I continue, I would like you to agree with me on the following principle: we are only prepared to show compassion towards the German people and to no one else on earth. The others did not show compassion towards us. As an old National Socialist, I must state that if the Jewish clan were to survive the war in Europe, while we had sacrificed our best blood in the defence of Europe, then this war would only represent a partial success. With respect to the Jews, therefore, I will only operate on the assumption that they will disappear.[2]

The Wannsee Conference took place on 20 January 1942. The minutes, prepared by Adolf Eichmann, record the nature of the discussion:

The chief of the Security Police and SD, *SS Obergruppenführer* Heydrich, began by announcing his appointment by the Reich Marshal as the person responsible for the preparation of the final solution of the European Jewish question and pointed out that this meeting was being held to achieve clarity on basic questions. The Reich Marshal's wish that he should be sent a draft on the organizational, technical, and material matters regarding the final solution of the European Jewish question made it necessary that all central authorities directly concerned with these questions should deal with them together in advance so as to ensure the coordination of the lines to be taken. ...

The Chief of the Security Police and SD then gave a brief review of the struggle which had been waged hitherto against these opponents. The basic elements were

(a) the exclusion of the Jews from the individual spheres of German life.

(b) the exclusion of the Jews from the living space of the German people. In pursuit of these efforts, the acceleration of the emigration of Jews from the Reich territory was increased and systematically adopted as provisionally the only feasible solution.

In January 1939, on the orders of the Reich Marshal, a Reich Central Office for Jewish Emigration was established and the Chief of the Security Police and SD was appointed to head it ... the objective was to purge Germany's living space of Jews in a legal fashion. ...

The financing of the emigration was undertaken by the Jews or rather Jewish political organizations themselves. To avoid the proletarianized Jews remaining behind, the principle was followed that the wealthy Jews had to finance the emigration of the propertyless Jews ... foreign Jewish financial institutions were requested by our domestic Jewish organizations to ensure the provision of sufficient foreign exchange ... in view of the dangers involved in emigration during the war, and in view of the opportunities provided by the east, the *Reichsführer SS* and Chief of the German Police had later banned emigration.

The evacuation of the Jews to the east has now emerged, with the prior permission of the Führer, as a further possible solution instead of emigration. These actions, however, must be regarded only as an alternative solution, but already the practical experience is being gathered which is of great importance to the coming final solution of the Jewish question. ...

In pursuance of the final solution, the Jews will be conscripted for labour in the east under appropriate supervision. Large labour gangs will be formed from those fit for work, with the sexes separated, which will be sent to these areas for road construction and undoubtedly a large number of them will drop out through natural wastage. The remainder who survive – and they will certainly be those who have the greatest powers of endurance – will have to be dealt with accordingly. For, if released, they would, as a natural selection of the fittest, form a germ cell from which the Jewish race could regenerate itself.[3]

The minutes of the Wannsee Conference were circulated to a wide range of government departments and SS head offices – the language used was designed to disguise the true intentions of those gathered at the conference. As is clear from the interrogation of Adolf Eichmann by the Israelis in 1960, the Final Solution of the Jewish problem was understood by the participants at the conference as referring to extermination:

> What I know is that the gentlemen sat together, and then in very blunt terms – not in the language that I had to use in the minutes, but in very blunt terms – they talked about the matter without any circumlocution. I certainly could not have remembered that if I had not recalled saying to myself at the time: look, just look at Stuckart, who was always regarded as a legal pedant, punctilious and fussy, and now what a different tone! The language being used here was very unlegalistic. I should say that this is the only thing from all this that has still stuck clearly in my mind.
> *Presiding Judge*: What did he say on this matter?
> *Answer*: In particular, Mr President, I would like to ...
> *Question*: Not in particular – in general!
> *Answer*: The talk was of killing, elimination, and annihilation.[4]

Following the Wannsee Conference, Hitler in his annual address to the *Reichstag* on the anniversary of his appointment as Reich Chancellor stated his intentions regarding the Jewish community:

> We are clear about the fact that the war can only end either in the extermination of the Aryan nations or in the disappearance of Jewry from Europe. On 1 September 1939, I already announced in the German *Reichstag* – and I avoid making premature prophecies – that this would not end as the Jews imagined, namely with the extermination of the European-Aryan nations, but rather that the war will result in the destruction of Jewry. This time, for the first time, the old and typical Jewish law will be applied 'An eye for an eye, a tooth for a tooth'.
>
> And the more the fighting spreads, the more – and world Jewry should take note of it – anti-Semitism will spread. It will find nourishment in every prisoner-of-war camp, in every family which becomes aware of the reason why it has had to make its sacrifice. And the hour will come when the most evil enemy of the world of all time will for at least a thousand years have played his last role.[5]

In the months that followed, the Nazis rounded up Jews for deportation to their deaths. Aware of their eventual fate, these innocent victims sought to hide or escape from their oppressors. 'We tremble at the mention of Lublin,' Chaim Kaplan wrote in his diary. 'Our blood turns to ice when we listen to tales told by refugees from the city. Even before they arrived in the Warsaw ghetto, the rumours reaching us were so frightful that we thought they came from totally unreliable sources.' Yet there was no escape. As Kaplan recorded in his diary:

> As Jews tried to escape, the Nazis hunted them down. Heeding the advice of the prophet, 'Wait a little until the danger is past', some Jews tried to conceal themselves in obscure holes and corners. Perhaps God would have mercy and spare them? Perhaps the Keeper of Israel would take pity? But the killers discovered the hiding places and swiftly put to death anyone they found. Some of the Jews suffocated in these airless holes even before the Nazis discovered them, for the doors could not be opened from within and there was no one to open them from without because everyone above ground had been arrested.[6]

Such a round-up of Jews was often undertaken with lightning speed. On 11 April 1942, for example, an eye-witness of such an event in Zamosc recalled:

> The SS, SD and the mounted police fell like a pack of savages on the Zamosc Jewish quarter. It was a complete surprise. The brutes on horseback in particular created a panic; they raced through the streets shouting insults, slashing out on all sides with their whips. Our community then numbered 10,000 people. In a twinkling, without even realizing what was happening, a crowd of 3000 men, women and children, picked up haphazardly in the streets and in the houses, were driven to the station and deported to an unknown destination.
>
> The spectacle which the ghetto presented after the attack literally drove the survivors mad. Bodies everywhere, in the streets, in the courtyards, inside the houses; babies thrown from the third or fourth floors lay crushed on the pavements. The Jews themselves had to pick up and bury the dead.[7]

When the Gestapo entered the Warsaw ghetto the same month, they went from one building to the next. As Chaim Kaplan noted:

> At 36 Nowolipki Street a man by the name of Goldberg was killed. He was a barber in peacetime, and when the war broke out he went to work in the quarantine house. His wife worked there too. When he was killed, his wife set up a terrible wailing and would not leave his side. To silence her, they killed her too. Both were left lying by the gate. In death as in life they remained inseparable.
>
> The baker, David Blajman, on Gesia Street, was murdered in the same

way. They came to take the husband but the frantic wife ran after him. To rid themselves of this hindrance, the murderers killed her along with her husband. The morning light revealed both bodies at the gate.[8]

In her diary, Mary Berg recalled the events that took place on 17 April:

All the bakers were terrified. Epstein and Wagner, who own the bakery in our house, no longer sleep at home. The Germans come to various houses with a prepared list of names and addresses. If they do not find the persons they are looking for, they take another member of the same family instead. They lead him a few steps in front of the house, politely let him precede them, and then shoot him in the back. The next morning these people are found lying dead in the streets. If a janitor fails to open the door for the Germans as quickly as they want him to, he is shot on the spot. If a member of the janitor's family opens the door the same fate befalls him, and later the janitor is summoned to be killed, too.[9]

On 8 May Jews in the White Russian village of Radun discovered that the ghetto had been sealed off. Several days later, a group of Jews were given spades, marched out of the ghetto, and forced to dig pits. Fearing for their lives, some Jews attempted to flee. As Avraham Aviel related, he had tried to escape from the ghetto to meet his father in a nearby wood. Yet, it was feared he was too small to join the others as partisans, and he returned to the ghetto:

I tried to hide my smaller brother and my mother and the people who were with us in the house. I tried to hide them in the attic. I covered them with rags and boxes, then I went down and I tried to find out what was happening. As soon as I went down from the attic, I heard a terrible noise. Motorcycles were coming in. There were shouts. Germans came in from the direction of Lida in battle uniform equipped with automatic weapons as if they were marching out to the front. It was a different uniform from what we had seen before. They had about the same uniform as that very first group had when they killed those 40 people. I left the house and I saw a great mass of Jews being pushed from the edge of the ghetto, being driven on in the direction of Grodno. ... At that moment a number of Germans entered our house. One of them stood at the entrance blocking it and the others scattered in the rooms and began searching and driving out people who were not yet in hiding. ... Unfortunately, however, I saw my mother, my small brother, an uncle and other Jews included in the group of those people who were found and my little brother then told me later that they were beaten severely. Then we marched together in this direction in which we were driven.[10]

Resistance against the German onslaught was seen as futile. On 10 June 1942 Jews of Biala Podlaska were deported to Sobibor. Later Emanuel Ringelblum spoke to the head of the Jewish Social Relief Organization in Biala Podlaska. 'How much longer will we be slaughtered?', he asked. This question, he continued,

> haunts all of us, but there is no answer to it because everyone knows that resistance, and particularly if even one German is killed, its outcome may lead to a slaughter of a whole community, or even of many communities. The first who are sent to slaughter are the old, the sick, the children, those who are not able to resist. The strong ones, the workers, are left meanwhile to be, because they are needed for the time being.
>
> The evacuations are carried out in such a way that it is not always and not to everyone clear that a massacre is taking place. So strong is the instinct of the workers, of the fortunate owners of work permits, that it overcomes the will to fight, the urge to defend the whole community, with no thought of consequences. And we are left to be led as sheep to a slaughterhouse. This is partly due to the complete spiritual breakdown and disintegration caused by the unheard-of terror which has been inflicted upon the Jews for three years and comes to its climax in times of such evacuations.[11]

Despite such despair, there were numerous acts of resistance. In Warsaw, for example, two porters were suspected of smuggling and taken to be executed. In his diary, Chaim Kaplan depicted their struggle against these murderers:

> In the dark of the night a wrestling match began between those who were defending their lives and the killers. The porters fought with the strength of their bodies, without weapons; the killers were armed and confident of their superiority.
>
> At such times there is no rational thought. Instinct comes in its stead. In time of danger the latent, hidden powers of a man burst out and are exposed; and in particular when one finds oneself in a condition of 'in any case we will die'. And therefore, before the killers had time to act, the condemned men pounced on them and tried to seize the pistols. One of the pistols went off and wounded the tailor in the leg. Then the porters grabbed the Nazis by the throat and tried to strangle them. The two sides wrestled until their strength waned, and in the end the killers,

who still had their weapons, were victorious. ... On the morrow, the Nazis avenged the mutiny of the two porters with 100 Jews. They were put to death for the sins of men who had never laid eyes on them.[12]

Discussion: The annihilation of the Jews

The Wannsee Conference marked a turning-point in the Nazi quest to ensure that Europe was *judenrein* (free of Jews). In Poland terror squads were responsible for the elimination of the Polish elite, and haphazardly for Jews as well. With the conquest of Russian territory, the *Einsatzgruppen* were officially instructed to follow the German army into the Soviet Union and protect its rear from partisan attack. Yet, as we have seen, their real aim was to eliminate the Jewish population. Between 1½ and 2 million Jews were slaughtered by these mobile killing units. All Jews were perceived as supporters of Bolshevism, and thus dangerous subversives. In addition, since the children of Jews were destined to become enemies of Germany, they were to be annihilated as well. At times, commanders told their troops that killings were necessary to prevent typhus and other diseases.

In general the *Einsatzgruppen* were accepted by the army so long as they did not interfere with army activities. Despite the claim after the war that the mobile killing units acted without the compliance of the military, there is substantial evidence to illustrate that there was ample collaboration between the *Einsatzgruppen* and the *Wehrmacht* in rounding up victims as well as in the shootings themselves. In this connection, it was policy for the army to hand over all Jewish prisoners of war to the SS for execution.

Who were those individuals who made up the *Einsatzgruppen*? In general the commanders of these killing units were middle-class in origin. Many were professionals: doctors, lawyers and intellectuals. Organized into four units, Group A consisted of 900 men and operated in the Baltic states; B was operative in the north-central region of Russia; C was located in the vicinity of Kiev; and D had a strength of 500 men and advanced behind the most southern army in the Crimea. Each of these groups was augmented by auxiliary troops of native eastern Europeans including ethnic Germans in Poland. A sizeable contingent of volunteers were from the Baltic States and Romania.

Innocent of the intentions of the Nazis, the people in conquered territories were totally unprepared for the ferocity of the German onslaught. When told that Jews were to be resettled, these Russian Jews believed the victors. When they were ordered to assemble in the town square, they complied. Told to climb aboard trucks, they were obedient. However, once the first wave of killings took place, rumours were rife and the round-up of victims became more difficult. Hundreds of thousands of Jews fled to the east. During the next few months of the operation, however, the numbers of individual Jews killed by the Germans was overwhelming. In the first five months of the operation approximately half a million men, women and children were killed, and a second wave was instructed to kill those who remained.

Records of the action of the *Einsatzgruppen* reveal the barbarity of their methods. Commanders of these groups adopted different approaches in the killing process: some desired that their victims should kneel before the were shot; others wanted them standing. In some cases Jewish victims were compelled to hand over their possessions; other Nazi soldiers wanted houses to remain intact before they were confiscated by SS personnel. Yet, despite such differences in approach, the pattern of murder remained much the same. Once the German army had passed through a Russian town, those who had fled to the woods came back to their homes. In a short time, *Einsatzgruppen* troops appeared. The officer in charge asked for the rabbi or head of the Jewish town council. All Jews were then instructed to assemble in the town square; a roll-call was then conducted with the alleged intent of resettling the community.

When the black-shirted commander appeared, he told the assembled multitude that there was to be a change in plan. Everyone was told to go to a hillside several kilometres outside the town. Groups of about 100 were to leave every ten minutes; those who were too weak to walk were taken by truck. When these individuals arrived at the hill they were met by a squad of SS men who told families to get undressed. Eventually the *Einsatzkommando* opened fire on these individuals and they plunged into mass graves. Not all were killed in this onslaught, however, and those who survived attempted to climb out of this grave. In time more victims arrived who were shot in turn and fell upon the wounded who were struggling to escape.

This process of mass slaughter was too laborious. What was required was a more efficient and less emotionally demanding method. Initially the use of gas vans was designed to resolve these dilemmas. At first the vans were used in Chelmno. There an isolated mansion had been converted into a killing site: three vans were equipped to asphyxiate Jews from Lodz. Allegedly these vans were to be used as de-lousing quarters. Approximately 50 men, women and children were ordered to climb into each van, unaware that a hose had been attached to the exhaust pipe of the diesel motor so that carbon monoxide fumes would be directed into the interior. After 15 minutes, all those inside would have died and the driver stopped near a pit where a group of Jews, the *Sonderkommando*, emptied the van.

The gas vans were a short-lived solution. In their place, fixed killing centres were established at Chelmno, Belzec, Sobibor, Treblinka, Majdanek, and Auschwitz, adopting similar methods to those used during the euthanasia programme. In place of carbon monoxide, Zyklon-B gas was used. With this machinery in place, ghettos were emptied and trainloads of Jews from Nazi-occupied territory made their way to Poland. Under SS Major-General Odilo Globocnik, the Final Solution was carried out in accordance with the plans laid at the Wannsee Conference.

Notes

1   Nuremberg Document PS-709.
2   W. Präg and W. Jacobmeyer (eds), *Das Diensttagebuch des deutschen Generalgouverneurs in Polen 1939–1945*, Stuttgart, 1975, pp. 457–8 in J. Noakes and G. Pridham, *op. cit.*, p. 1126.
3   L. Poliakov and J. Wulf, *Das Dritte Reich und die Juden*, Frankfurt, 1983, pp. 119–26 in J. Noakes and G. Pridham, *op. cit.*, pp. 1127–31.
4   G. Fleming, *Hitler and the Final Solution*, London, 1985, pp. 91–2.
5   M. Domarus, *Hitler, Reden 1932 bis 1945*, Wiesbaden, 1973, pp. 1828–9 in J. Noakes and G. Pridham, *op. cit.*, p. 1135.
6   Kaplan diary, 7 April 1942, in Abraham Katsch (ed.), *The Warsaw Diary of Chaim A. Kaplan*, New York, 1973, pp. 312–13.
7   Testimony of David Mekler, *Miriam Novitch Collection*, Kibbutz Lohamei Hagettatot, Israel, in Gilbert, *op. cit.*, pp. 319–20.
8   Kaplan diary, 18 April 1942, in Katsch, *op. cit.*, p. 314.
9   Mary Berg diary, 28 April 1942, in S. L. Schneiderman (ed.), *Warsaw Ghetto: A Diary by Mary Berg*, New York, 1945, pp. 142–3.
10 Testimony of Avraham Aviel, Eichmann Trial, 5 May 1961, session 29.
11 Joseph Kermish, 'Emanuel Ringelblum's Notes Hitherto Unpublished', *Yad Vashem Studies, VII*, Jerusalem, 1968, pp. 178–80.
12 Kaplan diary, 3 July 1942, in Katsch, *op. cit.*, pp. 368–369.

16. Transportation and arrival at the camps

Chelmno was the first death camp to operate: between December 1941 and the spring of 1943, over 200,000 Polish Jews and thousands of Soviet prisoners and gypsies died there. The second camp established by the Nazis was located at Belzec where approximately 500,000 Jews were exterminated between March 1942 and May 1943. At Sobibor about 250,000 Jews who had been transported from throughout Europe lost their lives in the gas chambers which were disguised as shower and disinfectant installations between May 1942 and October 1943. At Treblinka Jews from Warsaw numbering about 800,000 died between 1942 and August 1943. During this period another 130,000 Jews were killed at Majdanek. Finally, about 1,250,000 Jews were murdered at Auschwitz between 1942 and November 1944. Such mass killing could only be accomplished by the transportation of Jewish victims by heartless Nazi soldiers.

The journey to the camps

As deportations took place throughout Europe, rumours constantly circulated about what fate awaited those who travelled eastward. As Zygmunt Klukowski noted in his diary of 26 March 1942:

> There is great unhappiness and fear among the Jews. From everywhere comes the news about the incredible violence against the Jews. They are bringing trainloads of Jews from Czechoslovakia, Germany, and even from Belgium. They are also resettling the Jews from various towns and villages and taking them somewhere towards Belzec. Today I heard a story about what they did to the Jews in Lublin. It is difficult to believe

it's true. Today they deported Jews from Izbica – they were also taken to Belzec where there is supposed to be some monstrous camp.[1]

The next month Klukowski recorded that the Jewish community was overwhelmed by what they learned about these deportations. 'We know now for certain,' he wrote, 'that one train every day from the direction of Lublin, and one from the direction of Lvov of twenty-odd waggons, each are going to Belzec. Here, they are taking the Jews out of the trains, pushing them behind barbed-wire fences and killing them either by electrocution or poisoning with gas, and after that they burn the remains.' Describing the journey to Belzec, he stated:

On the way to Belzec people can see horrifying scenes – especially the railwaymen – because the Jews know very well why they are being taken there, and on the journey they are given neither food nor water. On the station in Szczebrzeszyn the railwaymen could see with their own eyes, and hear with their own ears Jews offering 150 zlotys for a kilo of bread, and a Jewess took off a gold ring from her finger and offered it in exchange for a glass of water for her dying child. The inhabitants of Lublin told me of some incredible scenes which are happening there among the Jews, shooting the sick on the spot, and outside the town – shooting the healthy ones and transporting thousands of others to Belzec.[2]

Repeatedly Jews were hounded by the Nazis and forced to assemble at meeting-points before being taken to the railway station and sent off to unknown destinations. A typical occurrence of this nature took place on 6 June 1942 in Cracow. According to an eye-witness of this event:

Old people, women and children pass by the pharmacy windows like ghosts. I see an old woman of around 70 years, her hair loose, walking alone, a few steps away from a larger group of deportees. Her eyes have a glazed look; immobile, wide open, filled with horror, they stare straight ahead. She walks slowly, quietly, only in her dress and slippers, without even a bundle, or handbag. She holds in her hands something small, something black, which she caresses fondly and keeps close to her old breast. It is a small puppy – her most precious possession, all that she saved and would not leave behind.

Laughing, inarticulately gesturing with her hands, walks a young, deranged girl of about 14, so familiar to all the inhabitants of the ghetto.

She walks barefoot, in a crumpled nightgown. One shuddered watching the girl laughing, having a good time. Old and young pass by, some dressed, some only in their underwear, hauled out of their beds and driven out. People after major operations and people with chronic diseases went by. ...

Across the street from the pharmacy, out of the building at 2 Harmony Square, walks a blind old man, well known to the inhabitants of the ghetto; he is about 70 years old, wears dark goggles over his blind eyes, which he lost in the battles on the Italian front in 1915 fighting side by side with the Germans ... immediately after him, another elderly person appears, a cripple with one leg, on crutches. The Germans close in on them; slowly in a dance step, one of them runs towards the blind man and yells with all his power: *'Schnell!'* 'Hurry!' This encourages the other Germans to start a peculiar game.

Two of the SS men approach the old man without the leg and shout the order for him to run. Another one comes from behind and with the butt of his rifle hits the crutch. The old man falls down. The German screams savagely, threatens to shoot. All this takes place right in the back of the blind man who is unable to see, but hears the beastly voices of the Germans, interspersed with cascades of their laughter. ...

For a moment we think that perhaps there will be at least one human being among them unable to stand torturing people one hour before their death. Alas, there was no such person in the annals of the Cracow ghetto.[3]

The horrors of the deportations were described by various witnesses. A local Pole, Stanislaw Bohdanowicz, for example, recalled the nature of the trains that transported victims through Zwierzyniec:

The trains looked terrible. The small windows were covered with planks or lots of barbed wire, and in some places planks were missing from the walls, which was proof of desperate struggles taking place inside. Through the cracks in the planks, and through the wired-up windows peered scared human faces. Sometimes we could tell that a train was approaching, although it was still afar off, because of the shooting by the guards; they were standing on the buffers of the waggons and shooting those who tried to escape.

When such a train stopped at Zwierzyniec station in order to allow another train to pass through, screams, laments and cries could be heard from all the waggons, 'Water, water!' The Jews were holding out bottles and money fastened to sticks or parts of broken planks – but no one was allowed to approach the waggons. The Germans were shooting without warning all those who begged for water, as well as those who tried to give it to them. Soldiers were marching along the train breaking the bottles with sticks and pocketing the money. Women were throwing rings, ear-rings and jewellery through the windows and cracks, begging for a glass of water for their children who were dying of thirst.[4]

One of the deportees from Lvov to Belzec, Rudolf Reder, depicted the terrors accompanying the arrival of his train:

About mid-day the train entered Belzec, a small station surrounded by small houses inhabited by the SS men. Here, the train was shunted off the main track on to a siding which ran for about another kilometre straight to the gates of the death camp. Ukrainian railwaymen also lived near the station and there was a post office nearby as well.

At Belzec station an old German with a thick, black moustache climbed into the locomotive cab. I don't know his name, but I would recognise him again, he looked like a hangman; he took over command of the train and drove it into the camp. The journey to the camp took two minutes. For months I always saw the same bandit.

The siding ran through fields, on both sides, there was completely open country; not one building. The German who drove the train into the camp climbed out of the locomotive, he was 'helping us' by beating and shouting, throwing people out of the train. He personally entered each waggon and made sure that no one remained behind. He knew about everything. When the train was empty and had been checked, he signalled with a small flag and took the train out of the camp.[5]

According to Reder, the entire area of Belzec was occupied by the SS. Anyone who accidentally entered the area was immediately shot. Describing the entry of the train into the yard, he continued:

The train entered a yard which measured about one kilometre by one kilometre and was surrounded by barbed wire and fencing about two metres high, which was not electrified. Entry to the yard was through a wooden gate covered with barbed wire. Next to the gate there was a guard house with a telephone and standing in front of the guard house were several SS men with dogs. When the train entered the yard the SS men closed the gate and went into the guard house. At that moment, dozens of SS men opened the doors of the waggons shouting, 'Los!' ['Out!'] They pushed people out with their whips and rifles. The doors of the waggons were about one metre above the ground. The people, hurried along with blows from whips, were forced to jump down, old and young alike, it made no difference. They broke arms and legs, but they had to obey the orders of the SS men.[6]

Once Jews had arrived at Belzec, they were told that they were going to the bath house and then would be sent to work. Fearing the worst, they were filled with hope. As Reder recalled, the crowd went quietly into a building on which there was a sign: 'Bath and inhalation room':

> The women went about 20 metres farther on – to a large barrack hut which measured about 30 metres by 15 metres. There they had their heads shaved, both women and girls. They entered, not knowing what for. There was still silence and calm. Later, I knew that only a few minutes after entering, they were asked to sit on wooden stools across the barrack hut, and Jewish barbers, like automatons, as silent as the grave, came forward to shave their heads. Then they understood the whole truth, none of them could have any doubts any more. All of them – everyone – except a few chosen craftsmen – were going to die.
>
> The girls with long hair went to be shaved, those who had short hair went with the men – straight into the gas chambers. Suddenly there were cries and tears, a lot of women had hysterics. Many of them went cold-bloodedly to their deaths, especially the young girls.[7]

As a member of the *Sonderkommando* of about 500 Jews who were selected from previous transports, Reder was responsible for dealing with those who had been killed:

> We dug huge mass graves and dragged bodies. We used spades, but there was also a mechanical excavator which dug up the sand and piled it into mounds and later covered over the graves already full of bodies. About 450 of us worked at the graves. It took a week to dig one pit.
>
> The most horrible thing for me was that there was an order to pile the bodies up to a level one metre above the edge of the graves, and then cover them with a layer of sand, while thick, black blood flowed out and flooded the ground like a lake. We had to walk along the ledges from one pit to the next, and our feet were soaked with our brothers' blood. We walked over their bodies and that was even worse. ...
>
> The brute Schmidt was our guard; he beat and kicked us if he thought we were not working fast enough. He ordered his victims to lie down and gave them 25 lashes with a whip, ordered them to count out loud. If the victim made a mistake, he was given 50 lashes. No one could withstand 50 lashes. Usually they managed somehow to reach the barrack hut afterwards, but the following morning they were dead. ... 30 or 40 of us were shot every day. A doctor usually prepared a daily list of the weakest men. During the lunch break they were taken to a nearby grave and shot.[8]

Some of those who were transported to their deaths were unaware of what awaited them in the camps. As a member of the Jewish station commando recalled:

> The transports from Germany, Austria and Czechoslovakia arrived in luxury carriages with all their personal luggage and the people were convinced that they were coming to be resettled. Their naivety was such that some people from the transport turned to us workers of the so-called 'station commando' and offered us tips to help them carry their luggage. I assume that even when they were led naked into the gas chambers they were still convinced they were going to have a bath.[9]

Most Jews, however, were keenly aware of their fate, and the Nazis employed terror to subdue these victims. As an eye-witness recalled:

> When the train arrived in Treblinka I can remember seeing great piles of clothing. Now we feared that the rumours really had been true. I remember saying to my wife more or less: this is the end.
>
> We were transported in goods waggons. The goods waggons were overcrowded. When the train arrived in Treblinka a considerable number of people had already died of exhaustion. I can no longer remember how many there were ... one of the worst things about the transport was the lack of air. There was only a small window covered with a grille and there were no sanitary facilities. I can remember confusion when the doors were pulled open in Treblinka. The Germans and Ukrainians shouted 'Get out, out'. The members of the so-called Jewish Red Commando also shouted and yelled. Then the people who had arrived began to scream and complain. I can remember too that whips were used on us.[10]

Once Jews arrived at the camps, they were separated into groups. Such scenes of horror were depicted by the few who survived. As Chaim Hirszman, a 29-year-old metal worker, recalled:

> Other SS men took us off the train. They led us all together – women, men and children – to a barrack. We were told to undress before we went to the bath. I understood immediately what that meant. After undressing we were told to form two groups, one of men and the other of women and children. An SS man, with the strike of a horse whip, sent the men to the right or to the left, to death – to work. I was selected to death. I didn't know it then. Anyway, I believed that both sides meant the same – death. But, when I jumped in the indicated direction, an SS

man called me and said: 'You have a military bearing, we could use you'. We, who were selected for work, were told to dress. I and some other men were appointed to take the people to the kiln. I was sent with the women. The Ukrainian Schmidt, an Ethnic German, was standing at the entrance to the gas chamber and hitting with a knout every entering woman. Before the door was closed, he fired a few shots from his revolver and then the door closed automatically and 40 minutes later we went and carried the bodies out to a special ramp. We shaved the hair of the bodies, which was afterwards placed in sacks and taken away by Germans. The children were thrown into the chamber simply on the women's heads. In one of the 'transports', taken out of the gas chamber, I found the body of my wife and I had to shave her hair.[11]

Discussion: Jewish complicity

Like the *Judenräte*, the *Sonderkommandos* consisting of Jewish men were used by the Nazis to implement the process of mass killing. When Jewish deportees from Germany, the Low Countries, France, Greece, the Balkans, Italy and Hungary arrived at the death camps, they were met first by Death's Head SS units accompanied by groups of Jewish prisoners, the *Sonderkommandos*. When the railway cars were opened, those who survived the journey staggered out unaware of their destination. Some jumped out; others were pushed. In this mass confusion, the SS beat and often killed these bewildered victims.

When the cars were cleared the *Sonderkommandos* hauled away those who had died on the journey and then hosed down the waggons. Before the gassing other *Sonderkommandos* shaved women's hair or sorted out the belongings of the dead; others worked in offices where they kept voluminous records. The most horrific duty involved handling the bodies of those who had been gassed. They were cleaned of excrement, and then stripped of any gold in their teeth or jewels hidden in bodily orifices. The corpses were then either burned in the crematoria, buried in mass graves or burned in pits.

How could Jews have cooperated in such activities? It could be argued that any collaboration with Nazi authorities is morally contemptible. An obvious response to this challenge is that such cooperation was unavoidable. Refusal resulted in certain death for oneself, and in many cases for others. In his account of the camps,

Reder for example recalled how the *Sonderkommandos* were themselves shot:

> 30 or 40 of us were shot every day. A doctor usually prepared a daily list of the weakest men. During the lunch break they were taken to a nearby grave and shot. They were replaced the following morning by new arrivals from the first transport of the day. Our *Kommando* always numbered 500 – we know, for example, that although Jews had built the camp and installed the death engine, not one of them now remained alive. It was a miracle if anyone survived for five or six months in Belzec.[12]

In such circumstances, it is understandable why the Nazis were able to manipulate the *Sonderkommandos* into complicity with their murderous intentions.

Yet, it should be noted that striking cases of rebellion among the *Sonderkommandos* took place in the camps. Such heroism in the face of death serves as a powerful counter-argument to the charge of Jewish passivity as a contributor to the Nazi success in killing six million Jews. In Birkenau, for example, the *Sonderkommandos* led a revolt against their captors. In the explosives factory a group of Jewish girls had collected explosives and gave them to the plotters hidden in the bottom of a food tray. As an eye-witness recalled:

> When I was standing near my friend he told me that there was a search going on. He told me that he had not had time to put the explosives in the saucers and that the explosives were only on his body in a cigarette package. I knew quite well that not only we would be killed as retaliation, but that all the underground of Auschwitz was jeopardized.[13]

On 7 October 1944 the senior *Sonderkommando* at Crematorium IV was told to draw up a list for evacuation of 300 men. Fearing that this would lead to their deaths, he refused to comply. An SS Staff Sergeant then called out the names, but only a few men responded. Eventually one of the *Sonderkommandos*, Chaim Neuhof, stepped forward and engaged in conversation with the SS Staff Sergeant. When the SS man reached for his gun, Neuhof yelled the password 'Hurrah', and hit the SS man on the head with his hammer. The other prisoners then threw stones at the SS. Describing this incident, one of the *Sonderkommandos* related:

They showed an immense courage refusing to budge. They set up a loud shout, hurled themselves upon the guards with hammers and axes, wounded some of them, the rest they beat with what they could get at, they pelted them with stones without further ado. It is easy to imagine the upshot of this. Few moments had passed when a whole detachment of SS men drove in, armed with machine guns and grenades. There were so many of them that each had two machine guns for one prisoner. Even such an army was mobilized against them.[14]

There is no doubt, however, that many of those who were compelled to serve as *Sonderkommandos* felt enormous guilt. They had been selected to perform horrifying deeds. Surrounded by suffering and death, they were complicit witnesses to the most grotesque acts of barbarity. Despite the death rate in the camps, some of these individuals managed to survive. It is not surprising therefore that many of the survivors of the Holocaust have found it impossible to discuss what they endured in the camps. Racked by memories of their own actions, these haunted figures have sought to erase the past through silence. Even though we can understand their cooperation with the authorities, they may not be able to forgive themselves.

Such guilt has in all likelihood been reinforced by the memories of accusations made in the camps. In Birkenau, for example, an eye-witness recalled an incident which took place after the children of the Siauliai ghetto in Lithuania had been deported:

There a girl of five stood and undressed her brother who was one year old. One from the *Kommando* came to take off the boy's clothes. The girl shouted loudly, 'Be gone, you Jewish murderer! Don't lay your hand, dripping with Jewish blood, upon my lovely brother! I am his mummy, he will die in my arms, together with me'. A boy of seven or eight stood beside her and spoke thus, 'Why, you are a Jew and you lead such dear children to the gas – only in order to live? Is your life among the band of murderers really dearer to you than the lives of so many Jewish victims?'[15]

Notes

1 Klukowski diary, 26 March 1942, in Dziennik, *z lat okupacji Zamojszczyzny*, Lublin, 1959, in Gilbert *op. cit.*, p. 308.
2 Klukowski diary, 8 April 1942, in Gilbert, *op. cit.*, p. 317.
3 Testimony of Tadeusz Pankiewicz in Eisenberg, *Witness to the*

Holocaust, pp. 194–203 in Gilbert, *op. cit.*, pp. 356–7.

4 'Testimony of Stanislaw Bohdanowicz of Zwierzyniec', *Tregenza Collection*, in Gilbert, *op. cit.*, pp. 408–9.

5 Rudolf Reder, 'Belzec', *Tregenza Collection*, trans. Maria Rozak, Cracow, 1946, pp. 4–6 in Gilbert, *op. cit.*, p. 413.

6 *Ibid.*, pp. 413–414.

7 *Ibid.*, p. 415.

8 *Ibid.*, pp. 416–17.

9 A. Rückerl (ed.), *NS Vernichtungslager im Spiegel der deutscher Strafprozesse. Belzec, Sobibor, Treblinka, Chelmno*, Munich, 1977, pp. 174–5 in J. Noakes and G. Pridham, *op. cit.*, p. 1154.

10 *Ibid.*, p. 218 in J. Noakes and G. Pridham, *op. cit.*, pp. 1154–5.

11 Testimony of Chaim Hirzsman, Lublin, 20 March 1946, archive of the Jewish Historical Institute, Warsaw.

12 Reder, *op. cit.*, pp. 11–12 in Gilbert, *op. cit.*, p. 417.

13 Testimony of Israel Gutman, Eichmann Trial, 2 June 1961, session 63.

14 Gilbert, *op. cit.*, p. 745.

15 'The Manuscript', J. Bezwinska and D. Czech, *Amidst a Nightmare of Crime*, pp. 118–19 in Gilbert, *op. cit.*, p. 633.

17. The concentration camps

Officially the purpose of concentration camps was to re-educate those who were politically opposed to the aims of the State. Under provisions which permitted the government to place troublemakers in protective custody for the restoration of law and order, the Nazis had the legal right to imprison suspects without trial. Initially Dachau, Buchenwald and Sachsenhausen housed labour union leaders, Communists, Socialists, pacifists and others. Of those imprisoned Jews constituted the majority. Eventually, however, the original purpose of concentration camps was superseded by other concerns: these institutions became large prisons where enemies of the State were incarcerated. In time some of these became killing centres where the Nazis attempted to exterminate European Jewry.

Life in the camps

On their way to the camps, prisoners suffered from hunger, thirst and beating. On arrival they were forced to undress and surrender their belongings. They were then taken to the barber, and all hair on a prisoner's head, face and body was shaved. The shaved areas were then scrubbed with rags which had been soaked with disinfectant. Men were then given old overalls, a set of underwear, a shirt and cap and wooden clogs. Women were issued with a striped cotton dress, a shirt, a pair of pants, a slip and long stockings. Each prisoner was then given a number and assigned to sleeping quarters. Prisoners were normally sent to separate quarantine blocks where new arrivals were held for two or three weeks.

In general prisoners were housed in two basic types of block. The standard barracks was approximately 50 metres long and 8 metres wide, divided into two wings. In each wing there was a dayroom measuring 9 metres by 6 metres which was furnished with tables, benches, stools, lockers and a stove. Doors led from the hall to the washroom, toilet, and broom cupboard. The dormitory was 12 metres by 8 metres, containing two or three tiered iron bunk beds or wooden frames. This facility was planned to house about 150 prisoners. From 1939, most of the blocks were much more crowded. Generally two prisoners were compelled to share a single bunk, a berth about 89 centimetres across. In periods of extreme over-crowding, the mattresses were placed on the bare floor; in this way over 400 prisoners could be confined in a single block.

Army stables were also used for mass housing. These barracks were made of thin, wooden boards and cardboard roofs. Latrine buckets were placed in a corner near the exit. The stalls contained three-tiered wooden bunks 2 metres high measuring 280 centimetres by 185 centimetres. These were designed for 15 prisoners each. Originally these structures had been planned to house between 250 and 400 individuals, but in some cases 1000 persons were confined there. Instead of 15, some 40 prisoners were crowded into a single bunk in sardine fashion.

Although inmates were confined in the same conditions, space was a privilege in the barracks. The pariahs of the camps – Jews, Soviet prisoners of war and Slavs – were placed in dilapidated wooden barracks or tents; new arrivals were put into the quarantine blocks. Prominent blocks were reserved for German and Austrian *Kapos*, clerks, and those who worked for the SS; only they had their own beds and lockers. In addition, they were permitted to wash regularly and change their linen and underwear. Block chiefs and their assistants were also able to expand their territory, taking over the entire dayroom and restricting others to the dormitories.

The course of the day in the camps followed a highly-structured pattern. Prisoners were awakened at 4 a.m. or 4:30 a.m. by bells, whistles or sirens. Those who did not rise quickly were beaten by block personnel. Beds had to be made, the block cleaned, breakfast distributed, and visits made to the latrine. 45 minutes later prisoners lined up for the morning roll-call. Block personnel counted the prisoners and passed on their reports to the SS leaders. After roll-call prisoners ran to the assembly points for work columns. They were then marched to work. At noon there was a break and roll-call, and prisoners were fed with soup. Work finished at dusk, or in summer at 5 p.m. or 6 p.m.

After work, prisoners were again counted and the bodies of the dead were placed on wheelbarrows or taken back to the camp on the shoulders of inmates. When the prisoners returned to the camp, another roll-call was taken including those who had died during the day. This roll-call normally took 1½ to 2 hours. Afterwards, the prisoners were released for the evening meal and free time. After 8:30 p.m. it was forbidden to leave the block; lights out began at 9 p.m.

Initially concentration camps were under the SA, the general SS, and in certain cases the police. In Dachau SS units took over the function of guards in mid-April 1933; later they were under the direction of the police, and subsequently they were in full control. In 1934 the Dachau commandant Eicke reorganized the entire concentration camp system. In the autumn of 1934 the guard formations were separated from the general SS. Beginning in 1936 the units responsible for the camps were termed SS Death's Head Formations. During the next year, the battalions were regrouped into three Death's Head Regiments and attached to the three main camps of Dachau, Sachsenhausen and Buchenwald.

By January 1938 the units numbered 5371 men; by April it reached 7847, rising to 9172 by December. In May 1939 Himmler was authorized to bring the units to 40,000. Of these, 14,000 constituted the minimum strength for Eicke's guard units, and 25,000 were categorized as 'police reinforcements'. By mid-1939 the Death's Head units had 22,033 men. After the invasion of Poland, Eicke set up the Death's Head Division. At the beginning of the war Eicke's office was divided into the Directorate of Concentration Camps and the General Directorate of the Reinforced SS Death's Head Regiments.

Within the camp, there was a privileged class of prisoners; beneath them was the general mass of individuals compelled to live in squalor and misery. With no access to privilege or power within the camps, they were housed in mass blocks, worked outside, and lacked any form of protection. As helpless objects of power, they were surrounded by suffering and death. Repeatedly, from waking until falling asleep in the evening, prisoners were treated as members of a collective whether when counted in a roll call, at work, during meals, or at night in their wooden bunks. In this way any sense of individuality or personal worth was crushed.

Despite the motto above the camp gates, *Arbeit Macht Frei* (Work makes free), inmates were given no remuneration for their efforts. In essence they became slaves. The purpose of work was to shatter prisoners, driving them to despair and death. Within the camp system, Jews and others were not regarded as human beings, but rather objects at the disposal of their masters. Repeatedly prisoners were exposed to arbitrary decisions, controlled by an apparatus that had hounded them down, deported them from their homes, and degraded them. Within this context, terror determined the structure and activities within the camp.

In the various camps prisoners engaged in a variety of tasks including levelling the ground, laying terraces and streets, building barracks, and hauling away track. In the workshops artisans used their skills, whereas outside prisoners drained moors, ploughed fields, dug canals, quarried stone, and created tunnels. Yet, despite the variety of the nature of the work, prisoners were universally overburdened, exposed to a regime that was designed to destroy their physical capacities. Even the strongest were reduced to exhaustion within weeks. In stone quarries, for example, prisoners were forced to smash rocks and boulders with picks, and then lug the blocks on their shoulders or on wooden frames. They had to push waggons uphill and over difficult terrain while being continually struck by the *Kapos*. When building canals or constructing brickworks, prisoners were given only primitive implements including saws, shovels, and wheelbarrows. Sacks of cement as well as bricks and machines were to be hauled at double time.

In some places inmates were compelled to construct underground tunnels. In Ebensee, for example, the tunnels were as high as a two-storey house in the side of the mountains whereas in Melk six tunnels of several hundred metres were dug out. Because no safety precautions existed, there was constant danger from falling stones as well as the inrush of mud or water. In Porta-Barkhausen, prisoners on 12-hour shifts had to expand a tunnel system for an underground refinery. Here prisoners were forced to excavate and lay concrete.

Not surprisingly prisoners were continually exhausted by such labour. Inadequate rations, long marches to and from the work site, extended working hours and constant brutality led to collapse and death. In addition, the threat of punishment caused extreme stress. Even though tasks were frequently repetitive in character, vigilance was constantly necessary. Faced with labour-intensive tasks, the work appeared unceasing and unending. Faced with such excruciating work and surrounded by *Kapos*, prisoners lost all sense of purpose, becoming *muselmänner* (the living dead).

In the camps the *muselmänner* were totally devastated individuals, victims of a system of degradation and humiliation. In the final stages of life, such persons were skeletons. Their eyes had sunk deep into their sockets, and they moved slowly with hesitation. Rapacious with hunger, they ate anything they could find including mouldy bread, cheese infested with worms, and garbage found in bins. As shadows of their former selves, they only reacted when shouted at or struck.

Without the will to live, the *muselmänner* became resigned to death. Many of these persons lay in their excrement in the bunk. When they sat upright, their bodies rocked back and forth. When they became unable to lift their legs, they slowly shoved their feet forward; eventually they had to use their hands in order to put one foot in front of the other. Lost in memory, they were unable to concentrate. Some did not even know their own names. Only able to experience what occurred in front of them, their perception became increasingly narrow. When beaten, they ceased to resist. Turning inward, these individuals moved like ghosts in the camps.

Due to overcrowding, inmates in the camps were repeatedly ravaged by epidemics. In Dachau from 1941 to 1942, for example, approximately 259 prisoners suffered from scabies and were isolated in quarantine blocks. Left standing naked in front of showers, many contracted pneumonia and died. At the end of 1942 typhus and typhoid fever broke out in the camps, resulting in the death of 526 prisoners. In 1939 a dysentery epidemic occurred in Flossenburg. In Majdanek typhoid continually raged during its existence. In Auschwitz, prisoners suffered from paratyphoid fever, malaria, diphtheria, dysentery and tuberculosis.

Accompanying such plagues, psychological terror continually took its toll. Without the constraints of rules and punishments, those incarcerated in the camps were subject to brutality and cruelty. Under the control of the SS, prisoners were constantly vulnerable. Alongside official prohibitions, there were a host of informal regulations which prescribed proper behaviour in the camps. Such rules were not explained to new arrivals, leading to excessive punishments being inflicted on innocent victims. At the same time, prohibitions were often vague, enabling supervisors to define what correction was needed for various infractions. Further, in some cases rules contradicted one another, thereby ensuring that prisoners would be punished no matter what their actions.

In the camps, anything could be construed as an offence. Thus prisoners had only one course of action: in order to survive, one had to become as invisible as possible. Any contact with camp personnel was to be avoided. At roll-call, inmates sought to disappear into the middle rows and suppress any cough. When marching, prisoners attempted to position themselves in the middle of a column. In the barracks, a top bunk was safest. If one passed in front of guards, it was advisable to move as normally as possible without calling attention to oneself. In the courtyards, it was important not to appear to be loitering. By becoming invisible, life became safer.

In addition to individual punishment, collective penalties were imposed on prisoners even if they were not personally responsible. In the case of minor infractions, inmates were forced to run across the yard until they collapsed from exhaustion. If someone was absent from a barracks at roll-call, all the others were compelled to wait until the person was found. In this fashion collective punishment directed terror to the group, putting pressure on each individual.

Those punishments carried out at the end of the evening roll-call had a particular purpose: they served as ritual dramas for all the prisoners. Once a verdict was given by the camp leadership, and a medical report was given by the camp doctor, two prisoners were taken to the whipping block, called forward, tied down, and then beaten. Surrounding the culprits were SS guards with steel helmets and rifles. In this way, thousands of prisoners were forced to witness the utter defencelessness of those found guilty. This ordeal symbolized the powerlessness of those in the concentration camp.

Alongside corporal punishment, public execution also served a symbolic purpose. As a punishment for such acts as resistance, mutiny, sabotage or attempted escape, this event served to highlight the futility of rebellion. In most cases, prisoners were executed by hanging. In the absence of a gallows, workers used a portable frame. After roll-call had been completed, the prisoner was led to the execution site. If a prisoner had escaped and had been recaptured, he had to wear a sign proclaiming his pleasure at returning to the camp. The band then played, and the commandant gave a speech warning inmates what would happen to them if they acted in a similar fashion. Afterwards an executioner was selected from among the prisoners. The victim was forced to stand on boxes; the executioner tied a noose around his neck; the cover of the box was opened by a lever; and the prisoner plunged abruptly. In most cases, death came slowly.

In the camps excessive violence was a constant feature of daily life. From the inception of the concentration camp system, violence was viewed as a necessary means of disciplining prisoners. To ensure conformity to camp rules, prisoners were whipped, clubbed and killed. If a prisoner stumbled along the path of camp officials, he was immediately struck. At Sachsenhausen, for example, victims were seized at roll-calls, or in chance encounters. Usually they were beaten, kicked to death, or killed by blows. One Jew was drowned in a latrine; two others were seized and a water hose placed in their mouths on full blast. In February 1942 over 60 Jewish prisoners were forced several times to leave their barracks; on each occasion they were hit on the head with a club. Subsequently the men were forced to lie down on their stomachs in the snow, and two SS men ran over their backs. In the infirmary, prisoners suffering from diarrhoea were removed from their bunks by shovel handles, dropped and trampled to death.

In the camps, torture also became a routine practice. In Buchenwald, for example, prisoners were handcuffed to heating pipes before interrogation and subsequently beaten with truncheons or whipped. Those who fainted were doused with cold water. During questioning, prisoners were strung up on a grate door with their arms tied behind their backs and their feet a few centimetres from the floor. In some cases inmates were hung upside down by their feet. Another form of torture involved tying a rope to an inmate's genitals and swinging him back and forth as he hung on the door. In some cases his genitals were dipped into cold and then boiling water. In Auschwitz, victims were forced to sit down with their knees pulled closely together on the floor; they then clasped their bound hands up over their knees. A rod was then inserted below the hollows of the knees and above the lower arms. These were then lifted and fixed to a wooden frame. Prisoners then hung with their heads down and were swung back and forth while they received a blow to the buttocks or the genitals.

Such acts of torture took place in secret in concealed areas of the bunker or crematorium. Alone with the prisoners, the SS tormented their victims without remorse. Those block leaders who were able to kill without compunction were praised by the authorities. In this environment of continual violence, those who were able to demonstrate their zeal became objects of respect. To choke a person with one hand or kill with a single sharp blow was viewed as a mark of distinction. For the SS, Jews and others were no more than objects whose deaths could contribute to their personal glory.

It was also a frequent occurrence for mass shootings to take place in the camps. In Auschwitz in July 1941, for example, about 300 Soviet prisoners of war were murdered in a gravel pit near the kitchen. SS officers at the end of the pit fired on the prisoners working beneath; anyone not killed was beaten to death by *Kapos*. In Majdanek in November 1943 about 18,000 Jews were shot: prisoners were forced to climb down in rows of ten into graves and lie down. They were then fired upon from machine guns surrounding the pit. The next group was then forced to descend into the pit, and lie upon the dead. Eventually this mass grave was covered with earth.

In this process, the anonymity of victims became a contributing factor to such acts of barbarity. As one among countless prisoners, the inmate was a nameless figure. Viewed as sub-human, degraded and humiliated by camp life, these individuals ceased to possess any form of individuality. Stripped of human attributes, they evoked feelings of repugnance. In general the dehumanization of prisoners took place over several weeks, but in some cases this could occur within hours. At the transition camp Neue-Bremm in Saarbrücken, for example, such a transformation took place quickly:

One morning they brought in a German Jew. First they beat him brutally with a rubber truncheon: then the panther (deputy of the camp commandant) shoved him into the water pool. After this spectacle in the swimming pool, he was pulled out of the water, beaten once again, and then placed in a disinfection block. ... He left the block in a very sorry state, naturally covered all over with burns. But only in order for the entire sequence to be repeated once again, without a break, down to the middle of the afternoon. The poor Jew could no longer stand, he was burned all over his body. The man nearly drowned after he had been tossed once more into the pool. ... He now was just a poor wretched figure – trying desperately, as they beat him, to keep his head above the water. In the span of five hours, this man who had a rather robust constitution, had been reduced to a wreck and hounded to death.[1]

In this way, prisoners ceased to be recognizably human; as a result, it became easier for camp guards to dispense with them without compunction.

In addition to the various forms of murder that took place in the camps, it was not uncommon for excesses of violence to occur without bloodshed. In these instances, the forces of nature killed the victims. In Sachsenhausen, for example, the broom cupboard next to the washroom functioned in this way. The leader of the punishment company forced eight prisoners into this tiny space, one square metre in area with no windows. Clutching at each other, climbing over one another until the door was closed, they suffocated. As in gas chambers, death took place behind locked doors. Again, it was not uncommon to force prisoners to shower in ice-cold or hot water, and then let them stand naked for hours. In winter, prisoners were doused with water until they became blocks of ice. In washrooms, they were sprayed with streams of cold water against their hearts or carotid arteries until they died. In stone quarries, prisoners were crushed under rockfalls.

Subject to such barbarity, the inmates of the camps became victims of absolute power exercised without inhibition. The grotesque character of actions taken against Jews and others testifies to the lack of human restraint of the camp guards. Such inhumanity was seen as necessary to the discipline of camp life, and justified as a necessary feature of control. Driven by racial theories, the Nazis put into practice a ruthless form of torment and murder directed towards powerless victims who had been dehumanized and deindividualized. Seen as enemies of the Third Reich, these individuals were regarded as nothing more than vermin to be eliminated from society in pursuit of the creation of an Aryan civilization.

Discussion: Dehumanization in the camps

What was the aim of the regime in the camps? As we have seen, absolute power was used to humiliate, degrade, and ultimately destroy the personalities of prisoners. As a process of organized terror, Nazi despotism crushed the individual, eradicating all traces of humanity. Surrounded by suffering and death, inmates lost all sense of personal worth. Describing this process of degradation, a Polish Catholic, Pelagia Lewinska, recounted what she perceived as the aim of the Nazis:

> At the outset the living places, the ditches, the mud, the piles of excrement behind the blocks, had appalled me with their horrific filth . . .

and then I saw the light! I saw that it was not a question of disorder or lack of organization but that, on the contrary, a very thoroughly considered conscious idea was in the back of the camp's existence. They had condemned us to die in our own filth, to drown in mud, in our own excrement. They wished to abase us, to destroy our human dignity, to efface every vestige of humanity ... to fill us with horror and contempt towards ourselves and our fellows. ... From the instant when I grasped the motivating principle ... it was as if I had been awakened from a dream. ... I felt under orders to live. ... And if I did die in Auschwitz, it would be as a human being. I would hold on to my dignity. I was not going to become the contemptible disgusting brute my enemy wished me to be.[2]

From the moment of arrival, prisoners were stripped of their human dignity. Living in a world of suffering and namelessness, they were overwhelmed by hunger, disorientation and powerlessness. As helpless objects, they were surrounded by disease and death. Day by day, they feared for their lives, aware that their fellow prisoners who had been with them one day might disappear the next. As part of the social mass, individuals were isolated, separated from friends and loved ones. In the block, individuals were crowded together to the point of motionlessness. In these conditions, other people were not individuals, but fellow inmates trapped without a means of escape.

In this milieu, the *muselmänner* symbolically represented the hopelessness of camp existence. As we have seen, these shattered wrecks were the victims of a systematic annihilation of selfhood. In the final stages of emaciation, their skin was parchment-like, oedema had formed on their feet and thighs, their posterior muscles had collapsed, their noses dripped constantly, their gaze was glazed. In this state of decay, they issued a fetid odour, and sweat, urine and faeces covered their legs. The rags they wore were full of lice; their skin was covered with lice; and they suffered from diarrhoea. Such individuals were no more than shadows of their former selves; as living corpses, the *muselmänner* illustrated the triumph of the Nazi will against those who were perceived as pollutants of the human race.

Unable to cope, the *muselmänner* withdrew from the world; unable to remember or concentrate, they were indifferent to what happened to them. Unable to think or feel, they were powerless to think or act. Unable to perceive pain, they ceased to eat or speak. All defence mechanisms had collapsed, and they retreated into a world of vacuousness and apathy. Oblivious of others, they were constantly in the way; as a consequence, they were shouted at and beaten. Initially they were chased away by other prisoners, and later ignored. Vegetating at the margin of camp society, their spirit was extinguished and their bodies expired. The *muselmann* thus characterized the process of personal disintegration which became a common feature of camp life. He was the victim of absolute power which destroyed human beings through starvation, humiliation and murder.

Notes

1 Wolfgang Sofsky, *The Order of Terror: The Concentration Camp*, Princeton, 1997, p. 236.
2 Dan Cohn-Sherbok, *God and the Holocaust*, London, 1989, pp. 49–50.

18. The gas chambers

For Himmler the elimination of undesirable segments of the population was a glorious task. Unrestrained by moral compunction, the Nazi onslaught against the Jews and others was facilitated by the creation of death camps in which innocent victims were gassed. For Himmler, this task was to be carried out bravely in the quest to create an Aryan civilization which would endure for over a thousand years. Not just civilians, but men, women and children, were to be killed so that no future generation would pollute the race. This was a life and death struggle between the German people and sub-human, corrupting elements of society. The six death factories were all located in Polish territory where prisoners were deported until the end of the war.

The Final Solution

The first extermination site, Chelmno, was created in December 1941 in the woods 40 miles northwest of Lodz. This was not strictly a camp, but a site equipped with mobile vans which used exhaust fumes. Belzec, Sobibor and Treblinka, on the other hand, were solely death centres with no organizational link to the concentration camp system. Approximately 225,000 Jews were killed in Chelmno; 250,000 in Sobibor; 600,000 in Belzec; and 974,000 in Treblinka. At Majdanek about 200,000 died including about 60,000 Jews. In Auschwitz more than 1 million were murdered.

Belzec, Sobibor and Treblinka were located on several hectares of land with an area set off for the guards' barracks, and the camp administration centre. The reception area including a railway ramp and disrobing barracks and storeroom sheds were located nearby. There was a narrow passage leading from the reception area to the annihilation facilities. This path was bordered on both sides by barbed wire covered with brushwood. At the start of the path or further on, there was a barracks for shaving prisoners' hair. The annihilation area was surrounded by 6-foot-high fences, and the gas chambers were disguised as showers.

Initially no camp had more than three gas chambers. In the summer of 1942 Sobibor and Belzec increased their number to six, and Treblinka had ten. At Treblinka a ceremonial curtain taken from a synagogue was hung with the inscription: 'This is the gate through which the righteous enter'. Each factory was equipped with a diesel engine which emitted exhaust fumes into the gas chambers. The dead were then put on rail waggons that were pulled to a grave by Jewish *Kommandos*. From 1942, however, bodies were dug up and burned on massive grilles; the ashes and remains of bones were then dumped into empty graves about ten metres deep and covered with sand and refuse.

Those who worked in the camps were recruited from the euthanasia programme and had previously gained experience with gassing. The senior officials in each camp consisted of about 20 to 40 German SS officers and non-commissioned officers. The guard personnel consisted of units of Ukrainian and ethnic Germans. In Treblinka the staff numbered between 90 and 120; at Sobibor it was about 90. These guards went on patrols, took up positions in watchtowers, supervised Jewish *Kommandos*, and served as sentries at the ramp and along the path to the gas chambers.

Majdanek and Auschwitz were part of the central concentration camp administration; as a result, there was no need to bring in extra staff from the outside. A large number of Majdanek personnel were recruited from Buchenwald to construct the camp, but because there was a constant lack of supplies the camp was subject to permanent improvisation. For some time Soviet prisoners of war as well as Jewish and non-Jewish Poles were shot. In July 1942, however, a small crematorium was built and in September a gassing facility. Later three gas chambers were constructed. In September 1943 the mass shootings were replaced by gassing. New arrivals were usually confined to barracks, to await selection. On 3 November 1943 when the gas chambers ceased functioning, all Jews in the camp were killed in a major massacre.

The largest death facility was built at Auschwitz; this was done because of the increasing number of transports and overcrowding in the camps. The first gassings took place in September 1941 in the basement of Block 11 in the main camp. Subsequently, the morgue near the crematorium was used as a gas chamber. In 1942 operations were shifted to Birkenau where two farmhouses were converted into gas chambers. Corpses were then transported by rail to pits about several hundred metres away where they were buried. In the autumn of 1942 they were exhumed and burned. In July 1942 work began on four large death facilities which came into operation from March to June 1943. Each of these centres had disrobing rooms, gas chambers and furnaces.

In order to function properly, the organization of the death camps had to be highly efficient. After selection, prisoners were taken to the disrobing rooms; simultaneously the ovens were ignited in the crematoria and wood was piled up next to the burning pits. Victims were informed that after showering they would be given their clothing or told they would have warm soup. After handing over their valuables, they were moved in groups divided by sex through the passage to the gas chambers. When the first groups were pushed into the gas chambers, the *Kommandos* were already bringing clothing to the sorting site and packing it for shipment.

A Ukrainian assistant then turned on the motor. In cases where it did not start, victims stood sometimes for half an hour. At Auschwitz, prisoners noticed that the shower heads were fake. Lights were turned off, and the executioner who wore a gas mask shook Zyklon B crystals into shafts; after fifteen minutes all had been killed. Fans were then turned on to clear the gas chamber. The door was then unbolted, and members of the *Sonderkommando* hosed down the corpses and took them out. The members of the transport *Kommando* then hauled the dead to the freight elevator or the morgue where dentists pulled the gold teeth and fillings from their jaws and barbers cut off their hair. They were then put into crematoria.

This process ensured that while those who had been murdered were being burned, the next group was gassed. In this fashion, killing became a mechanized function of the camps. Gassing and cremation became stages in an efficient series of murderous acts. To facilitate the smooth operation of the death camps, deception became a central feature of the Nazi onslaught. Victims were kept ignorant of the consequences of following orders on their arrival at the camps. Trees surrounded the crematoria, and innocent signs were put up so that the final stop appeared to be a train station. In Sobibor special barracks were constructed for baggage; in Treblinka prisoners were instructed to deposit their documents and valuables. In disrobing rooms, numbers were put up for clothes and deportees were told to remember the number so they would find their belongings after showering. In Sobibor an SS squad leader wore a white doctor's coat and explained that hygienic measures were necessary before entering the camp. In Treblinka the sick were told they would receive medical treatment.

Yet despite these measures, victims were often aware of what lay ahead. At Treblinka, for example, new arrivals were able to see masses of decomposing bodies. As a consequence, many suffered nervous collapse. After one arrival of a transport from Bialystok, one woman who had been told about the death camps ran screaming from group to group. Initially she was not believed, but eventually the inmates began to panic and were eventually pacified by reassuring words and the appearance of armed SS sentries and their dogs.

Invariably when deception failed, the SS used violence against the victims. Deportees were compelled to hurry and struck by blows; the sick were dragged from the trains and thrown with the dead onto waggons. In some cases bloodhounds were released on the ramp and hesitant prisoners were dragged away. At Sobibor some of the guards grabbed small children left behind in the boxcars and smashed their skulls against the walls. At Auschwitz, the SS frequently herded victims immediately on arrival into the gas chambers. Any form of resistance was dealt with severely. In the view of the SS, all inmates were doomed, and therefore could be killed without restraint.

The effectiveness of the death camps was further facilitated by the use of the Jewish *Sonderkommandos*. As we have seen, these Jews were compelled to participate in the murder of fellow Jews and the cremation of the dead. Dentists, barbers, corpse bearers, stokers and gravediggers performed the most appalling tasks out of fear of death. These inmates were allowed to live so that they could dispose of the other Jews. Such individuals were chosen during selection. In Sobibor, new arrivals were received by the station *Kommando* dressed in uniform; another *Kommando* group took their possessions; another sorted and packed items. At Treblinka, a Jewish *Kommando* was made up of goldsmiths, jewellers and bank clerks.

In most cases corpse workers in the extermination camps consisted of about 150 workers who were housed in separate barracks – their job was to empty the gas chambers, examine the orifices of victims in the search for valuables, extract gold from their teeth and stack the dead in pits. Another group – the forest *Kommando* – were responsible for chopping down wood and bringing it to the camp for burning in the crematoria.

In Auschwitz the first *Sonderkommando* group consisted of about 80 prisoners; it was responsible for burying victims gassed in bunkers 1 and 2. This was liquidated in August 1942. The second *Sonderkommando* group was made up of about 150–300 members; it was responsible for exhuming corpses buried until November 1942 and burning them. On 3 December 1942 gravediggers were gassed in the crematorium of the main camp. The SS then recruited workers in the men's camp, isolating them in bunker 11. Subsequently, young men were selected on arrival without being processed for admission. From mid-1944 the *Sonderkommando* was housed in the crematorium itself.

The horrors of the camps have been described by both victims and perpetrators. At his trial Adolf Eichmann recalled his visit to Chelmno to witness the gassing of Jews:

> There was a room – if I remember correctly – perhaps five times as large as this one. Perhaps it was only four times as big as the one I am sitting in now. And Jews were inside. They were to strip and then a truck arrived when the doors opened, and the van pulled up at a hut. The naked Jews were to enter. Then the van was making for an open pit. The doors were flung open and corpses were cast out as if they were animals – some beasts. They were hurled into the ditch.[1]

The person chosen by Christian Wirth, the person in charge of the gas chambers at Belzec, to organize the death camp at Sobibor was Franz Stangl; subsequently he recalled his first visit to Belzec.

> 'The smell,' he stated, 'was everywhere. Wirth wasn't in his office; they said he was up in the camp. I asked whether I should go up there and they said, "I wouldn't if I were you – he's mad with fury. It isn't healthy to be near him". I asked what was the matter. The man I was talking to said that one of the pits had overflowed. They had put too many corpses in it and putrefaction had progressed too fast, so that the liquid underneath had pushed the bodies on top up and over and the corpses had rolled down the hill.'[2]

Another visitor to Belzec, Kurt Gerstein, recalled the smell of the camp and the terrifying scene of new arrivals:

Next morning, shortly before seven, I was told: 'the first transport will arrive in ten minutes. ... Behind the barred hatches stared the horribly pale and frightened faces of children, their eyes full of the fear of death. ... The train arrives: 200 Ukrainians fling open the doors and chase the people out of the waggons with their leather whips. Instructions come from a large loudspeaker: 'Undress completely, including artificial limbs, spectacles, etc. Give your valuables up at the counter without receiving a ticket or a receipt. Tie your shoes together carefully', because otherwise in the 25-metre-high pile of shoes no one can sort out which shoes belong together. Then, the women and girls have to go to the hairdressers who, with two or three snips of the scissors, cut off their hair and put it in potato sacks. ... Then the procession starts to move. They all go along the path with a very pretty girl in front, all naked men, women, and children, cripples without their artificial limbs. ... For some of these poor people a ray of hope which suffices to persuade them to walk the few steps to the chambers but the majority understand what is happening, the smell reveals their fate to them. And so they climb the staircase and then they see it all: mothers with children at their breasts, little naked children, adults, men, and women, all naked. They hesitate but they enter the death chambers, driven on by the others behind them or by the leather whips of the SS. ... A Jewess of about 40, eyes blazing, curses the murderers. She receives five or six lashes with his riding whip from Captain Wirth personally and then disappears into the chamber. Many people pray. ... The chambers fill up. 'Pack them in' – that is what Captain Wirth has ordered. People are treading on each other's toes. 700–800 in an area of 25 square metres, in 45 cubic metres! The SS push them in as far as possible. The doors shut; in the meantime, the others are waiting outside in the open, naked. ... After 28 minutes, only a few are still alive. At last, after 32 minutes, they are all dead. Men from the work detail open the wooden doors from the other side. Even though they are Jews, they have been promised their freedom and a small percentage of all the valuables which are found as a reward for their frightful duty. The dead stand like basalt pillars pressed together in the chambers. There is no room to fall or even to lean over. Even in death one can tell which are the families. They are holding hands in death and it is difficult to tear them apart to empty the chambers for the next batch. The corpses are thrown out wet with sweat and urine, smeared with excrement and with menstrual blood on their legs. The corpses of children fly through the air. There is no time. The riding whips of the Ukrainians whistle down on the work details. Two dozen dentists open mouths with hooks and look for gold. ... Some of the workers check genitals and anus for gold, diamonds and valuables. Wirth calls me over. 'Just lift up this tin full of gold teeth, that is only from yesterday and the day before!' In an incredibly vulgar and phoney voice he tells me: 'You have no idea what we find every day in the way of gold and diamonds and dollars. But see for yourself', and then he takes me over to a jeweller who is responsible for looking after all the treasures and shows me everything. The naked corpses are carried on wooden stretchers only a few metres to the ditches. ... After a few days the corpses swell up and then collapse so that one can throw another layer on top of this one.[3]

Horrific scenes of murder were depicted by other witnesses. At Auschwitz a German surgeon, Johann Kremer, watched as Jews from France were killed:

When the transport with people who were destined to be gassed arrived at the railway ramp, the SS officers selected from the new arrivals, persons fit to work, while the rest – old people, all children, women with children in their arms and other persons not deemed fit to work – were loaded on to lorries and driven to the gas chambers.

I used to follow behind the transport till we reached the bunker. There people were first driven into the barrack huts where the victims undressed and then went naked to the gas chambers. Very often no incidents occurred, as the SS men kept the people quiet, maintaining that they were to bathe and be deloused.

After driving all of them into the gas chamber, the door was closed and an SS man in a gas-mask threw contents of a Cyclon tin through an opening in the side wall. The shouting and screaming of the victims could be heard through the opening and it was clear that they were fighting for their lives.[4]

Discussion: Holocaust denial

Despite the massive historical evidence demonstrating the use of gas chambers by the Nazi regime, historical revisionists have argued that such material is unreliable. One of the most notorious cases concerning the denial of the existence of gas chambers concerns a report produced by Fred A. Leuchter, an engineer from Boston who specialized in constructing and installing execution equipment. In *The Leuchter Report: An Engineering Report on the Alleged Execution Gas Chambers at Auschwitz, Birkenau and Majdanek,*

Poland, he stated that the design and function of these facilities made it impossible for them to have served as execution sites. According to Leuchter, the size and usage rate of these facilities prevented them from having been used for mass killing. In his view, it would have required 68 years for the facilities at Auschwitz and Majdanek to have executed 6 million individuals.

In 1984 the Canadian government called Leuchter as an expert witness in a trial against an anti-Jewish agitator, Ernst Zundel, for provoking anti-Semitism through the publication and distribution of false material. At his trial, Leuchter gave evidence about the gas chambers which brought enormous relief to other Holocaust deniers such as Robert Faurisson who believed such testimony brought an end to the myth of the gas chambers. Yet during the trial it became clear that Leuchter's expertise in the field was questionable. After removing the jury, the court began to assess whether Leuchter was qualified as an expert witness. When questioned about his knowledge of the field, he acknowledged that he had only basic college training in chemistry and physics. Further, he revealed that he was not a toxicologist and that he had no degree in engineering. When questioned how he could function as an engineer without a degree he stated:

> Well, I would question, Your Honour, what an engineering degree is. I have a Bachelor of Arts degree and I have the required background training both on the college level and in the field to perform my function as an engineer.[5]

Ruling that Leuchter could not serve as an expert witness, the judge declared:

> I'm not going to have him get into the question of what's in a brick, what's in iron, what is in – he has no expertise in this area. He is an engineer because he has made himself an engineer in a very limited area.[6]

During the trial, the judge also refused to allow Leuchter to testify about the effect of Zyklon-B on humans since he was not a toxicologist nor a chemist and had not worked with the gas. Remarking on Leuchter's report, the judge maintained:

> His opinion in this report is that there were never any gassings or there were never any exterminations carried on in this facility. As far as I am concerned, from what I've heard, he is not capable of giving that

opinion. .... He is not in a position to say, as he said so sweepingly in this report, what could not have been carried on in these facilities.[7]

The judge was also critical of Leuchter's lack of awareness of historical documents regarding the gas chambers and crematoria. Further, doubts were raised about Leuchter's claims about the residues left by Zyklon-B. The samples Leuchter took from the delousing chambers contained a far higher residue of hydrogen cyanide than those from the homicidal gas chambers. Moreover, the bricks of the delousing chambers generally showed more blue coloration often left by hydrocyanic acid than those in the homicidal gas chambers. On this basis, Leuchter argued that this lower-level residue and stain demonstrated that the structures allegedly used for killing could not have in fact been used in this way.

Yet it was pointed out that lice which were killed in the delousing chambers were much more resistant than humans to hydrogen cyanide. This could well account for the blue stain in the delousing chambers. In addition, it was noted that because of the intensity of hydrogen cyanide in the homicidal chambers, only a limited amount was inhaled and the remainder was extracted by the ventilation system. As a consequence, this gas was in contact with the walls of the chamber for only a very short time. In the delousing chambers, on the other hand, hydrogen cyanide was in contact with the walls for an extended period. Thus, one would expect to find a higher residue there.

Another argument used by Leuchter at the trial was that it would have been insane to operate a gas chamber close to the crematoria because of the danger of explosion. Records, however, illustrate that the amount of gas used was below what would have caused an explosion. In this connection, the Crown pointed out that it was necessary to use far more substance to kill beetles than humans. Hence, if it was safe to kill beetles without the danger of an explosion, then it would have been safe to use a much smaller amount for human beings.

The Zundel case illustrates the dangers of drawing conclusions about the Holocaust on the basis of flawed evidence. Increasingly, scholars have drawn attention to the weakness of Holocaust denial and its political motivation. Pre-eminent among these critics, Deborah E. Lipstadt has warned about those who seek to challenge incontrovertible evidence about the gas chambers:

The impact of Leuchter's work is difficult to assess. Rationally, one would assume that, since Leuchter has been exposed as a man without the qualifications necessary to perform this analysis, and since his work has been demonstrated to be scientifically and methodologically fallacious, the destiny of the Leuchter Report would be the dust-bin of history. But the Holocaust and, to only a lesser degree, Holocaust denial itself remind us that the irrational has a fatal attraction even to people of goodwill. It can overwhelm masses of evidence and persuade people to regard the most outrageous and untenable notions as fact. This is easier to accomplish when the public does not have the historical and technical knowledge necessary to refute these irrational and inherently fantastic claims. Ultimately the deniers' ability to keep repeating Leuchter's conclusions even though they have been discredited is another indication that truth is far more fragile than fiction and that reason alone cannot protect it.[8]

Notes

1 Eichmann Testimony, Eichmann Trial, 19 April 1961, session 10.
2 Gitta Sereny, *Into the Darkness: From Mercy Killing to Mass Murder*, 1974, in Martin Gilbert, *Holocaust*, London. 1987, pp. 311–12.
3 L. Poliakov and J. Wulf, *Das Dritte Reich und die Juden*, Frankfurt, 1983, pp. 103–8 in J. Noakes and G. Pridham, *op. cit.*, pp. 1151–2.
4 Kazimierz Smolen (ed.), *From the History of K. L. Auschwitz*, Oswiecim, 1967, p. 212 in Gilbert, *op. cit.*, p. 438.
5 Deborah Lipstadt, *Denying the Holocaust*, New York, 1993, p. 114.
6 *Ibid.*, p. 165.
7 *Ibid.*, p. 166.
8 *Ibid.*, p. 182.

19. SS doctors and medical experiments

In their quest to carry out the Final Solution, SS doctors played a central role in the functioning of the camps. When deportees arrived after their long journeys, it was the doctors who were instrumental in implementing the process of selection. In addition, such individuals carried out a ruthless and barbaric programme of medical experimentation in line with Nazi racial ideology.

Doctors and the death camps

In the running of the camps, SS doctors were crucially important. Rather than engage in direct medical work, their function was to carry out the Nazi project of racial segregation and mass extermination. When Jewish prisoners arrived, these doctors performed initial large-scale selections. These were undertaken according to a fixed pattern: old and debilitated people, children and women with children were chosen to be sent to the gas chamber. Young adults, on the other hand, were allowed to survive, at least for a short time. After this selection took place, the presiding doctor with a medical technician was driven in an SS vehicle usually marked with a red cross. As leader of his team, the doctor had responsibility for carrying out the killing programme. In addition, it was up to him to allow twenty minutes or so to pass before the doors of the gas chamber could be opened and bodies removed.

SS doctors also engaged in two other types of selection: Jewish inmates were ordered to line up at short notice to make room for arrivals from new transports. In other selections individuals who were viewed as significantly ill or who required more than two or three weeks for recovery were sent to the gas chambers. This process was deeply influenced by the euthanasia programme where those who were judged as lacking worth for society were eliminated. In addition, racial ideology provided the rationalization for such wanton killing. Himmler's vision of biological pollution served as the justification for those who participated in such actions. In his view:

> Jews are the eternal enemies of the German people and must be exterminated. All Jews within our grasp are to be destroyed without exception, now, during the war. If we do not succeed in destroying the biological substance of the Jews, the Jews will some day destroy the German people.[1]

Embracing such racial theories, Nazi doctors called forth an absolutized conception of good and evil as a justification for their actions. As one Nazi doctor explained:

> Precisely because they were convinced of the justness ... or of the ... National-Socialist 'world blessing' and that the Jews are the root evil of the world – precisely because they were so convinced of it did they believe, or were strengthened, that the Jews, even existentially, had to be absolutely exterminated.[2]

For those who arrived at the camp, the role of the SS doctors was not always apparent. Amidst mass confusion, deportees did not realize that doctors were carrying out a selection. As one victim explained:

> We arrived at night. ... Because you arrived at night, you saw miles of lights – and the fire from the ... crematoria. And then screaming and the whistles and the 'Out, out!', and the uniformed men and the SS with the dogs, and the stripped prisoners. ... They separated you and then lined up everybody in fives, ... and there were two men standing. ... On one side, was the doctor, one was Mengele ... and on the other side was the ... Arbeitsführer, which was the ... man in charge of the work Kommando.[3]

For the SS doctors such selections were simply part of concentration camp life. Whatever reservations they might have initially had, they soon came to view their role as a regular job. In addition, doctors were responsible for various technical aspects of the gas chambers. In particular, they were preoccupied with the technical problem of burning large numbers of corpses. As one doctor explained:

> The gas chambers were sufficient, you see, that was no problem. But the burning, right? The ovens broke down. And they (the corpses) had to be burned in a big heap. ... The problem is really a large technical difficulty. There was not too much room, so first one thought one would have to take small piles. ... Well, ... that would have to be tried out. ... And then everyone contributed his knowledge of physics, about what might possibly be done differently. If you do it with ditches around them, then the air comes up from below and wooden planks underneath and gasoline on top – or gasoline underneath and wood in between – these were the problems.[4]

Paralleling selection for the gas chambers, inmates were killed by phenol injections. At Auschwitz from September 1941, this technique was used when patients became debilitated or a medical block was overcrowded. Initially phenol was injected into a prisoner's vein. As a Polish non-Jewish doctor explained:

> This time there was a table prepared with syringes. The phenol was in a bottle. There was cotton – everything you needed for an injection. There was also alcohol, as with ordinary injections – and rubber tourniquets. There was just one table ... and the right hand (of the victim) was put out on a kind of support table (to hold the arm steady), as with a regular intravenous injection, (and) the rubber tourniquet on the arm to apply the pressure to make the vein visible – all in the usual way. ... Mengele (who performed the killing) then rubbed alcohol on the spot, just under the elbow, that he was using for the injection, and then injected the phenol. ... He did it as though he were performing regular surgery.[5]

Although most inmates died immediately after the injection, some survived for a short period:

> The executioners used to boast about their records. 'Three in a minute'. ... And they did not wait until the doomed person really died. During his agony he was taken from both sides under the armpits and thrown into a pile of corpses in another room opposite. And the next took his place on the stool.[6]

In addition to such activities, SS doctors also participated in various types of experimental research. On 7 July 1942 Himmler chaired a meeting of the head of the Concentration Camp Inspectorate, the hospital chief, and various professors to discuss the use of medical experiments on women at Auschwitz. It was decided that such scientific investigations should be done secretly; three days later 100 Jewish women were taken to the hospital block. Two Dutch doctors who had been prisoners at Auschwitz described four such experiments:

1. These were performed by Professor Samuel who was forced to do them. Three to four operations a day. The abdomen was opened and an incision made in the uterus, whereupon neoplastic cells were implanted. The origin of these neoplastic cells is unknown. Three to six operations were performed after this at three to four weekly intervals and pieces of tissue from the uterus were taken and frozen sections made. The discharge which occurred through the cervix was clear and gave no indication of any change occurring. The women were unaffected by the actual operation.

2. Fifteen girls aged seventeen to eighteen years old. The girls who survived the following operations are in German hands and little is known about them. The subjects were placed in an ultra-short-wave field. One electrode was placed on the abdomen and another on the vulva. The rays were focused on the ovaries. The ovaries were consequently burned up. Owing to faulty doses several had serious burns of the abdomen and vulva. One died as a result of these burns alone. The others were sent to another concentration camp where some were put in hospital and others made to work. After a month they returned to Auschwitz where control operations were performed. Sagittal and transverse sections of the ovaries were made. The girls altered entirely owing to hormonal changes. They looked just like old women. Often they were laid up for months owing to the wounds of the operations becoming septic. Several died as a result of sepsis.

3. The women were put on a table. With the assistance of an electrically driven pump a white cement-like fluid (possibly barium) was driven into the uterus. As the white fluid was pumped in, Röntgen photos were taken. The women were extremely ill under this experiment. They felt as though the abdomen was going to burst. After getting up from the table they rushed to the laboratory where the fluid came out again. The pains caused by this experiment were equivalent to labour pains. The fluid which was evacuated was often mixed with blood. The experiments were repeated several times. Those patients that could not be used owing to a small Os Uteri or those patients upon whom the experiments were completed, were sent to Birkenau, another camp, where they were killed. This was practised on practically all women at Auschwitz, about 400 all told.[7]

Other operations were performed on the bodies of those who were selected for various scientific purposes. A typical example was witnessed by Dr Miklos Nyiszli from among the Lodz ghetto Jews who reached Birkenau in August 1944:

> When the convoys arrived, Dr Mengele espied, among those lined up for selection, a hunchbacked man about 50 years old. He was not alone; standing beside him was a tall, handsome boy of fifteen or sixteen. The latter, however, had a deformed right foot, which had been corrected by an apparatus made of a metal plate and an orthopaedic, thick-soled shoe. They were father and son.
>
> Dr Mengele thought he had discovered, in the persons of the hunchback father and his lame son, a sovereign example to demonstrate his theory of the Jewish race's degeneracy. . . . Scarcely half an hour later SS Quartermaster Sergeant Mussfeld appeared with four *Sonderkommando* men. They took the two prisoners into the furnace room and had them undress. Then the *Obergruppenführer*'s revolver cracked twice. Father and son were stretched out on the concrete covered with blood, dead.[8]

Later in the day Dr Mengele arrived and ordered that the bodies of the father and the son be boiled in water so that flesh could be removed from their bones. When this was completed, the lab assistant took up the bones of the skeletons and placed them on the work table. The skeletons were subsequently transported to the Anthropological Museum in Berlin.

Other examples of Mengele's cruelty were recorded by survivors – at Auschwitz over 1000 medical experiments were carried out on Jews whom Mengele took from the barracks. Following his arrival in May 1943, Mengele joined other SS officers and doctors in selecting victims for experimentation. From May 1943 to March 1944 he took part in 64 selections of deportees at the railway station, and also played an important role in at least 31 selections in the camp infirmary. Among those who were chosen for medical research were more than 1500 Jewish inmates. One of the survivors, Verak Kriegel, recalled that when she and her sister arrived at Birkenau, 'children were having their heads beaten in like poultry by SS men with gun butts, and some were being thrown into a smoking pit. I was confused: I thought that this was some sort of animal kingdom or perhaps I was already in Hell'.[9] Mengele's interest in these twins was genetic: he wanted to know why their eyes were brown and their

191

mother's were blue. Forced to live in a cage for 10 days, their eyes were injected with a burning liquid. In Auschwitz, she continued, she had entered a laboratory where she was confronted by a collection of human eyes used in experiments of which she, her sister and her mother were a part.

In addition to Jewish patients, gypsies were also used for experimental purposes. Another survivor, Vera Alexander, recounted how two gypsy twins, one of whom was a hunchback, were sewn together and had their veins connected. 'Their wounds were infected,' she said, 'and they were screaming in pain. Their parents managed to get hold of some morphine and used it to kill them in order to end their suffering.'[10] Mengele also experimented on Jews with physical deformities, particularly dwarfs. Among the Jews deported to Birkenau in the summer of 1944 were seven dwarfs and three children of normal size from the Ovitch family. Later one of the dwarfs, Elizabeth Moshkovitz, explained that Mengele rescued the dwarfs from the gas chambers to use for various experiments. On one occasion Mengele exhibited the Ovitch family naked at an SS hospital. Various experiments were also carried out on the bodies of dwarfs.

Paradoxically those who were chosen for experiments were more likely to survive the harsh conditions of the concentration camps. By October 1944 there were about 200 surviving children. As the guardian of the dwarfs, Ernst Spiegel, stated:

> The twins were looked after by Mengele. He needed them so he took great care of them. He would receive questions about the twins from the Kaiser Wilhelm Institute in Berlin, and he would send them the answers. He needed the twins alive, and they would receive white bread. When the rains came, he made sure that they worked in shelter, that is, in the washrooms.[11]

Other children, however, were selected for death. Recalling an event in Auschwitz that took place before Yom Kippur, Josef Kleinmann described the process which Mengele employed as a game:

> All of a sudden a tremble passed through the parade ground like an electric current. The angel of death appeared. Dr Mengele appeared on his bicycle. Somebody approached him, took his bicycle and leaned the bicycle near the barrack. ... He put his hand behind his back, his lips as usual were tightly closed, he went to the centre of the parade ground,

lifted his head so that he could survey the whole scene and then his eyes landed on a little boy about fifteen years old. Perhaps only fourteen years old or something like that. ... He was blond, very thin, and very sunburnt. His face had freckles. He was standing in the first line when Mengele approached him and asked him, 'How old are you?' The boy shook and said, 'I am eighteen years old.'

I saw immediately that Dr Mengele was furious and started shouting, 'I'll show you. Bring me a hammer and nails and a little plank.' So somebody ran immediately and we were standing and looking at him completely silent. A deathly silence prevailed on the parade ground. He was standing in the middle and everyone was watching him. In the meantime, the man with the hammer and nails arrived.

When the man with the tools was standing near Dr Mengele, Mengele approached another boy. He was a tall boy in the first row. His face was round and he looked quite well. Mengele approached him, grabbed him by the shoulder and led him to the goal post which was on that field. It was a regular football field. There were two goal posts. He led this boy by the shoulder and the man with the plank and the tools and the hammer also followed them. He put the boy near the goal post and gave orders to nail the plank above the boy's head so that it was like the letter L only in reverse. Then he ordered the first group to pass under the board. The first group of boys started going in single file.

We had no explanations. We understood that the little ones who did not reach the board, who were not tall enough, would be taken to their deaths.[12]

Nazi biomedical research also included anthropological investigations; many of these projects took place in Block 10 in Auschwitz. One of the SS doctors explained its origins:

There appeared (in Block 10) a new protagonist of racial theories. He chose his material by having naked women of all ages file ... in front of him. He wanted to do anthropological measurements. ... He had measurements of all the parts of the body taken ad infinitum. ... They were told that they had the extraordinary good fortune to be selected, that they would leave Auschwitz to go to an excellent camp, somewhere in Germany.[13]

These women were taken to a concentration camp at Natzweiler near Strasbourg which possessed its own gas chamber. There they were given a physical examination and then gassed; their corpses were then transported to the anatomy pavilion of the Strasbourg University Hospital. Two shipments of men were also sent to the

Hospital from whom the left testicle had been removed and sent to an anatomy lab under the direction of Dr August Hirt. Such projects were sponsored by the ancestral heritage office of the SS, which Himmler created in 1939 to encourage historical and scientific studies of the Nordic Indo-Germanic race.

Elsewhere in Block 28, another experimental area was created for other types of research. There Jewish inmates were taken to have toxic substances rubbed into their arms and legs – this procedure caused severely infected areas and extensive abscesses. The purpose of these experiments was to gather information that would help one recognize attempts by those who deliberately created such responses in order to avoid military service. A second type of experiment involved the application of lead acetate to various parts of the body: this caused painful burns as well as discoloration. After such experiments were undertaken, specimens were sent to laboratories for investigation, and photographs were taken to provide records of the conditions caused. A final type of experiment required ingestion of a powder in order to study the symptoms of liver damage. Such research was undertaken in accordance with Himmler's interest in liver disease and jaundice. Surgical experimentation was also undertaken in the camps. In Block 41 of Birkenau, for example, vivisections designed to expose leg muscles took place. Elsewhere surgery was performed by medical students in a female hospital block – this was undertaken so that they would gain experience as doctors.

Discussion: Nazi medicine

How were SS doctors able to reconcile themselves to this murderous act? As we have seen, they were deeply influenced by racial ideology. Such a justification appears to have nullified all moral and religious scruples. Josef Mengele, for example, was committed to the Nazi world view, and believed the camps offered ample opportunities for research. Arriving in Auschwitz on 30 May 1943, he had previously embraced right-wing nationalism, joining the SA in 1934. In 1937 he applied for Party membership, and for membership of the SS once he was admitted to the Party. After studying at the Universities of Munich, Bonn, Vienna and Frankfurt, he concentrated on physical anthropology and genetics, eventually working under Otmar von Verschuer at the Frankfurt University Institute of Hereditary Biology and Racial Hygiene.

Prior to arriving in Auschwitz, he had published various anthropological studies dealing with heredity. Anxious to continue such investigations, he viewed Auschwitz as providing human specimens for his work. In the opinion of many inmates, Mengele symbolized the selection process. Standing on the ramp, he deliberately looked for individuals who would be suitable for experimental research. As we have seen, his particular passion was for twins. Once he had found them, they became part of an elaborate structure. Identical twins were of particular significance. As one survivor related:

It was like a laboratory. First they weighed us, then they measured and compared. ... There isn't a piece of body that wasn't measured and compared. ... We were always sitting together – always nude. ... We would sit for hours together, and they would measure her, and then measure me, and then again measure me and measure her.[14]

Ruthlessly, Mengele murdered those on whom he wished to experiment. As one eye-witness explained:

In the work room next to the dissection room, fourteen gypsy twins were waiting, guarded by SS men, and crying bitterly. Dr Mengele didn't say a single word to us, and prepared a 10 cc and 5 cc syringe. From a box he took evipan and from another box he took chloroform, which was in 20 cubic-centimetre glass containers, and put these on the operating table. After that, the first twin was brought in, ... a 14-year-old girl. Dr Mengele ordered me to undress the girl and put her on the dissecting table. Then he injected the evipan into her right arm intravenously. After the child had fallen asleep, he felt for the left ventricle of the heart and injected 10 cc of chloroform. After one little twitch the child was dead, whereupon Dr Mengele had it taken into the morgue. In this manner all fourteen twins were killed during the night.[15]

How can one understand doctors like Mengele? It is obvious that he was dedicated to scientific investigation; yet he was oblivious to the human factor. Fanatical in approach, he was committed to Nazism. As one witness related:

If you think that the German race, or any race, is absolutely superior, and that means it has the right to destroy a weaker race, that is already a limitation. ... He didn't like to think about or ... go deeply into a problem that contradicts his own. He was like a religious man ... absolutely so committed that he will only consider the people going to church as the right people – or those who have the same face as he has.[16]

195

Driven by ideological convictions, Mengele was able to transcend normal human feelings. As one doctor explained, Mengele was a double man, driven by contradictory impulses:

> The double man. The double, that is to say he had all the sentimental emotions, all the human feelings, pity, and so on. But there was in his psyche a hermetically closed cell, an impenetrable, indestructible cell, which is obedient to the received order. He can throw himself in the water to go and save a gypsy, try to give him medication . . . and then as soon as they are out of the water . . . tell him to get in a truck and quickly off to the gas chamber.[17]

Imbued with the Auschwitz mentality, doctors such as Mengele were able to encase themselves in a shell of insensitivity to the suffering of those whom they treated. Such detachment accounts for the lightning-fast changes doctors underwent from being attentive and compassionate to becoming unfeeling and brutal. By encasing themselves in this fashion, SS doctors acted without emotion, indifferent to pain. Surrounded by death, they exemplified the Nazi ideology of hardness, determined that the Aryan race triumph over its enemies.

In the camps, Jewish doctors were occasionally compelled to work as collaborators with the Nazis. How are we to understand such complicity? Unlike the SS doctors, they repudiated racial doctrine; they were driven instead by the desire to survive or protect others. Maximilian Samuel, for example, was an academic gynaecologist in Cologne. On his arrival in Auschwitz, he was treated with special consideration, working first at Buna. Later he was transferred to Block 10 where, as we have seen, he became involved with the experiments on women. Some inmates asserted that he was more considerate than Nazi doctors, but he was nonetheless diligent in carrying out orders.

A broken man, his wife was killed on arrival in Auschwitz. His daughter, however, was selected for work, and it appears that his activities were part of an effort to save her life. As with other prisoners, such aspirations were futile. Both Samuel and his daughter were killed. Such self-delusion was characteristic of prisoner medical collaborators as well as those who served in the *Sonderkommando*. In assessing the moral complexities of such behaviour, one Polish doctor remarked:

> It is difficult to pass judgement on the behaviour of inmates. It's difficult

to accuse the Jews of the *Sonderkommando* of helping to kill their fellow Jews by pushing them into the gas chambers. It was done under pressure which deprived them of their will. But there were times when a man went over the border of what we could expect from him – did more than what was demanded or required – when he performed functions with sadistic satisfaction or even did certain things before he received any orders and in that way anticipated the Nazis. These things we may consider as crimes. ...

Perhaps the doctor's case is a little different because doctors are bound by their professional ethic, and physicians are people with higher education. ... Samuel was a Jew, which meant a person 100 per cent condemned to death in the camp. So he had the right to prolong his life – week by week, month by month.[18]

Notes

1   Robert Jay Lifton, *The Nazi Doctors*, New York, 1986, p. 157.
2   *Ibid.*, p. 205.
3   *Ibid.*, pp. 164–5.
4   *Ibid.*, p. 177.
5   *Ibid.*, p. 258.
6   *Ibid*, p. 259.
7   P. D. C. MacKay to the *British Medical Journal*, 19 August 1945: Foreign Office Papers, 371/50989 in Gilbert, *op. cit.*, pp. 373–375.
8   Miklos Nyiszli, *Auschwitz: A Doctor's Eye-Witness Account*, London, 1973, pp. 128–30 in Gilbert, *op. cit.*, pp. 719–720.
9   Testimony of Vera Kriegel, in David Horowitz, '40 Years of Despair', *Jerusalem Post International Edition*, 16 February 1985 in Gilbert, *op. cit.*, p. 687.
10 Report from a Tribunal held at Yad Vashem, Jerusalem in February 1985, *Jewish Chronicle*, 8 February, 1985; *Jerusalem Post International Edition*, 16 February 1985, in Gilbert, *op. cit.*, p. 689.
11 Gilbert, *op. cit.*, p. 756.
12 Testimony of Joseph Zalman Kleinmann, Eichmann Trial, 7 June 1961, session 68.
13 Lifton, *op. cit.*, p. 284.
14 *Ibid.*, p. 349.
15 *Ibid.*, p. 350–1.
16 *Ibid.*, p. 365.
17 *Ibid.*, p. 375.
18 *Ibid.*, pp. 252–3.

20. The euthanasia programme

From 1939 to 1945 the Nazis instituted a euthanasia programme designed to eliminate over 100,000 mentally-ill and handicapped persons. Such decisions were undertaken by the government rather than an individual's family. The aim of this policy was to rid society of those individuals who were deemed to have no value to the community.

Murdering the innocent

The policy of killing worthless members of society was initiated by Professor Karl Binding, former President of the *Reichsgericht*, and Professor Alfred Hoche, President of Psychiatry at Freiburg University. In their book, *Permission for the Destruction of Worthless Life, its Extent and Form*, they argued that Germany had been overdrained by what they referred to as living burdens who were draining the resources of society.

In this work Binding argued that there are individuals who have lost their human characteristics to the extent that they are of no value either to themselves or society.

> 'It cannot be doubted,' he wrote, 'that there are people for whom death would come as a release and, at the same time, for society and the state in particular would represent liberation from a burden which, apart from being an example of great self-sacrifice, is not of the slightest use.'[1]

For Binding there were three types of individuals who could be killed. The first consisted of those who were terminally ill, in full possession of their mental capabilities, and had expressed a desire to die.

The second category consisted of incurable lunatics regardless of whether they were born as such or were in the final stage of their condition. Such individuals, he stated:

> have neither the will to live nor to die. Thus, they are unable to approve of their killing; on the other hand, it will not clash with any will to live which would have to be broken. Their life is completely useless, but they do not find it intolerable. They represent a terribly heavy burden for their relatives as well as for society. Their death would not have the slightest impact except perhaps on the feelings of their mothers or their loyal nurses.[2]

According to Binding, there was no reason why these persons should not be killed. In fact, he noted, in times of a higher morality, these poor people would in all likelihood have been released from their miseries.

The third category, Binding continued, comprised mentally healthy individuals who through tragic events had permanently lost consciousness, or would awaken to misery if they regained it. Since the Weimar Republic could never take the initiative for such killings, such decisions would have to be made by the sick themselves, their doctors, or their relatives. In Binding's view, requests should be made to a state authority consisting of a doctor, a psychiatrist and a lawyer. If a mistake were made, Binding maintained,

> then mankind would be one fewer. But after successfully overcoming this catastrophe (the physical disability), this life might have become very expensive to maintain; in most cases its value would have been hardly more than mediocre. The relatives would of course feel the loss badly. But mankind loses so many of its members through mistakes that one more or less hardly matters.[3]

Following similar lines, Hoche emphasized the cost of keeping the mentally deficient alive:

> The question of whether the resources of all kinds devoted to these living burdens is justified was not an urgent one in the prosperous days gone by; but now things are different and we must deal with it seriously. ... The task before us Germans for many years to come will be to achieve

the most intense concentration of our potential and to liberate every capacity at our disposal in order to advance our goals. The fulfilment of this task runs counter to the modern concern to preserve as far as possible even the weaklings of every kind and to devote increasing care and protection to those who, while not mentally dead, are congenitally inferior elements ... one day we may reach the mature opinion that the elimination of those who are mentally completely dead is not a crime, not an immoral act, not brutal, but a permissible and beneficial act. ... There was a time which we regard as barbaric, in which the elimination of those who were born or became unviable was regarded as natural. Then came the phase we are in now, in which finally the maintenance of any, even the most worthless, existence was considered to be the highest moral duty; a new period will come which, on the basis of a higher morality, will cease continually implementing the demands of an exaggerated concept of humanity and an exaggerated view of the value of human life at great cost.[4]

Although Binding's and Hoche's work was met with severe criticism, the assumption that human life should contribute to society gained increasing acceptance. Once the Nazis had gained control of German society, this approach to human life was endorsed by the government. Under the Nazi regime the individual was totally subordinated to the community. Embracing the principles of Social Darwinism, Nazi officials stressed that human life should be perceived as a struggle for the survival of the fittest. The value of individual citizens was thus to be measured by their contribution to the nation. Such attitudes were earlier expressed by Hitler in a speech to the Nuremberg Party Rally on 5 August 1929:

If Germany was to get a million children a year and was to remove 700–800,000 of the weakest people, then the final result might even be an increase in strength. The most dangerous thing is for us to cut off the natural process of selection and thereby gradually rob ourselves of the possibility of acquiring able people. ... As a result of our modern sentimental humanitarianism we are trying to maintain the weak at the expense of the healthy. It goes so far that a sense of charity, which calls itself socially responsible, is concerned to ensure that even cretins are able to procreate while more healthy people refrain from doing so, and all that is considered perfectly understandable. Criminals have the opportunity of procreating, degenerates are raised artificially and with difficulty. And in this way we are gradually breeding the weak and killing off the strong.[5]

After 1933 eugenic principles became incorporated in various laws such as the Sterilization Law of 14 July 1933 which introduced compulsory sterilization for inferiors. At first the mentally handicapped and mentally ill were sterilized; such a policy was accompanied by propaganda which sought to persuade the public that such people were of no worth to society at large. Eventually the next step was taken in this campaign: rather than simply prevent such individuals from reproducing, it was suggested that they should be eliminated. Promoting such ideas, the SS journal *Das Schwarze Korps* printed a letter on 18 March 1937 from a reader dealing with the topic of mercy deaths. In response to an article in the previous issue, this person wrote:

> If people say that human beings have no right to kill them then one must reply that humans have a hundred times less right to interfere with nature and keep something alive which was not born to live. That has nothing whatever to do with Christian love of one's neighbour. For, under the term 'neighbour', we can only understand our fellow human beings who are capable of responding to the love which we give them. Anyone who has the courage to carry these considerations to their logical conclusion will make the same demand as our reader.
>
> A law should be passed which would give nature its due. Nature would let this unviable creature starve to death. We can be more humane and give it a painless mercy death. That is the only humane act which is appropriate in such cases and it is a hundred times more noble, decent and humane than that cowardice which hides behind a sentimental humanitarianism and imposes the burden of its existence on the poor creature, on its family and on the national community.[6]

In August 1939 a Reich Committee was formed to deal with the euthanasia of children who possessed hereditary or congenitally-based diseases. Such individuals were starved to death or given lethal injections in hospital clinics. One of these clinics was established in the asylum of Egelfing-Haar near Munich which was described by a visitor in 1940:

> After some brief introductory remarks Dr Pfannmüller approached one of the fifteen cots which flanked the central passage to right and left.
>
> 'We have here children aged from one to five', he pontificated. 'All these creatures represent for me as a National Socialist "living burdens" ... a burden for our nation. ... In this sense, the Führer's action to free the national community from this overburdening is quite simply a

201

national deed, whose greatness non-medical men will only be able to assess after a period of years if not decades. We do not carry out the action with poison, injections or other measures which can be recognized'. ... With these words he pulled a child out of its cot. While this fat, gross man displayed the whimpering skeletal little person like a hare which he had just caught, he coolly remarked: 'Naturally we don't stop their food straight away. That would cause too much fuss. We gradually reduce their portions. Nature then takes care of the rest.'[7]

At about the same time Hitler gave instructions that a euthanasia programme be established for adults. In response to the question who should be killed, the official policy was that those who were simply animals in human form were to be eliminated. As one of the chemists related, this was to be done by gassing the patients:

I was ordered by Brack to attend the first euthanasia experiment in the Brandenburg asylum near Berlin. ... There were already two mobile crematoria in the asylum with which to burn the corpses. There was a rectangular peephole in the entrance door, which was constructed like an air raid shelter door. ... The first gassing was carried out by Dr Widmann personally. He turned the gas tap and regulated the amount of gas. ... For the first gassing about 18–20 people were led into this 'shower room' by the nursing staff. These men had to undress in an anteroom until they were completely naked. The doors were shut behind them. These people went quietly into the room and showed no signs of being upset. ... I could see through the peephole that after about a minute the people had collapsed or lay on the benches.[8]

Once the euthanasia programme had been established, those in asylums had to be transported to their deaths. According to a nurse in the district asylum of Jestetten in Württemberg:

The vehicles ... were like Post omnibuses, only the windows had been painted so that one could neither see in nor out ... the patients who were to be transported ... had numbers written in ink on their wrists which had been previously dampened with a sponge. In other words, the people were transported not as human beings but as cattle.[9]

One of those who worked in such extermination centres related what fate awaited those who were transported:

Captain Wirth called us together ... 'Comrades, I have called you together to explain to you what is going to happen. I have been ordered by the Reich Chancellery to take charge here. I, as Captain, am in overall command. We have got to build a crematorium here in order to burn the mentally ill from the Ostmark. Five doctors have been assigned to examine the mentally ill to establish who is capable of being saved and who is not. Those who aren't will be put in crematoria and burnt. The mentally ill are a burden on the state.[10]

Describing the euthanasia process, he stated:

About six weeks after 2 April 1940 the preparations and the buildings were ready and the plant began to operate. The mentally ill were, as far as I know, brought from the various asylums by train and bus to Hartheim at very different times of the day. Sometimes the numbers arriving were large, sometimes small. The numbers arriving varied between 40 and 150. First, they were taken to the undressing room. There they – men and women in different sections – had to undress or were undressed. Their clothes and luggage were put in a pile, labelled, registered and numbered. The people who had undressed then went along a passage into the so-called reception room. In this room there was a large table. A doctor was there together with a staff of 3–4 assistants. . . . Those people who had gold teeth or a gold bridge were marked with a cross on their backs. After this procedure, the people were led into a nearby room and photographed. Then the people were led out of the photography room through a second exit back into the reception room and from there through a steel door into the gas chamber. The gas chamber had a very bare interior. It had a wooden floor and there were wooden benches in the chamber. Later, the floor was concreted and finally it and the walls were tiled. The ceiling and the other parts of the walls were painted with oil. The whole room was designed to give the impression that it was a bathroom. Three showers were fixed in the ceiling.[11]

Continuing this narrative, he recalled:

When the whole transport had been dealt with, i.e. when the registration had been carried out, the photographs taken, people's numbers stamped on them, and those with gold teeth marked, then they all went into the bath-gas room. The steel doors were shut and the doctor on duty fed gas into the gas chamber. After a short time the people in the gas chamber were dead. After around an hour and a half, the gas chamber was ventilated.[12]

The gassing of patients was not always painless as an employee who observed a gassing at Hadamar recalled:

> I ... looked through the peephole in the side wall. Through it I saw 40–45 men who were pressed together in the next room and were so slowly dying. Some lay on the ground, others had slumped down, many had their mouths open as if they could not get any more air. The form of death was so painful that one cannot talk of a humane killing, especially since many of the dead men may have had moments of clarity.[13]

Such killing was intentionally kept secret from relatives. Normally a letter would be sent expressing sympathy such as the following from Brandenburg:

> As you are no doubt aware, your daughter Fraülein ... was transferred to our institution on ministerial orders. It is our sad duty to have to inform you that she died here ... of influenza in conjunction with an abscess on the lung. All attempts by the doctors to keep the patient alive were unfortunately unsuccessful. We wish to express our most heartfelt condolences for your loss and hope that you will find comfort in the knowledge that the death of your daughter has released her from her great and incurable suffering.[14]

Discussion: Euthanasia policy

The euthanasia policy was not a radical departure from previous plans for selective breeding. As early as 28 June 1933 Reich Minister of the Interior Wilhelm Frick established a Committee of Experts for Population and Racial Policy. The aim of this body was to propose a law sanctioning sterilization. On 14 July 1933 clause 12 of the Law for the Prevention of Progeny with Hereditary Diseases stipulated those considered hereditarily ill could be sterilized; according to this law, the range of sicknesses included in this category included those suffering from congenital feeble-mindedness, schizophrenia, manic depression, hereditary blindness, hereditary deafness, and serious physical deformities.

The reasons given for such a law related to the aims of the Party:

> Since the National Revolution public opinion has become increasingly preoccupied with questions of demographic policy and the continuing

decline in the birth rate. However, it is not only the decline in population which is a cause for serious concern but equally the increasing evident genetic composition of our people. Whereas the hereditarily healthy families have for the most part adopted a policy of having only one or two children, countless numbers of inferiors and those suffering from hereditary conditions are reproducing unrestrainedly while their sick and associate offspring burden the community.[15]

On 26 June 1935 this law was amended so as to sanction abortions within the first six months of pregnancy in the case of women who had been designated as hereditarily ill by the Hereditary Health Courts.

These laws served as the background to development of the euthanasia programme. According to the Reich Physicians Leader, Dr Wagner, Hitler stated in 1935 that in the event of war he would initiate a policy of euthanasia. It was not until the winter of 1938–9 that the euthanasia programme commenced. At this a father petitioned Hitler, requesting that his deformed child be put to death. In response Hitler sent a physician to investigate this matter, empowered to terminate the child's life if required. Subsequently, this doctor, Karl Brandt, and Philipp Bouhler formed the Reich Committee for the Scientific Registration of Serious Hereditarily and Congenitally-based Illnesses; this body scrutinized reports on deformed births sent by physicians and midwives which were passed on to three paediatricians who determined whether the child was to die. These children were then sent to paediatric clinics where, as we have seen, they were starved or given lethal injections. This was followed by adult euthanasia.

In October 1939 Hitler gave formal authorization to this policy. Backdated to September 1939, the document stated:

> Reich Leader Bouhler and Dr. med. Brandt are charged with responsibility to extend the powers of specific doctors in such a way that, after the most careful assessment of their condition, those suffering from illnesses deemed to be incurable may be granted a mercy death.[16]

To support this policy, films were made which stigmatized the mentally and physically handicapped. In October 1939 Victor Brack, Bouhler's deputy, commissioned Hermann Schweninger to make propaganda films dealing with euthanasia. In pursuit of this end, he sought to depict some of the most shocking types of cases including idiotic and deformed children. This programme, however, was superseded by a more indirect approach. The film, *I Accuse*, which was released in August 1941, depicts a professor of pathology whose wife Hanah developed multiple sclerosis. Faced with the agonizing spectre of his wife's illness, the doctor resolved to help his wife die. When his wife's brothers brought a lawsuit against him for murder, the spokesman for the jurors argued that the law needed to be changed so that mercy killings would be allowed. In the jury scene, a retired Major stated:

> When one deploys hundreds of thousands of physicians, sisters and nurses, and puts up vast buildings with laboratories and medicaments and God knows what, simply in order to keep a few pitiful creatures alive, who are either too crazy to get anything out of life, or a threat to the community or in general just like animals – and that at a time when one doesn't have enough people, room or the wherewithal to keep the healthy in health, or to properly provide for the mothers of newborn babies – then that is the most hare-brained nonsense! The State has the duty firstly to look after the people who in general are the State – namely the workers – and as far as those are concerned who would like to die, because they were once healthy and now cannot endure any longer – my view is that the State, which demands from us the duty to die, must give us the right to die.[17]

Despite such propaganda, there was a concerted attempt to keep the euthanasia programme a secret. Nonetheless, knowledge of this policy spread. As a consequence, relatives contacted clergy and judicial authorities who sought information about patients who were wards of court. In response, the Reich Ministry of Justice passed on such complaints to the Ministry of the Interior and the Reich Chancellery. At the same time, church leaders such as the Bishop of Münster, Clemens August Count von Galen, denounced the Nazis' quest to rid society of those perceived as useless. In a passionate address given on 3 August 1941, he condemned the wanton killing of innocent victims; his words are a chilling warning given the destruction of human life which was to take place in the ensuing years:

> If you establish and apply the principle that you can kill 'unproductive' fellow human beings then woe betide us all when we become old and frail. If one of us is allowed to kill the unproductive people then woe betide the invalids who have used up, sacrificed and lost their health and strength in the productive process. If one is allowed forcibly to remove one's unproductive fellow human beings then woe betide loyal soldiers

who return to the homeland seriously disabled, as cripples, as invalids. If it is once accepted that people have the right to kill 'unproductive' fellow humans – and even if it only affects the poor defenceless mentally ill – then as a matter of principle murder is permitted for all unproductive people, in other words for the incurably sick, the people who have become invalids through labour and war, for us all when we become old, frail and therefore unproductive. Then it is only necessary for some secret edict to order that the method developed for the mentally ill should be extended to other 'unproductive' people, that it should be applied to those suffering from incurable lung disease, to the elderly who are frail or invalids, to the severely disabled soldiers. Then none of our lives will be safe any more. Some commission can put us on the list of the 'unproductive', who in their opinion have become worthless life. And no police force will protect us and no court will investigate our murder and give the murderer the punishment he deserves.[18]

Notes

1 K. Binding and A. Hoche, *Die Freigabe der Vernichtung lebensunwerten Lebens. Ihr Mass und ihre Form*, Leipzig, 1920, pp. 27ff in J. Noakes and G. Pridham, *op. cit.*, p. 998.
2 *Ibid.*, pp. 27ff.
3 *Ibid.*, p. 40.
4 *Ibid.*, pp. 55ff
5 *Völkischer Beobachter*, 7.8. 1929 in J. Noakes and G. Pridham, *op. cit.*, p. 1002.
6 J. Tuchel (ed.), *'Kein Recht auf Leben.' Beiträge und Dokumente zur Entrechtung und Vernichtung 'lebensunwerten Lebens'* in *Nationalsozialismus*, Berlin, 1984, pp. 48–9 in J. Noakes and G. Pridham, *op. cit.*, p. 1003.
7 F. K. Kaul, *Die Psychiatrie im Strudel der 'Euthanasie'*, Frankfurt, 1979, p. 33 in J. Noakes and G. Pridham, *op. cit.*, p. 1008.
8 E. Klee, *'Euthanasie' im NS-Staat. Die Vernichtung 'lebensunwerten Lebens'*, Franfurt, 1983, pp. 110–12 in J. Noakes and G. Pridham, *op. cit.*, pp. 1019–20.
9 *Ibid*, pp. 179–80
10 *Ibid.*, pp. 124ff.
11 *Ibid.*, pp. 124ff.
12 *Ibid.*, pp. 124ff.
13 *Ibid.*, p. 148.
14 E. Kogon *et al.*, *Nationalsozialistische Massentötungen durch Giftgas*, Frankfurt, 1983, pp. 50–1 in J. Noakes and G. Pridham, *op. cit.*, p. 1028.

15 Michael Burleigh and Wolfgang Wippermann, *The Radical State: Germany 1933–45*, Cambridge, 1996, pp. 137–8.
16 *Ibid.*, p. 148.
17 *Ibid.*, pp. 156–7.
18 Nuremberg Document 3701-PS.

21. Gypsies, the asocial and homosexuals

Allied with the destruction of European Jewry, the Nazis were intent on eliminating other undesirable elements from the Third Reich. In their quest to purify German blood, the NSDAP perceived the Sinti and Roma communities as threatening the race; so, too, homosexuals and the asocial were regarded as a significant danger to Aryan civilization. Like the Jews, these three groups were persecuted, deported, and murdered by the state apparatus, and such barbarism was rationalized by racial ideology.

Persecution and death

As part of their racial programme, the Nazis adopted harsh measures against the gypsy communities living in Germany. In a circular issued by Himmler on 8 December 1938, he declared:

> Experience gained in the fight against the gypsy nuisance, and knowledge derived from race-biological research, have shown that the proper method of attacking the gypsy problem seems to be to treat it as a matter of race. ... Treatment of the gypsy question is part of the National Socialist task of national regeneration. A solution can only be achieved if the philosophical perspectives of National Socialism are observed. Although the principle that the German nation respects the national identity of alien peoples is also assumed in the fight against the gypsy nuisance, nonetheless the aim of measures taken by the State to defend the homogeneity of the German nation must be the physical separation of Gypsydom from the German nation, the prevention of miscegenation, and finally the regulation of the way of life of pure and part-gypsies. The necessary legal foundation can only be created through

209

a gypsy Law, which prevents further intermingling of blood, and which regulates all the most pressing questions which go together with the existence of gypsies in the living space of the German nation.[1]

On 21 September 1939 Heydrich organized a conference on racial policy in Berlin which appears to have produced a final solution to the gypsy problem. The discussion concerned several issues: the concentration of gypsies in towns, their relocation to Poland, and the systematic deportation of Jews from Germany. The next month a letter was sent by the Reich Main Security Office to local agents which stated that the gypsy question would be regulated throughout the Reich. Gypsies were restricted to particular locations. Those who attempted to flee were sent to concentration camps. At this time Adolf Eichmann recommended that the gypsy problem should be resolved alongside the Jewish question. In consequence about 2500 Sinti and Roma were sent to Poland from the western regions of the Reich between April and May 1940. However, the deportation of the gypsy population was eventually halted so as to give priority to the transportation of Jews. Instead, gypsies were compelled to endure the most horrific conditions in camps where they were subject to beatings, solitary confinement, poor food, manual labour, and various forms of persecution.

With the invasion of the Soviet Union, the Nazi policy regarding the gypsies underwent a transformation. As with the Jewish population, in Russia SS *Einsatzgruppen* and army units murdered gypsies en masse. On the assumption that such individuals were spies, about 250,000 Sinti and Roma were killed. Within the Nazi ranks, however, officials debated whether any gypsies should be kept alive. Himmler wished to preserve a few clans as ethnic curiosities; Martin Bormann, on the other hand, sought to eliminate these groups entirely. On 16 December Himmler signed an order which decreed that Sinti and Roma be sent to Auschwitz.

At Auschwitz the B II e camp measured about 1000 metres by 80 metres, consisting of a series of wooden barracks on waterlogged soil. Entire families were sent there where conditions were intolerable, with outbreaks of typhus, smallpox and ulcerous conditions. Both twins and dwarfs were subjected to medical experiments undertaken by Dr Mengele. Eventually those who were able to engage in work were relocated elsewhere leaving behind wives and families. On 2–3 August 1944 nearly 3000 individuals who remained in the camp were taken to the gas chambers. The few children who had hidden themselves were captured the next day by Dr Mengele who drove them to the gas chambers in his own car. Of the 23,000 gypsies who had entered the camp, 20,078 were murdered.

Elsewhere other Sinti and Roma were permitted to move around Germany. To resolve this contradictory policy, various ordinances were issued. Hence on 13 March 1942, the Reich Minister of Labour ordered that the special stipulations with regard to Jews in the field of welfare legislation should be applied to gypsies. On 25 April 1943, the Reich deprived both Jews and gypsies of their rights as German citizens:

> The Reich leadership of the NSDAP – Main Office for the Nation's Welfare – has decreed the following through a letter dated 21 May 1942 to the leaders of the offices for the nation's welfare in the *Gau* leadership of the NSDAP ... full gypsies, and part-gypsies with predominant or equal parts of gypsy blood, are to be equated with Jews with regard to labour legislation.[2]

Allied with the gypsy policy, the Nazis were determined to bring asocial elements in Germany under control. According to Nazi ideology, asocial behaviour was determined by genetic factors. Hence, they sought to fight against crime through sterilization or castration. Only in this way, they believed, would it be possible to sustain the purity of the race. Once the Nazis seized power, individuals who were accused of asocial or criminal behaviour were sterilized in accordance with the Law for the Prevention of Hereditarily Diseased Progeny.

In accordance with this policy, the National Socialists sought to exclude such individuals from the national community. In September 1933 raids against beggars and vagrants took place in line with the guidelines issued by the Ministry of Propaganda:

> The psychological importance of a planned campaign against the nuisance of begging should not be underestimated. Beggars often force their poverty upon people in the most repulsive way for their own selfish purposes. If this sight disappears from the view of foreigners as well, the result will be a definite feeling of relief and liberation. People will feel that things are becoming more stable again, and that the economy is improving once more. A successful action against the nuisance of begging can have important propaganda benefits for the 'struggle

against cold and hunger'. Once the land has been freed of the nuisance of beggars, we can justifiably appeal to the propertied classes to give all the more generously for the Winter Aid Programme now being set in motion by the State and the Party.[3]

Increasingly racial-biological criteria were used to deal with asocial elements in German society. From 1935 prisons and correctional institutions in Prussia were authorized to carry out criminal-biological investigations on inmates. Special criminal-biological collection points were established in various cities to carry out prescribed tests. Further, more radical steps were taken following Himmler's appointment as Chief of the Police in the Reich Ministry of the Interior on 17 June 1936. Seeking to remove responsibility for the solution of the asocial question from the courts, he decreed that about 2000 habitual criminals as well as those who offend against public decency should be taken into police custody and sent to concentration camps. In response to criticism of this action by justice authorities, Himmler issued a circular dealing with this matter on 14 December 1937:

> Those to be considered asocial are persons who demonstrate through criminal behaviour towards the community, which may not in itself be criminal, that they will not adapt themselves to the community. The following are examples of the asocial: (a) Persons who through minor but repeated infractions of the law demonstrate that they will not adapt themselves to the natural discipline of the National Socialist state, e.g. beggars, tramps, gypsies, whores, alcoholics with contagious diseases, particularly sexually transmitted diseases, who evade the measures taken by the public health authorities.[4]

Such a decree enabled the Criminal Police to take into preventive custody persons who had not actually been charged with criminal or political offences and extended the range of individuals who could be incarcerated. Between 21 and 30 April 1938 large numbers of arrests took place; those taken into custody were questioned and then deported to Buchenwald. Later Heydrich ordered that every regional district police headquarters should fill a quota of at least 200 arrests. These raids were coupled with the expansion of the Nazi work programme as emphasized by SS-Oberführer Ulrich Greifelt:

> The chief of the SS administration has created the ideal means in the concentration camps for achieving the productive deployment of the

labour potential of criminal and political prisoners. They have established, or are in the process of establishing, production centres for costly building materials which are needed for the major construction enterprises of the Führer. ... In view of the tight situation on the labour market, national labour discipline dictated that all persons who would not conform to the working life of the nation, and who were vegetating as work-shy and asocial, making the streets of our cities and countryside unsafe, had to be compulsorily registered and set to work. Prompted by the Office for the Four-Year Plan, the Gestapo intervened with considerable energy. Simultaneously, the Criminal Police took on tramps, beggars, gypsies, and pimps, and finally those who refused to pay maintenance. More than 10,000 of these asocial forces are currently undertaking a labour training cure in the concentration camps, which are admirably suited for this purpose.[5]

Like gypsies and the asocial, homosexuals were also put at risk. Reflecting on the change that occurred in 1933, a homosexual stated:

1933 was the starting point for the persecution of homosexuals. Already in this year we heard of raids on homosexual pubs and meeting-places. Maybe individual, politically uneducated homosexuals who were only interested in immediate gratification did not recognize the significance of the year 1933, but for us homosexuals who were also politically active, who had defended the Weimar Republic, and who had tried to forestall the Nazi threat, 1933 initially signified a reinforcing of our resistance. In order not to mutually incriminate ourselves, we decided to no longer recognize each other. When we came across each other in the street, we passed by without looking at one another. There were certainly possibilities for us to meet, but that never happened in public. For a politicized homosexual, visiting places which were part of the homosexual subculture was too dangerous. Friends told me that raids on bars were becoming more frequent.[6]

The same year students of the Berlin School for Physical Education demolished the Institute for Sexual Science – this institute had been founded in 1919 by Magnus Hirschfeld for the scientific discussion of sexuality including homosexual behaviour. The books in the library were burned on the Opernplatz to the singing of the *Deutschland-lied*, and a bust of Hirschfeld was hanged and thrown on a bonfire. As an eye-witness recalled:

On 6 May 1933 at 9:30 a.m., a few vans with about 100 students and a band with brass instruments appeared before the Institute. They took up

213

military formation and then, accompanied by music, forced their way into the building. ... The students demanded entrance to all the rooms; in so far as these were locked, like the reception rooms on the ground floor, which were no longer in use, or the present office of the World League for Sexual Reform, they broke through the doors. ... They emptied inkwells over papers and the carpets, and turned to private bookshelves. They took with them what appeared to be suspect. ... Most of the other pictures, photographs and representative types were taken off the walls. They played football with them, so that a great mess of broken glass and crumpled pictures remained ... at 3p.m. several vans arrived with SA men, who declared that the confiscation must continue, because the Squad in the morning had not had enough time to clear everything out totally. This second troupe once again searched the whole building and using a lot of baskets, loaded two large lorries with valuable books and manuscripts. ... The number of books from the Institute's special library which were destroyed amounted to over 100,000. The students carried a bust of Dr Magnus Hirschfeld in a torchlight parade and threw it on a bonfire.[7]

In 1935 the section of the Reich Criminal Code dealing with homosexual behaviour was expanded. Previously Paragraph 175 stated:

1. A male who indulges in criminally indecent activity with another male, or who allows himself to participate in such activity, will be punished with imprisonment.
2. If one of the participants is under the age of 21, and if the offence has not been grave, the court may dispense with the sentence of imprisonment.[8]

This was altered by Paragraph 175b so that any form of homosexual activity which caused public offence or stimulated sexual desire became punishable:

1. A term of imprisonment of up to ten years, or if mitigating circumstances can be established, a term of imprisonment of no less than three years will be imposed on:

1. Any male who by force or threat of violence and danger to life and limb compels another man to indulge in criminally indecent activities, or allows himself to participate in such activities;
2. Any male who forces another male to indulge with him in criminally indecent activities by using the subordinate position of

the other man, whether it be at work or elsewhere, or who allows himself to participate in such activities;

3. Any male who indulges professionally and for profit in criminally indecent activities with other males, or allows himself to be used for such activities or who offers himself for the same.[9]

In 1936 Himmler established a Reich Central Office for the Combating of Homosexuality and Abortion. This was in line with the view of the SS which was adamant in urging that the death penalty be imposed on those who were found guilty of homosexual activity. For example, in May 1935 the SS journal *Das Schwarze Korps* included an article by *SS-Untersturmführer* Professor Eckhardt which pointed out that Nordic-German states usually punished homosexual offenders more severely than western-Latin peoples. Such differences, Eckhardt argued, illustrated the purer consciousness of the concept of race among Nordic-Germanic peoples.

As a result of Himmler's appropriation of such police activities, the number of prosecutions increased: in 1934, 766 males were convicted; in 1938 the number rose to 8000. Further, from 1936 many of those convicted were sent to concentration camps after serving a prison sentence. On 18 February 1937 Himmler made his views clear about the evils of homosexuality in a speech to *SS-Gruppenführer*:

If you further take into account the facts I have not yet mentioned, namely that with a static number of women, we have two million men too few on account of those who fell in the war, then you can well imagine how this imbalance of two million homosexuals and two million war dead, or in other words, a lack of about four million men capable of having sex, has upset the sexual balance sheet of Germany, and will result in a catastrophe. ... A people of good race which has too few children has a one-way ticket to the grave, for insignificance in 50 or 100 years, for burial in 250 years. ... We must be absolutely clear that if we continue to have this burden in Germany, without being able to fight it, then that is the end of Germany, and the end of the Germanic world.[10]

How did such policies affect the life of homosexuals living in Germany? A typical reaction was recorded by a homosexual living in Reinbeck:

With one blow a wave of arrests of homosexuals began in our town. One of the first to be arrested was my friend, with whom I had a relationship since I was 23. One day people from the Gestapo came to his house and took him away. It was pointless to enquire where he might be. If anyone did that, they ran the risk of being similarly detained, because he knew them, and therefore they were also suspect. Following his arrest, his home was searched by Gestapo agents. Books were taken away, note- and address books were confiscated, questions were asked among his neighbours. ... The address books were the worst. All those who figured in them or had anything to do with him were arrested and summoned by the Gestapo. ... After four weeks my friend was released from investigative custody. The fascists could not prove anything against him either. However the effects of his arrest were terrifying. Hair shorn off, totally confused, he was no longer what he was before. ... We had to be very careful with all contacts. I had to break off all relations with my friend. We passed each other by on the street, because we did not want to put ourselves in danger. There were no longer any homosexual meeting places. When I wanted to meet people I went to Hamburg. Each time that was a clandestine undertaking, because I had to make sure that no one was following me. I went up to the platform, I got on to the next train. At Berliner Tor I got out, went over to the tram stop, and when everyone had got on, quickly ran over to the underground and went further. ... We lived like animals in a wild game park, always sensing the hunters.[11]

Other solutions to the homosexual problem were also proposed. A Danish SS doctor Carl Vaernet had been experimenting with artificial gland implants in mice. He then operated unsuccessfully on 180 human beings – he patented a hormonal implant capsule, and sought to sell his findings to the SS who provided him with laboratory facilities and access to concentration camp prisoners. The surgical operation involved inserting a capsule which released the male hormone testosterone. In a case history of a patient in Buchenwald, Vaernet revealed the aim of such procedures:

Patient No. 1
n. 21 666, S. Bernhard, born 1889, theologian, member of a religious order.
Prehistory:
Always sickly, rather withdrawn, but cheerful and helpful. Sexual maturity at 18. 1911-12 attempts to come close to a girl, but on account of fear nothing sexual came of it. At school, bad performance at first because of living conditions, then good. 1924–8 relations with young

men, touching their thighs, no feelings of fear. 1932–5 again with men, then normal relations with a girl, satisfaction the same. Last emission in February 1944. 8 years' imprisonment, nothing took place there. Implantation of the 'artificial male hormonal gland' on 19.6.44 (dose 3a).

Following the operation on:

16.9.44 Pains. Neurological, no findings.

17.9.44 No pains.

18.9.44 Erection.

19.9.44 Full erection in the early morning.

20.9.44 Once again full erection.

22.9.44 Erection again.

23.9.44 Erection in the morning and evening.

24.9.44 The same.

26.10.44 Surgical wounds fully healed without any reactions. No reactions to the implantation of an 'artificial gland'. Feels better and has dreamed of women.

His appearance has improved considerably. Looks younger, his features are smoother, today he came for an examination laughing and happy. During the first examination he was taciturn and only answered the questions obliquely; today he talks freely and in detail about his earlier life and about the changes which have taken place since the implant ... his entire erotic universe has altered – before, all of his erotic thoughts and dreams were aimed at young men, but now only at women. He thinks that life in the camp is unfavourable – thought about the women in the brothel, but for 'religious reasons' he cannot go there.[12]

Discussion: Nazi victims

In the Jewish world the Holocaust is frequently perceived as the outcome of centuries of persecution against Jewry. Repeatedly the claim is made that the Nazis' attempted annihilation of the Jewish people was a modern manifestation of the Christian onslaught against Jews and Judaism. Yet, there is a crucial distinction between previous forms of Judaeophobia and Nazi policy. As we have seen, from New Testament times to the modern period, the Church regarded itself as the true Israel. Accused of deicide, Jews were viewed as demonic in character, a wayward people destined to suffer rejection and misery because of their unwillingness to accept Jesus as the Messiah.

For the Nazis, however, such religious convictions were of little consequence. Instead, Hitler viewed the Jewish people as an evil race

217

seeking world domination. It was racial, not religious, antipathy which animated the Nazis in their quest to rid Europe of a Jewish population. The Third Reich was deeply ideological, committed to the creation of a new society devoid of pernicious influences. In this quest, the Jewish people were seen as the greatest threat to the future of Aryanism. Victory against the Jewish people was of the greatest importance, and Hitler saw himself as an agent of divine providence in carrying out this task.

In this light the Holocaust is often interpreted as exclusively concerned with Jewry. But, as this chapter illustrates, the Third Reich aimed to eliminate all undesirable elements from society in the quest to create a racial utopia. It was not just the Jews who were the target of Nazi policy – other undesirable groups suffered a similar fate. From the outset both academics and scientists were involved in the formulation of Nazi racial policy: anthropologists, biologists, economists, historians and sociologists helped to create the framework for an all-embracing racial theory. Applying knowledge, skill and technique, these ideologues sought to implement these policies in the life of the nation.

Pre-eminent among the organizations which sought to carry out Nazi plans was the German Society for Racial Hygiene. In 1933 this body had 1300 members composed largely of academics, some of whom worked in the Racial Political Office of the NSDAP. In addition, the German Society for Racial Research carried out similar programmes. The most important institute concerned with race was the Kaiser Wilhelm Institute for Anthropology, Heredity and Eugenics which was established in 1928; five years later its directors joined the Committee of Experts for Population and Racial Policy in the Reich Ministry of the Interior.

By July 1933 the directors assured the Interior Minister that the institute would serve the Reich in racial hygienic research; as a result, the institute was given considerable financial support so that medical students, physicians and others would be trained in racial and eugenic theory. Given its prominence in the field, the institute gave official advice concerning a variety of racial matters. Within the institute researchers such as Wilhelm Abel embarked on investigations of Jews as well as Sinti and Roma in Romania. One of the most notorious figures involved in such investigation was Josef Mengele who sent the eyes of gypsies and the internal organs of children to the institute.

Located near the institute was another centre which was intimately involved in racial policy – the Racial-Hygienic and Hereditary Research Centre. Established in 1936, its director, Robert Ritter, was concerned primarily with gypsies. From 1935 Sinti and Roma – like Jews – were perceived as carrying non-German blood. Yet this did not settle the question of who should be classified as gypsies. Utilizing genealogical, biological and anthropological criteria Ritter and his associates classified all Sinti and Roma in Germany. On the basis of degrees of racial purity, these individuals were either sterilized or sent to concentration camps. Supported by Himmler, Ritter became Director of the Criminal-Biological Institute of the Security Police.

Other institutions which engaged in racial research included the Provincial Office for Racial Questions in Jena, headed by Karl Astel. Another research institute, the Institute for Hereditary and Race Care in Giessen, was under the direction of Wilhelm Kranz. Two other institutions engaging in racial investigation were headed by historians: the *Publikationsstelle* in Dahlem, and the North-East German Research Community. Both of these bodies were involved in the establishment of research institutes in eastern Europe including the *Institut für Deutsche Ostarbeit* in Cracow, the *Reinhard-Heydrich-Stiftung* in Prague, and the *Reichsuniveristät* in Posen. The proliferation of such research centres illustrates the Nazis' overwhelming preoccupation with race.

In line with such policy, the Nazis from a very early stage created a variety of agencies which sought to put racial doctrine into practice. In June 1933 the Committee of Experts for Population and Racial Policy was established by the Interior Minister Wilhelm Frick. Among other issues, this committee was concerned with questions of racial hygiene, eugenics, compulsory abortion, castration and sterilization. Later a second working party was given the task of creating and implementing policy. Allied with these agencies, the Department for People's Health and subordinate public health offices were responsible for carrying out compulsory sterilization. issuing certificates for marriage, and assessing the German population on a hereditary-biological basis.

Such a massive apparatus was designed to ensure the racial purity of the German nation. The onslaught against Jews must thus be placed in the context of an overarching racial quest to purify German blood from any form of pollution. Like the Jews, the asocial, gypsies and homosexuals were perceived as a threat to the future of the German Reich – actions directed against these groups were undertaken so as to protect the German population from what was seen as a serious threat from corrupting influences. The Third Reich should thus be seen as pre-eminently a racial state whose actions against minority groups should be understood as an indivisible whole.

Notes

1 Michael Burleigh and Wolfgang Wippermann, *The Racial State: Germany 1933–45*, Cambridge, 1996. pp. 120–1.
2 *Ibid.*, pp. 126–7.
3 *Ibid.*, pp. 168–70.
4 'Grundlegender Erlass über die vorbeugende Verbrechensbekämpfung durch die Polizei des Reichs und Preussischen Ministers des Innern vom 14.12.1937; Reichssicherheitshauptamt-Amt V' (ed.), *Vorbeugende Verbrechensbekämpfung*, Berlin, 1942, p. 41 in Burleigh and Wippermann, *op. cit.*, p. 173.
5 *Ibid.*, p. 175.
6 Hans-Georg Stümke, Rudi Finkler, *Rosa Winkel, Rosa Listen, Homosexuelle und 'Gesundes Volksempfinden' von Auschwitz bis Heute*, Hamburg, 1981, p. 238 in Burleigh and Wippermann, *op. cit.*, p. 183.
7 *Ibid.*, pp. 163–6.
8 Richard Plant, *The Pink Triangle: The Nazi War Against Homosexuals*, Edinburgh, 1987, p. 206.
9 *Ibid.*, p. 206.
10 Stümke and Finkler, *op. cit.*, pp. 217–21 in Burleigh and Wippermann, *op. cit.*, pp. 192–193.
11 Hans-Georg Stümke, *Homosexuelle in Deutschland*, Munich, 1989, pp. 115–16 in Burleigh and Wippermann, *op. cit.*, p. 194.
12 BA (Koblenz) NS 4 Bu/50, Carl Varnet to the Reichsführer–SS, 30 October 1944, with attached notes on Patient No. 1 (No. 21, 686) in Burleigh and Wippermann, *op. cit.*, pp. 195–6.

22. Jewish resistance and the final stages of terror

According to some scholars, the Jewish people went to their deaths as innocent victims. In their view, the Jewish population was passive in the face of the Nazi onslaught. In addition, the *Judenräte* have been viewed as culpable for their collaboration with the German authorities. The murder of Jews, these critics have argued, would have been smaller if they had not provided assistance to the Nazis. There is no doubt that millions of victims went to their deaths without struggle. Yet this is not the complete picture. In the unfolding of events, Jews frequently resisted those who set out to destroy the Jewish community.

Jewish defence against the enemy

By September 1942 the German armies had conquered most of Europe. Yet, as mass killing continued, resistance increased. On 24 September the Jews of the White Russian town of Korzec set the ghetto on fire, and a number of Jews established a partisan band. On 25 September in Kaluszyn near Warsaw, the chairman of the Jewish Council in Lukow near Lublin collected money from Jews assembled in the main square in the hope that he could use the funds to ransom the Jewish community. But when he found that the deportation would take place, he shouted: 'Here is your payment for our trip, you bloody tyrant'. Tearing the money into shreds, he struck the German supervisor and was shot on the spot by the Ukrainian guards. In the same month a former Jewish soldier in the Polish army who was being held with several hundred other prisoners in Lublin escaped with seventeen Jews, forming a small partisan group.

In the Warsaw ghetto, the Jewish Fighting Organization prepared itself for action. On 29 October 1942, a member of the Organization killed the commander of the Jewish police in the ghetto. In the Bialystok ghetto resistance was also taking place with the assistance of German soldiers from whom they obtained weapons. Near Cracow six members of the Jewish Fighting Organization fled to the forests armed with pistols and a knife, but were betrayed by local peasants. The next month the Jewish Fighting Organization in Cracow sabotaged railway lines, raided a German clothing store, and killed several Germans. In Marcinkance the chairman of the Jewish Council called out to the Jews who had been brought to the railway station: 'Fellow Jews, everybody run for his life. Everything is lost!' As the Jews ran towards the ghetto fence, attacking the guards, over 100 were shot.

Nonetheless, despite the insurmountable odds, some Jews did manage to escape from the Nazis. As one survivor recalled:

> The moans of the elderly, the screams of the children ... were being drowned by the clatter of the death train as it moved through the French countryside of contrasting bucolic beauty and serenity. ... Two parallel iron bars in the rectangular opening in the corner of the cattle car represented the only obstacle to our escape. ... We took off our sweaters, soaked them in human waste, wrung them out, thereby giving the fabric greater tensile strength. We then wrapped them around the iron bars. ... Working feverishly, we applied that twisting method until the bars showed some inward bending. ... We chose the moment of escape very carefully. It had to come at a time when the train would slow down for a curve. It also had to avoid the floodlights which the guards were aiming over the entire length of the concave curvature of the train during the period of reduced speed. ... At this split second, we had to take our chances and leap before the beams of the floodlights would fall on us. We jumped.[13]

In November 1942 Polish Jews who had managed to escape the deportation to Treblinka established a small group to protect those Jews who went into hiding. The news of executions in the labour camps in December encouraged plans for resistance in Warsaw. As an eye-witness to these events, Emanuel Ringelblum, recorded:

> The community wants the enemy to pay dearly. ... They will attack them with knives, sticks, carbolic acid; they will not allow themselves to

be seized in the streets, because now they know that the labour camp these days means death.[14]

In the labour camp at Kruszyna near Radom Jews decided to resist with knives and fists in December 1942. When they were ordered to gather together, they attacked the guards. Three weeks later 400 Jews in the Kopernik camp in Minsk Mazowiecki barricaded themselves into the buildings and resisted the oppressors with sticks, stones and bricks. On 22 December 1942 in Cracow, the Jewish Fighting Organization attacked a cafe which was frequented by the SS and the Gestapo. In Czestochowa on 4 January 1943 members of the Jewish Fighting Organization wounded the German commander.

On 19 April 1943 German troops entered the Warsaw ghetto determined to transport Jews to Treblinka. Whereas they did not expect any resistance, preparations had been made in the ghetto by Jews who sought to defend themselves. Pistols and grenades had been obtained; those who had no weapons armed themselves with sticks, bottles and lengths of pipe. As German troops entered the ghetto, the Jews attacked. One of those who witnessed this battle, Zivia Lubetkin, recounted the events which took place:

> All of a sudden they started entering the ghetto, thousands armed as if they were going to the front against Russia. And we, what were our arms? The arms we had – we had a revolver, a grenade and a whole group had two guns, and some bombs, home-made, prepared in a very primitive way. We had to light it by matches, and Molotov bottles. It was strange to see those twenty men and women, Jewish men and women, standing up against the armed enemy glad and merry, because we knew that their end will come. We knew that they will conquer us first, but to know that for our lives they would pay a high price.[15]

According to Lubetkin, the Germans were initially repulsed by this small Jewish fighting force:

> When the Germans came up to our posts and marched by and we threw those hand grenades and bombs, and saw German blood pouring over the streets of Warsaw, and after we saw so much Jewish blood running in the streets of Warsaw before that, there was rejoicing. The tomorrow did not worry us. The rejoicing amongst Jewish fighters was great and, see the wonder and the miracle, those German heroes retreated, afraid and terrorized from the Jewish bombs and hand grenades, home-made.[16]

In the wake of this battle, the German Commander, SS General Jürgen Stroop, reported that he had lost six SS men and six Ukrainian auxiliaries. During the first evening of the ghetto uprising, the Passover *Seder* took place. One of the fighters, Tuvia Borzykowski, went in search of flashlights at 4 Kacza Street, only to find that Jewish life went on as usual:

> Wandering about there, I unexpectedly came upon Rabbi Maisel. When I entered the room, I suddenly realized that this was the night of the first *Seder*. The room looked as if it had been hit by a hurricane. Bedding was everywhere, chairs lay overturned, the floor was strewn with household objects, the window panes were all gone. It had happened during the day, before the inhabitants of the room returned from the bunker. Amidst the destruction, the table in the centre of the room looked incongruous with glasses filled with wine, with the family seated around, the rabbi reading the Haggadah. His reading was punctuated by explosions and the rattling of machine guns.[17]

During the Nazi onslaught against the ghetto on 20 April, Jewish defenders attacked the troops; in retaliation the buildings where these shots were fired were burned down. In the fire, hundreds of Jews jumped from the tenements. In his diary Leon Najberg recorded:

> Our brave defenders are holding their posts. Germans – in spite of everything – have to fight for access to each house. Gates of houses are barricaded, each house in the ghetto is a defensive fortress, each flat is a citadel – Jewish defenders are showering missiles from flats' windows and throwing shells at bandits. The defenders are passing over from one street to another through the garrets and recapturing places which are threatened by German bandits. The murderers have introduced flame-throwers into action. Houses in the ghetto are set on fire.[18]

Though outnumbered by German troops, Jewish fighters continued to engage in battle. Pleading for assistance, Mordechai Anielewicz wrote to Yitzhak Zuckerman who was attempting to obtain assistance from the Aryan side, complaining that what was needed were grenades, rifles, machine guns and explosives. Several days later Leon Najberg watched as several Jews perished in the fires started by the Germans. Observing this devastation, he described the plight of a German Jew, Hoch:

He had hidden in a hide-out on the fourth floor. He had started to be asphyxiated under the influence of the smell of burning carbon monoxide. When the first tongues of flame had reached Hoch's hide-out, the staircase was already destroyed. He had jumped from the fourth floor. He had his arms broken, his spine shattered, and coagulated blood on his face. Yesterday he was still conscious and crawled up to the cellar on his own. Today he is lying and dying.[19]

A similarly terrifying account was given by Feigele Peltel who observed the ghetto in flames:

On the balcony of the second floor a woman stood wringing her hands. She disappeared into the building but returned a moment later, carrying a child and dragging a feather bed, which she flung to the pavement to break her fall. Clutching her child, she started to climb over the railing. A spray of bullets caught her midway – the child dropped to the street – the woman's body dangled lifeless from the railing.[20]

Continuing this narrative, Peltel watched as building after building burned:

Dawn came quietly and ghastly to the ghetto, revealing the burnt-out shells of the buildings, the charred, blood-stained bodies of the victims. Suddenly one of those bodies began to move, slowly, painfully crawling on its belly until it disappeared into the smoking ruins. Others began to show signs of life. The enemy was on the alert, a spray of machine-gun fire – and all was lifeless again.[21]

On 29 Mila Street fighters were told to withdraw when their building was set on fire. As Tuvia Borzykowski related:

The unit commander went from hole to hole dragging out those who were afraid to move, warned the tardy that the convoy would start without them. When we finally started to move, a thin, childish voice heard from a distance stopped us. Then we saw a girl of about ten come out of a passage connecting two courtyards. She pleaded with us to save her mother who was still in the bunker with her clothes on. The girl herself was in severe pain from several burns. Several comrades immediately ran to the passage, but they were too late. In the few minutes since the girl had left her, the woman had been buried under burning debris. The child could not understand that her mother was gone; she cried and screamed, and refused to leave the place.[22]

By the first week of May 1943 the last stage of resistance in the ghetto was a bunker where 120 Jewish fighters gathered together. When attacked by German troops, the final Jewish enclave heroically resolved to take their own lives rather than die at the hands of the Nazis. As Zivia Lubetkin later recalled:

> Aryeh Wilner was the first to cry out: 'Come let us destroy ourselves. Let's not fall into their hands alive'. The suicides began. Pistols jammed and the owners begged their friends to kill them. But no one dared to take the life of a comrade. Lutek Rotblatt fired four shots at his mother but, wounded and bleeding, she still moved. Then someone discovered a hidden exit, but only a few succeeded in getting out this way. The others slowly suffocated in the gas.[23]

Reports of the resistance in Warsaw spread throughout Europe; nonetheless, pressure against the Jews continued. When the Red Army advanced on the Eastern Front, the Nazis decided to dig up the corpses of Jews and burn them. On 15 June at the Janowska death pits in Lvov Jewish labourers were compelled to dig up those who had been killed and extract gold teeth and rings. As an eye-witness, Leon Weliczker, later recalled:

> The fire crackles and sizzles. Some of the bodies in the fire have had their hands extended. It looks as if they are pleading to be taken out. Many bodies are lying around with open mouths. Could they be trying to say: 'We are your own mothers, fathers, who raised you and took care of you. Now you are burning us'. If they could have spoken maybe they would have said this, but they are forbidden to talk too – they are guarded. Maybe they would forgive us. They know that we are being forced to do this by the same murderers that killed them. We are under their whips and machine guns.[24]

The pace of murder was unrelenting. At Birkenau on Christmas Day 1943 Jewish women who had been starving were brought from the barracks. The victims knew they were going to the gas chambers and tried to escape. According to an account of this incident, when the lorry motors started, a terrible noise arose – the death cry of thousands of young women. As they struggled to escape, a rabbi's son cried out: 'God show them your power – this is against you'. When nothing happened, the boy cried out: 'There is no God'.

As the months passed, Jews continued to be subjected to equally terrible events. In Kovno several thousand children were rounded up, driven off in trucks and murdered. As an observer of this action related:

> I saw shattered scenes. It was near the hospital. I saw automobiles which from time to time would approach mothers with children or children who were on their own. In the back of them, two Germans with rifles would be going as if they were escorting criminals. They would toss the children in the automobile. I saw mothers screaming. A mother whose three children had been taken away – she went up to this automobile and shouted at the German, 'Give me the children', and he said, 'You may have one'. And she went up into that automobile, and all three children looked at her and stretched out their hands. Of course, all of them wanted to go with their mother, and the mother didn't know which child to select and she went down alone, and she left the car.[25]

By the summer of 1944 the last deportations took place. More than 67,000 were taken from the Lodz ghetto to Birkenau. There on 1 October, the Day of Atonement was celebrated with a sense of religious exaltation despite the terrors that had taken place:

> The moon shone through the window. Its light was dazzling that night and gave the pale, wasted faces of the prisoners a ghostly appearance. It was as if all the life had ebbed out of them. I shuddered with dread, for it suddenly occurred to me that I was the only living man among corpses. All at once the oppressive silence was broken by a mournful tune. It was the plaintive tones of the ancient *Kol Nidre* prayer. I raised myself up to see whence it came. There, close to the wall, the moonlight caught the uplifted face of an old man, who, in self-forgetful, pious absorption, was singing softly to himself. ... His prayer brought the ghostly group of seemingly insensible human beings back to life. Little by little, they all roused themselves and all eyes were fixed on the moonlight-flooded face.
>
> We sat up very quietly, so as not to disturb the old man, and he did not notice that we were listening.
>
> When at last he was silent, there was exaltation among us, an exaltation which men can experience only when they have fallen as low as we had fallen and then, through the mystic power of deathless prayer, have awakened once more to the world of the spirit.[26]

Discussion: The Jewish reaction

When compelled to register as Jews, Jewish communities complied. When forced to wear the Jewish star, Jews did not rebel. When told to form Jewish Councils and police forces, they did not offer resistance. When commanded to report to railway stations for deportation, they left their homes and waited in queues. When told to dig their own graves, they did so. When driven into the gas chambers, they did not revolt. Why did the millions of Jews who were massacred in the most gruesome way comply with these orders? Why did they cooperate with those who sought their deaths?

As we have seen, the incidence of rebellion was greater than was previously thought. In the Warsaw ghetto and elsewhere, Jewish men and women took up whatever arms they could against an overwhelming adversary. Yet there were numerous factors which militated against such resistance. First, the Nazis went to great lengths to deny access to any knowledge of what the evacuation to the east entailed. Despite occasional leaks of information as well as eye-witness reports, most Jews were misled into minimizing the Nazi threat. Reports of factories where Jews were being murdered were generally dismissed as unreliable scaremongering. In a state of confusion and demoralization, the community was unable to grasp the significance of the events taking place around them.

In addition, German Jews were deliberately isolated from the outside world. Even those who could communicate with relatives and friends in other countries were unable to remain in contact with those who had been deported to ghettos and labour camps. Because of such segregation, these Jews were in no position to obtain weapons from anti-Nazi groups within or outside the Third Reich. Such conditions made it virtually impossible to mount any form of resistance within Germany or to rouse sympathizers elsewhere to come to the defence of those who were being persecuted or killed.

The fear of collective punishment also seriously militated against any form of corporate action. Repeatedly the Nazis demonstrated that any form of resistance would be met by large-scale retribution. In the Vilnius ghetto, for example, the Nazis stated that if anyone attempted to escape from a work-party outside the ghetto walls, the entire group would be shot along with their families. A typical example of such reprisals occurred in the Bialystok ghetto in 1943 where 1000 Jewish children were murdered as a form of punishment.

Given such conditions, it was inevitable that the most fervent opposition to any form of resistance to the Nazis came from the leaders of the Jewish people. Disconcertingly, leaders of the community were convinced that Hitler would eventually be defeated – as a result, their primary task was to keep as many Jews alive as possible. Those who resisted were thus perceived as traitors to the Jewish cause; their actions were seen as endangering the lives of other Jews. The primary duty of being Jewish, these leaders believed, was to ensure the continuation of Jewry. In this quest, their strategy was to prove to their enemies that Jews could be productive citizens in the Nazi state. Such a policy demanded compliance in the face of the Nazi onslaught.

Another factor contributing to the Jewish lack of resistance was the constant presence of death. Faced with the loss of loved ones and living in constant fear, prisoners lapsed into a state of apathy. The unresisting behaviour of inmates was largely the result of the dehumanizing conditions of the camp life. As we have seen, many became *muselmänner*. In addition, even when victims contemplated resistance they lacked any confidence that they would be successful. In such conditions, it is not surprising that many Jews went to their deaths as lambs to the slaughter.

Finally, the fact that through the centuries Jews had endured constant persecution and suffering no doubt conditioned deportees to expect humiliation and degradation from the Nazis. Heroically, these individuals faced their deaths just as martyrs had done in previous ages. Pondering the question why there was such little resistance in the camps, Elie Wiesel concluded that resistance against the enemy could be perceived as a betrayal of those who had died:

Why did the Jews in the camps not choose a death with honour, knife in hand and hate on their lips? Putting aside the technical and psychological reasons which made any attempt at revolt impossible (the Jews knew they had been sacrificed, forgotten, crossed off by humanity), to answer we must consider the moral aspects of the question. The Jews, conscious of the curse weighing them down, came to believe that they were neither worthy nor capable of an act of honour. To die struggling would have meant a betrayal of those who had gone to their deaths submissive and silent. The only way was to follow in their footsteps, die their kind of death – only then could the living make their peace with those who had already gone.[27]

Notes

1 Martin Gilbert, *Holocaust*, London, 1987, pp. 496–7.
2 Ringelblum notes, 5 December 1942, in Jacob Sloan (ed.), *Notes from the Warsaw Ghetto: The Journal of Emanuel Ringleblum*, New York, 1958, p. 326.
3 Testimony of Zivia Lubetkin, Eichmann Trial, 2 May 1961, session 25.
4 *Ibid.*
5 Tuvia Borzykowski, *Between Tumbling Walls*, Tel Aviv, 1972, pp. 57–8.
6 Leon Najberg, diary entry for 20 April 1943, *Yivo Institute for Jewish Research* in Gilbert, *op. cit.*, p. 500.
7 Najberg diary, 25 April 1943, in Gilbert, *op. cit.*, p. 561.
8 Vladka Meed, *On Both Sides of the Wall*, Tel Aviv, 1972, pp. 180–1.
9 Ibid., pp. 180–1.
10 Borzykowski, *op. cit.*, p. 66.
11 Zivia Lubetkin, 'Last Days of the Warsaw Ghetto', *Commentary*, New York, May 1947.
12 Leon Weliczker Wells, *The Janowska Road*, New York, 1970, pp. 141–2.
13 Testimony of Dr Aharon Peretz, Eichmann Trial, 4 May 1961, session 28.
14 Leon Szalet, *Experiment 'E'*, New York, 1945, pp. 70–1 in Gilbert, *op. cit.*, p. 739.
15 E. Wiesel, *Legends of Our Time*, New York, 1968, in R. Landau, *The Nazi Holocaust*, London, 1992, p. 197.

23. Reactions to the Holocaust

Once Hitler came to power, anti-Semitism became a major feature of German life. How did ordinary Germans react to the racial policy which served as a framework of the Third Reich? Initially, most Germans were indifferent to racial ideology, yet there was little opposition to the regime. Similarly, both the Protestant and Catholic Churches largely failed to come to the rescue of those who were victimized in the Third Reich. A similar conclusion applies to the Allies – it appears that they did not consider it their duty to take action that went beyond the mainstream strategy of ensuring the defeat of the German nation.

Ordinary Germans, the Churches, and the Allies

How did the German public react to the Holocaust? In the early years of Nazi rule, it appears that there was general indifference to allegations about the Jewish threat to German society. Despite anti-Semitic propaganda and indoctrination, only a small minority of Germans participated in anti-Jewish activities such as physical attacks and the destruction of property. Most of those involved belonged to the SA or Hitler Youth whereas the majority of the population were simply bystanders. This was so even during the summer of 1935 when attacks against Jews intensified.

In Kiel, for example, a survey compiled in July 1935 by the Gestapo station reported:

> It is noteworthy that whenever there are actions against the Jews, these emanate chiefly from members of the Party and its affiliated

231

organizations, whereas the majority of the population hardly partici-
pates in the Jewish question.[1]

In other parts of the country similar conditions prevailed, as is
evidenced by a report about attitudes in the Rhineland: here the
majority of the population rejected the allegations of the Party's anti-
Semitic newspaper, *Der Stürmer*. In rural areas there was a
reluctance to disassociate with the local Jewish elements. In Bavaria,
for example, peasant attitudes were determined by economic
considerations; the local Gestapo described the peasants as having
no concern with racial issues. Likewise in Munich, the Gestapo
reported that the relationship between Jews and peasants continued
uninterruptedly despite the success of the NSDAP. In urban areas it
appears that anti-Jewish activities were fuelled by personal
antagonism rather than racial hatred.

Such apathy about the Jewish question was reflected in the
public's reaction to the anti-Jewish boycotts. In general Germans
were reluctant to participate actively in such activities. Despite the
Party's support for such discrimination, most citizens continued to
patronize shops owned by Jews. Among the poorer elements of
society, there was little support as well: most continued to shop in
Jewish-owned establishments. Industrialists, too, were largely
unaffected by Nazi propaganda; in their view, the Party's anti-
Jewish policy might endanger Germany's economic interests abroad.

Many in Germany questioned the wisdom of the anti-Semitic
campaign, fearing that this might harm their own interests. In
Kosslin, for example, the Gestapo reported that although the local
population harboured anti-Semitic attitudes, they did not wish to
suffer as a result of Nazi policy. A report in Hamburg in August 1935
similarly illustrated that there was little sympathy for attacks on
Jews because of the possible repercussions. In the district of Koblenz
a Gestapo survey for August and September 1935 revealed that a
township in the area requested that the anti-Semitic campaign be
lessened since those living there feared that the closure of a Jewish-
owned medical institution would seriously affect their economic
position. In Magdeburg a report in July 1935 illustrated public
disapproval for official Jewish policy. In Cologne, too, there was
concern about the anti-Semitic campaign which was viewed as
excessively brutal.

Despite such concern, there appears to have been little criticism of anti-Jewish legislation. In the early years of Nazi rule, the Law for the Restoration of the Professional Civil Service laid down racial criteria for all public positions, leading to the dismissal of thousands of Jewish officials. It appears that there was little public protest. Such a lack of opposition was no doubt due to the fact that ordinary Germans were able to take advantage of the jobs that immediately became available. As Jewish doctors, judges and teachers were dismissed from their positions, many were anxious to take their places.

Turning to the Nuremberg Laws, it appears that the majority of Germans accepted this legislation without complaint. Such acceptance seems to have been due to a general approval of racial policy. It appears that most Germans were in agreement that racial separatism was necessary to ensure the purity of the Reich. In addition, many believed that such regulation would curb violence directed against the Jewish population. In this regard, the law cancelling Jewish citizenship evoked little reaction; it was perceived as a logical development of Nazi rule. Further, the acceptance of the Law for the Protection of German Blood and Honour was generally welcomed since it too embodied Nazi doctrine.

Prior to the promulgation of these decrees, there had been terror and chaos on the streets. Fearing that such violence might spread to other segments of society such as the churches or those who maintained contact with German Jews, there was a sense of relief that such legislation had been enacted. As a report by the Gestapo in Berlin demonstrated, the public was disturbed by the lack of a clear policy towards Jews. Further, it added that since more complaints were being made about racial defilement, it had become impossible to prevent the renewal of anti-Semitic riots. The populace thus sought a legal settlement of the racial issue. In this light, the Nuremberg Laws as well as other laws about race provided a clear legal framework for the relationship between Jew and non-Jew.

Only rarely was such legislation challenged. Serious opponents of the Nazi regime criticized anti-Jewish enactments as did courageous churchmen, particularly Evangelical pastors who were hostile to Nazi ideology. Similarly, the Marxist underground admonished the Nazi party for its discriminatory policies and called for an extensive struggle against the Nazi regime. In addition, some members of the bourgeoisie as well as the liberal intelligentsia objected to the Nazis' treatment of minority groups within society. Ironically, other criticisms of the Nuremberg Laws stemmed from individuals employed by Jews who were faced with the prospect of unemployment. In the world of commerce, too, some believed that Jews abroad would stir up antagonism to Nazi Germany and thereby undermine the economy.

Again in 1938 the Jewish question came to occupy the German leadership. During the winter and spring of 1938, the Aryan process was intensified; simultaneously a new wave of anti-Semitism was unleashed upon the Jewish population. In the summer such antagonism towards Jews led to rioting in Berlin, culminating in the *Juniaktion* (June operation) when a significant number of German Jews were arrested. The reaction to these events was in essence no different from that of previous years.

During this period the German populace appears to have remained indifferent to the persecution of Jewry – this may have been due to the increasing apprehension about war. In addition, many Germans were unaware of the potential outcome of Nazi attitudes towards Jews in Europe. However, the events of *Kristallnacht* had an important impact on public opinion. Anti-Semitism had previously been widely accepted as a feature of the Third Reich. The destruction of Jewish property strengthened German morale but such acts of violence outraged many ordinary Germans, and highlighted the excesses of Nazi ideology. No longer were Germans able to sustain a stance of indifference to the events surrounding them. As the American counsul in Leipzig commented:

> The shattering of shop windows, looting of stores and dwellings of the Jews which began in the early hours of 10 November 1938 was hailed subsequently in the Nazi press as 'a spontaneous wave of righteous indignation throughout Germanys. ...' So far as a very high percentage of the German populace is concerned, a state of popular indignation that would spontaneously lead to such excesses can be considered as non-existent. On the contrary, in viewing the ruins and attendant measures employed, all of the crowds who observed were obviously benumbed over what had happened and aghast over the unprecedented fury of Nazi acts that had been or were taking place with bewildering rapidity throughout the city.[2]

As the war began in 1939, a state of isolation prevailed in the country. In addition, Jewish families were forced to live in overcrowded conditions. In the cities they were transferred from outlying areas to communal urban quarters occupied by fellow-Jews and forced to display Jewish stars on their homes. In this environment, Jews were expelled from public areas including museums, libraries and parks, and driven to buy all their goods at designated shops at set times. Further, all Jews between the ages of 16 and 65 were ordered to engage in forced labour, often in segregated companies. Eventually Jews disappeared from the world of commerce, and in the autumn of 1941 they were prevented from engaging in any form of business. The only exceptions were a limited number of physicians, dentists and lawyers who were given permission to carry on with their work. In this environment, Jews rarely appeared in public, and a curfew was established which required Jews to be off the streets by 8 p.m. in winter and 9 p.m. in summer. In general most Germans payed little attention to these restrictions. Such discriminatory policies were simply an integral part of the Nazi regime.

Supplementing Nazi policy, many ordinary Germans supported the legal restrictions imposed on the Jewish community. Criticisms were made of the apparent laxity in imposing such laws. Professional practitioners, for example, protested that Jewish doctors received pay for public holidays. Others objected that they were obliged to use the title of Jewish medical colleagues when corresponding with them. Other Germans were dismayed that Jewish children continued to receive the same milk rations as non-Jews. Another complaint was that Jews were able to use the same railway compartments as German workers and soldiers. Restrictions in shopping hours of Jews were also a source of contention – there were some who maintained that Jews should only be permitted to shop after hours, or that they be assigned to separate stores. Again, there was the feeling that clothing should be made in such a way that Jews would immediately be recognizable. A more radical suggestion was that Jews should be evacuated from Germany altogether.

There were, nonetheless, some Germans who were critical of Nazi policy and befriended their Jewish neighbours. Faced with such displays of compassion, the Nazi Party encouraged re-education. Thus, the Gestapo chief, Heinrich Müller, declared in October 1941:

It has repeatedly come to our notice recently that persons of German blood continue to maintain friendly relations with Jews and appear with them in public in a blatant fashion. Since such persons of German blood apparently even now still show a lack of understanding of the most elementary and basic principles of National Socialism and since their behaviour must be regarded as a flouting of official measures, my orders are that in such cases the person of German blood concerned is to be taken into protective custody for educational purposes or in serious cases to be transferred to a concentration camp, Grade 1.[3]

Turning to the reaction of the Church, various factors militated against sympathy to the Jewish plight. German Protestantism was identified with German nationalism and in some cases aligned with ultra-right Conservatism. Further, the Roman Catholic Church regarded Bolshevism as its main enemy between the wars, thereby encouraging Catholics to view the NSDAP with sympathy. Further, the German churches were anxious to retain an autonomous position within the Third Reich, an attitude which led to accommodation with the authorities. The churches' reaction to the Nazi regime was thus ambiguous, varying among priests, pastors and laity.

Within the Protestant Church there were serious divisions, and with the rise of Nazism a new movement emerged, the German Christians, which viewed itself as the SA of the Church. Professing a theology which combined evangelical piety and nationalism, this body claimed that the German nation had a divinely-ordained role to play in history. Attracting support from various academic theologians, the German Christians gained the support of both young pastors and theological students. Demanding a new people's church, they viewed the Nazi regime as the opportunity for religious renewal.

Responding to this development, the various Protestant denominations established a centralized constitution with a Reich Bishop. Initially Pastor von Bodelschwingh was appointed to this position; on 24 June 1933, however, he resigned and in the subsequent elections, German Christians won a majority, and Ludwig Müller, who was an acquaintance of Hitler became Reich Bishop while various German Christians assumed posts as state bishops and Church functionaries.

In opposition to these developments, a movement emerged based on a defence of the Protestant Confession. Reacting against the extreme views of the German Christian movement, the Swiss theologian Karl Barth called for a renewal of Christian values in his treatise *Theological Existence Today*. In addition, a group of pastors led by Martin Niemöller, the pastor of the Berlin suburb of Dahlem, formed the Pastors' Emergency League to resist German Christians as well as defend Lutheranism. In response, official German Christian authorities sought to stifle opposition. In the autumn of 1934, two Lutheran state bishops, Hans Meiser of Bavaria and Theophil Wurm of Württemberg, were arrested, leading to demonstrations on their behalf.

On 21 October 1934 the Pastors' Emergency League rejected the Reich Church, creating a Confessional Church government in a declaration issued in Dahlem:

1. We declare that the Constitution of the German Evangelical Church has been destroyed. Its legally constituted organs no longer exist. The men who have seized the Church leadership in the Reich and the states have divorced themselves from the Christian Church.

2. In virtue of the right of Churches, religious communities and holders of ecclesiastical office, bound by scripture and confession, to act in an emergency, the Confessional Synod of the German Evangelical Church establishes new organs of leadership. It appoints as leader and representative of the German Evangelical Church, as an association of confessionally determined Churches, the Fraternal Council of the German Evangelical Church and from among it the Council of the German Evangelical Church to the management and leadership. Both organs are composed in accordance with the confessions.

3. We summon the Christian communities, their pastors and elders to accept no directives from the present Church Government and its authorities and to decline cooperation with those who wish to remain obedient to this ecclesiastical governance. We summon them to observe the directives of the Confessional Synod of the German Evangelical Church and its recognized organs.[4]

Concerned about such criticism, Hitler decided not to attempt to control the Church directly through Reich Bishop Müller and the German Christians. As a result Meiser and Wurm were reinstated and German Christians were replaced by orthodox bishops and Church officials. This meant that in the early years of the Reich, there were three major bodies in the Protestant Church: (1) the German Christians; (2) the Confessional Church; and (3) the official Church establishment.

The Catholic Church, on the other hand, had initially come to terms with the Nazi regime through a Concordat signed between

Hitler and the Pope in 1933. In the preamble to this document, both parties declared a common desire to consolidate and enhance the friendly relations between the Holy See and the German State. In return for supporting the Enabling Law, the Catholic Centre Party assumed that Hitler would not seek to interfere with the affairs of the Church. Yet the Nazi regime did not desist from seeking to subvert the influence of the Roman Catholic Church, leading to protests from various Church officials. On 9 November 1936 Cardinal Faulhaber arranged a personal interview with Hitler. Although this meeting was cordial, relationships between the Church and the Nazi Party did not improve.

Several months later, Pope Pius XII issued an encyclical, *With Burning Anxiety*, condemning National Socialist attacks on the Church. The Nazis responded by continuing the onslaught against the Church. Monks and nuns were arrested, and Joseph Goebbels launched a smear campaign against the clergy. This led to a number of immortality trials designed to undermine the influence of Catholicism on German life. On 13 December 1936 the Bavarian bishops expressed their disillusionment with the government in a pastoral letter. Although critical of their treatment under the Nazis, the bishops nonetheless expressed their agreement with certain areas of Nazi policy:

After the deplorable fight carried on by Marxists, Communists, Free Thinkers and Freemasons against Christianity and the Church we welcomed with gratitude the National Socialist profession of positive Christianity. We are convinced that many hundreds of thousands are still loyal to this profession of faith and, indeed, we observe with sorrow how others tend to remove themselves from Christian belief and from the programme of the Führer, and by this means put the Third Reich on a new basis, a *Weltanschauung* [world view] standing in open contradiction to the commandments of Christianity. This formation of National Socialism into a *Weltanschauung* cuts it away from any foundation in religion in developing more and more into a full-scale attack on the Christian faith and the Catholic Church. All this bodes ill for the future of our people and our fatherland. Our Führer and Chancellor in a most impressive demonstration acknowledged the importance of the two Christian confessions to State and society, and promised the two confessions his protection. Unfortunately men with considerable influence and power are operating in direct opposition to those promises and both confessions are being systematically attacked.

Certain of those who lead the attack on the Churches wish to promote a united church in which the confession of faith will become meaningless. Most especially they seek to rid Germany of the Catholic Church and declare it to be a body foreign to our country and its people. ... In 1933 a Concordat was signed between the Holy Father and the German Reich. ... But instead of the much wished-for friendship, there has developed an ever-growing struggle against the Papacy.[5]

Turning to resistance outside of Germany, a number of scholars have argued that the Anglo-American Allies were in possession of knowledge about the atrocities committed by the Nazis; nonetheless, they were unwilling to take direct action to rescue victims from mass extermination. It appears that the first information about mass murder reached the West in May-June 1942, yet it was not until 17 December 1942 that the Americans and the British were prepared to announce that the Nazis sought to eliminate Jewry from Europe. Although other writers have stressed that the struggle against the Nazi regime was an all-consuming objective for the Allies, there is no doubt that they made no sustained attempt to rescue Jews and others who were being systematically killed in the camps.

Discussion: Bystanders and victims

As we have seen, within Germany there was a general acceptance of Nazi policy. With few exceptions, those who witnessed the persecution of the Jewish community did little to resist the racial policies of the Third Reich. The devastation of European Jewry was thus not brought about by a small elite within the Nazi Party; rather, the entire country was culpable in this tragedy. Furthermore, in recent years there has been a growing awareness that ordinary Germans were implicated in the barbaric actions taken against innocent victims in Germany and the East. In the attempt to create a utopian state, an entire nation appears to have suspended normal moral values and been blind to the horrors of the Holocaust.

In this context, scholars have emphasized that Church leaders within Germany were particularly culpable for their unwillingness to draw attention to the plight of Jews and others. The Catholic Church in particular has been censured for its attitudes. The primary criticism has been levelled at Pope Pius XII who consistently refused to speak out against Nazi policy. Had the Pope threatened to excommunicate those Catholics who participated in the onslaught against Jewry, such condemnation might have deterred the Nazi leadership. In June 1941 when the Vichy government in France introduced discriminatory legislation against the Jewish population, the Pope stated that such laws were not in conflict with Catholicism. Subsequent attempts to influence the Vatican to denounce the Nazi effort to exterminate European Jewry were similarly met with little enthusiasm. The cowardice of the Vatican and the German Catholic Church contrasts sharply with the attitudes of various Catholic bishops in other countries. In France, Belgium and Holland, for example, senior Church figures protested against the deportation of Jews and denounced the actions of German Catholics who participated in such barbaric acts.

Turning to the actions of the Allies, a number of writers have stressed that various important factors should be considered. First, it appears that the Allies were disinclined to intervene on behalf of those victimized inside enemy territory. The prior need was to defeat the enemy militarily – all other considerations were of secondary importance. Furthermore, it is difficult to envisage how the Allies could have prevented the murder of hundreds of thousands of Jews by the *Einsatzgruppen* during the invasion of Russia in 1941–2 or the deaths of those who perished in the ghettos of Poland. As far as the bombing of the death camps and the railway lines are concerned, it has been alleged that knowledge of the activities taking place at Auschwitz were not known until 1944. Only when three escaped prisoners were able to reveal the true purpose of the camp did the Allies have an awareness of the tragedy taking place.

Other excuses for Allied inaction relate to military strategy. Allegedly, the necessary fleets for rescuing hundreds of thousands of Jews were not available. Moreover, there was the fear that there might have been foreign agents placed among Jewish refugees which could have seriously undermined the war effort. Another factor which affected Allied intervention was the determination of the American State Department and the British Foreign Office not to acknowledge the special case of the Jews. Again, the fear of an anti-Semitic reaction in Britain and America if mass emigration took place deterred the Allies from seeking to save European Jewry. In addition, there was considerable concern that if time and resources were used to rescue victims of Nazism the war effort could be badly affected. A final factor was British anxiety about the effect such a rescue operation would have on the Arab population in Palestine.

Critics of Allied policy, however, have stressed that a successful bombing operation could have saved the lives of possibly hundreds of thousands of Jews and other victims of the Nazi regime. Further, the Allies could have encouraged neutral countries such as Sweden or Switzerland to take in refugees on a temporary basis. At the very least, war-time visa quotas could have been filled for entry to the United States and Palestine. In addition, the British who had irrefutable evidence of Nazi atrocities could have abandoned their restrictive policy of emigration to Palestine during the war. In addition, the Allies could have broadcast more information about the Nazis' policy towards European Jewry into occupied Europe – such information would have dispelled any illusions held by Jews living under the Nazi regime.

Notes

1 David Bankier, 'German Society and National Socialist anti-Semitism', unpublished PhD thesis, Hebrew University of Jerusalem, 1983, p. 126 in R. Landau, *The Nazi Holocaust*, London, 1992, p. 224.
2 Nuremberg Document L-202.
3 K. Pätzold (ed.), *Verfolgung, Vertreibung, Vernichtung Dokumente des faschistischen Antisemitismus, Leipzig*, 1984, pp. 311–12 in J. Noakes and G. Pridham, *op. cit.*, p. 1111.
4 *Kirchliches Jahrbuch 1933-1944*, Gütersloh, 1948, p. 70 in J. Noakes and G. Pridham, *op. cit.*, p. 584.
5 *The Persecution of the Catholic Church in The Third Reich*, London, 1940, p. 170 in J. Noakes and G. Pridham, *op. cit.*, pp. 587–8.

24. The Nuremberg Trials

Following the war the International Military Tribunal considered the issue of the Nazis' planned extermination of the Jewish people as a crime against humanity. Held in Nuremberg on 20 November 1945, the Nuremberg Trials interrogated captured leaders of the Nazi regime including Hermann Göring, Rudolf Hess, Joachim von Ribbentrop, Ernst Kaltenbrunner, Alfred Rosenberg, Julius Streicher and Hans Frank. Indictments were jointly submitted by the four main prosecutors representing the United States, the Soviet Union, Britain and France. After nearly a year, the proceedings concluded on the Jewish Day of Atonement. Twelve defendants were sentenced to death, three to life imprisonment, four were given prison sentences, and three acquitted.

Prosecuting the persecutors

In May 1945 the German government signed a document of unconditional surrender. Writing on behalf of the government, General Alfred Jodl, formerly Chief of the Wehrmacht Operations Staff, stated: 'With this signature the German people and the German Armed Forces are, for better or worse, delivered into the hands of the victors. ... In this hour I can only express the hope that the victors will treat them with generosity.'[1] The Allies, however, were intent on bringing the Nazis to trial for what they perceived as crimes against humanity.

After considerable discussion, the date for the Nuremberg Trials was set for 20 November 1945. The procedure on the first morning was for the defendants to enter the court first; they were followed by the defence and prosecution counsels, and the judges. Once the judges were seated, Sir Geoffrey Lawrence, President of the

Tribunal, raised the gavel, and the International Military Tribunal commenced at 10 o'clock. In his opening statement, Lawrence reminded the public of the need for order and decorum and called on all those involved in the trial to discharge their duties without fear or favour in accordance with the principles of law and justice.

The first day was taken up with the reading of the indictment; this was essentially a formality since the defendants had had copies of this document since 19 October. On the second day of the trial, the defendants had to plead guilty or not guilty to the indictment. Göring was the first to respond. Standing at the microphone in the dock, he stated: 'I declare myself in the sense of the indictment not guilty'. This formula was similarly adopted by Ribbentrop, Rosenberg, Schirach and Fritzsche. Sauckel declared himself not guilty 'in the sense of the indictment, before God and the world and particularly before my people'. Similarly Jodl added to his plea of not guilty, 'for what I have done or had to do I have a pure conscience before God, before history and my people'. The others gave a formal reply.

Judge Robert Jackson for the prosecution then began his speech. Beginning with the history of the Nazi party, he outlined its programme: a range of social measures, the destruction of the Versailles settlement, the union of the German people, and the acquisition of new territory. These, he stated, were legitimate aims, but only if attained peacefully. The Nazis, however, continually used violence, disregarded the law, and continually contemplated war. When Hitler became Chancellor in 1933, he suspended civil liberties, later declaring ruthless war upon those whose activities were injurious to the common interest. Such individuals included trade unionists, members of the churches, and the Jewish people. The Nazis dominated German life, he went on, through legislation, imprisonment in the camps, vandalism and physical violence.

Jackson continued by describing the organized persecution of the German Jews through disenfranchisement, discrimination, obstacles to economic activity, and the Nuremberg Laws. Such a policy was accompanied by physical attacks culminating in *Kristallnacht* on 9–10 November 1938. Several days later the Nazi government imposed a fine of a billion Reichsmarks on the Jewish community. In this context he quoted Hans Frank who had declared: 'The Jews are a race which has to be eliminated'. This, however, was not the sole aim of the Nazis; Aryan supremacy was to be established over gypsies, Slavs, Greeks and Frenchmen.

According to Jackson, once Germany had been terrorized, the Nazis turned their attention to Europe. In this process, they militarized the nation, trained and equipped the troops, and placed the economy on a war footing. The practical consequences of this policy resulted in what Jackson referred to as 'experiments of aggression'. During this period the Rhineland was occupied, Austria annexed in the *Anschluss*, the Sudetenland captured, and Bohemia and Moravia seized. All this was accomplished without armed resistance.

This, however, was not the end of Hitler's plans. On 23 May 1939, he declared: 'We cannot expect a repetition of the Czech affair. There will be war.' This occurred in September. Once a non-aggression pact had been concluded with Russia, Hitler was able to move against Denmark, Norway, the Low Countries and France. In 1941 German troops invaded Greece and Yugoslavia; this was followed by an attack against Russia. In each case assurances of peace were given before an assault was launched. This was in line with Hitler's military strategy; as he told his military commanders: 'Agreements are to be kept only as long as they serve a certain purpose.'

Such a cynical attitude dominated German politics in the Third Reich. During the war Allied captives lost the protection of prisoner-of-war status, and civilians were encouraged to lynch captured pilots. The Commando Order of 1942 stated that all captured commandos were to be slaughtered. According to Jackson, the Nazi treatment of prisoners of war transgressed every convention. He went on to explain that the Nazi treatment of civilians was equally brutal. In this regard the policy of Night and Fog allowed for the arrest of ordinary citizens. Any form of opposition was crushed: hostages were taken and killed, and entire villages were burned. Further, Nazi troops systematically plundered their enemies; they took money, art treasures and food when possible, leaving whole populations to die. In this process the Nazis stripped Europe of its population – 5 million foreign workers were brought to Germany, including children between ten and fourteen who were taken away to work as slave labourers.

Turning to Himmler's activities, Jackson described the nature of the concentration camp system, explaining that those unfit for work were sent to the gas chambers. Others died of starvation, torture, disease or experimentation. In some cases deportees were compelled to execute one another; others were worked to death. In the East pogroms took place resulting in the loss of thousands of lives. In many cases the local population was rounded up by the *Einsatzgruppen* and murdered: they were shot, burned or forced into gas vans. Summarizing the case against those being tried, he stated:

> The privilege of being the first trial in history for crimes against the peace of the world imposes a grave responsibility. ... The wrongs which we seek to condemn and punish have been so calculated, so malignant and so devastating that civilization cannot survive their being repeated. That four great nations, flushed with victory and stung with injury, stay the hand of vengeance and voluntarily submit their captive enemies to the judgement of the law is one of the most significant tributes that Power has ever paid to Reason.[2]

During its subsequent presentation, the prosecution was anxious to illustrate Nazi atrocities by showing a film of the concentration camps as discovered by the Allies. According to one viewer:

> The impression we get is an endless river of white bodies flowing across the screen, bodies with ribs sticking out through the chests, with pipe-stem legs and battered skulls and eyeless faces and grotesque thin arms reaching for the sky. ... On the screen there is no end to the bodies, tumbling bodies and bodies being shoved over cliffs into common graves and bodies pushed like dirt by giant bulldozers, and bodies that are not bodies at all but charred bits of bone and flesh lying upon a crematory grate made of bits of steel rail laid upon blackened wood ties.[3]

As the trial proceeded, the prosecutors turned to the alleged crimes against humanity. Regarding the forced labour programme, a speech by Erich Koch, the Commissar of the Ukraine, to a party meeting in 1943 was read out:

> I will draw the very last out of this country. I did not come to spread bliss. I have come to help the Führer. The population must work, work and work again. ... We are a master race, which must remember the lowliest German worker is racially and biologically a thousand times more valuable than the population here.[4]

Evidence was produced to show that the population of nearly 5 million people were set to work at home or removed to Germany.

The prosecution then produced evidence concerning the concentration camps. Tales of mass executions, gas vans and gas chambers were followed by a report from Eichmann announcing the death of 4 million Jews in the camps and a further 2 million at the hands of the police in the East. Added to this material were SS films depicting girls running naked and terrified through the streets, old women dragged by their hair, and men beaten senseless while the SS stood by. Other horrific illustrations of Nazi barbarism included the shrunken head of a Polish officer used as a paperweight, and strips of tattooed skin taken from the bodies of prisoners which the commandant of Buchenwald had used as lampshades.

Witnesses of Nazi brutality also testified during the trial. Otto Ohlendorff, for example, served as the leader of *Einsatzgruppe D*, organizing the murder of 90,000 people. At the trial he testified that he believed shooting parties constituted less of an emotional strain on his men than unloading bodies from gas vans. In his defence, he stated that it was inconceivable that a subordinate should not carry out orders given by the leader. In a similar vein Dieter Wisliceny, a friend and colleague of Eichmann, stated he knew everything about the Final Solution. He related that he had seen Eichmann's order from Hitler to deal with the Jewish question, stating that he could quote from subsidiary orders concerning this policy. Moreover, he could repeat the comment that Eichmann had made to him that if Germany lost the war he would leap laughing into his grave because the 5 million dead Jews were a source of consolation to him.

Among the witnesses of Nazi atrocities, Alois Hollriegel, a simple Austrian peasant, recounted watching men worked to death in stone quarries at Mauthausen, and dropped 100 feet to their deaths as a punishment. Franz Blaha, a Czech doctor, explained that he had been drafted to a concentration camp. In Dachau, he was subjected to typhoid experiments. When he refused to perform operations on healthy prisoners, he was sent to the autopsy room where by 1945 he had performed 12,000 post-mortems. In his account, he described filthy experiments, executions, squalor, and death from exhaustion and hunger.

During the trial, Russian films portrayed Nazi atrocities in Eastern Europe. At Majdanek, 800,000 pairs of shoes were neatly stacked along with piles of skulls, broken bodies and mutilated corpses. The film showed naked women driven to mass graves where they lay down and were shot. In Blagorschine Forest massive bone crushers worked on 150,000 corpses. There the women bent over bodies stiffened by cold, trying to identify their husbands and children. Remorselessly, the Russians went on to produce the destruction of human beings. Severina Shmaglerskaya, who had spent three years in Auschwitz, recounted scenes of women sent to work within minutes of giving birth, of babies taken, and of children sent to the gas chambers.

Samuel Rajzman had been taken from the Warsaw ghetto to Treblinka. On his arrival, the camp had the appearance of an ordinary railway station with signs for the restaurant and ticket office. However, on the platform prisoners were stripped, and women shaved so that their hair could be used for mattresses. The deportees then walked up Himmelfahrt Street to the gas chambers. In his view, about 10,000–12,000 victims were murdered each day. In addition to such evidence, the Russians supplied documents on tortures, beatings, castrations, injections with poison, and infections with cancer and other diseases.

One of the witnesses, Jacob Vernik, a Warsaw carpenter, described the year he spent at Treblinka:

Awake or asleep I see the terrible visions of thousands of people calling for help, begging for life and mercy. I have lost all my family, I have myself led them to death. I have myself built the death chambers in which they were murdered. I am afraid of everything. I fear that everything I have seen is written on my face. An old and broken life is a very heavy burden, but I must carry on and live to tell the world what German crimes and barbarism I saw.[5]

During the three months of prosecution evidence, the defendants were subjected to a barrage of information about the Nazi regime. Few were able to watch films or listen to detailed accounts of the suffering of the victims. Each of them described the tortures and murders as terrible and shocking. Yet they remained largely undisturbed when faced with their own crimes. Repeatedly they used euphemisms for the horrors depicted. In addition their documents spoke of the Jewish problem rather than hatred for Jews. Such vocabulary protected the defendants from having to face the reality of their deeds. In some cases, they justified their actions by appealing to the officers' tradition of obeying orders. At other times, they simply stated that they did not know about what was happening during the war or in the camps. Fritz Sauckel, Plenipotentiary-

General for Labour Mobilization, for example, stated: 'I knew absolutely nothing of these things and I certainly had nothing to do with it'. Similarly, Walther Funk, Minister of Economic Affairs, asked, 'Do you think I had the slightest notion about gas waggons and such horrors?' In the same vein the ideologist Alfred Rosenberg observed:

> Of course it's terrible, incomprehensible, the whole business. I would never have dreamed it would take such a turn. . . . We didn't contemplate killing anyone in the beginning, I can assure you of that. I always advocated a peaceful solution.[6]

In their defence, one of the commonest charges was that Himmler was ultimately responsible. Thus when Baldur von Schirach asked Göring who had given orders to destroy the Warsaw ghetto, the answer was 'Himmler, I suppose'. Göring added: 'Himmler had his chosen psychopaths to carry these things out and it was kept secret from the rest of us. But I would never have suspected him of it. He didn't seem to be the murderer type.' Similarly, Joachim von Ribbentrop, Minister of Foreign Affairs, declared: 'Himmler must have ordered those things. But I doubt if he was a real German. He had a peculiar face.' Julius Streicher, too, blamed Himmler: 'That was done by Himmler,' he stated. 'I disapprove of murder.' He then went on to deprecate Himmler's understanding of racial ideology: 'He didn't know anything about it. He had Negro blood himself. . . . I could tell by his head shape and hair. I can recognize blood.'[7]

Others blamed Hitler. Hans Frank, Governor General of Poland, stated: 'At some moments Hitler and Himmler must have simply sat down and Hitler gave him orders to wipe out whole races and groups of people.' Constantin Neurath, Reich Protector of Bohemia and Moravia, reached the same conclusion – Hitler, he believed,

> must have done his conspiring with his little group of henchmen late at night. But I couldn't stay up so late. Sometimes he would call up at one, two or three in the morning. That is probably when these secret discussions with Himmler and Bormann took place.[8]

After months of evidence, the Nazis accepted that the Nazi government had propagated atrocious policies. Yet all the defendants claimed to have known nothing about the actions of the government, nor to have noticed that large sums were being diverted to exterminate the Jews and others. They insisted that they were not implicated either legally or morally.

At the end of the trial, individual verdicts were given by the Court. Despite a robust defence, Hermann Göring was charged under all four counts; as both the summary of the case and the final judgement pointed out, he had performed every form of criminal act that the Tribunal regarded as punishable. He participated in the preparation of every aggressive war plan, and helped establish and carry out programmes for looting art and plundering the economies of the occupied territories, and for maltreating and killing prisoners of war. All the judges held Göring guilty on four counts and sentenced him to death by hanging.

Like Göring, Rudolf Hess had risen to a high position in the party and was named by Hitler as his alternative successor if he and Göring had died. Yet his flight to Scotland in 1941 in an attempt to persuade the British government of Hitler's peaceful intentions affected the trial. Further, his unstable mental condition raised questions about his fitness to be tried. In any event, the Tribunal found him guilty of crimes against peace and conspiracy to commit other crimes, and he was given a life sentence to be served in the Allied military prison in Berlin-Spandau.

Unlike Göring and Hess, Joachim von Ribbentrop was not an early member of the Nazi party; rather, he joined the party in the early 1930s. After holding a series of advisory posts, he became ambassador to England, and later Foreign Minister. Found guilty on all four counts, he was sentenced to death by hanging. Field Marshal Wilhelm Keitel was also a late recruit, becoming chief of staff to the Minister of War in 1938, and subsequently chief of the High Command. He, too, was found guilty on all four counts and sentenced to death by hanging.

Ernst Kaltenbrunner was an Austrian lawyer who served as Himmler's chief deputy. As a long-time party member, SS man, and Nazi police official, he gradually took over the position of secret police chief and executioner following Heydrich's assassination. As chief of the Central Security Office, he presided over the SD and the Gestapo. Three days before the trial began, he suffered a brain haemorrhage. In his absence, other defendants had detailed the atrocities committed by Kaltenbrunner and his associates. Charged with conspiracy, war crimes and crimes against humanity, he was not held responsible for crimes against peace. None of the judges had any question about Kaltenbrunner's guilt for war crimes and crimes against humanity, but there was division about whether he was guilty of conspiracy. In the event, he was sentenced to death by hanging.

Alfred Rosenberg was the ideologist of the Third Reich, and head of the Nazi Party's Foreign Affairs Department. Found guilty on all four counts, he was sentenced to death by hanging. Similarly Hans Frank, chief administrator of the General Government, was found guilty and sentenced to death by hanging. So, too, Wilhelm Frick, Reich Minister of the Interior, was convicted and sentenced to hang. Along with these men, Julius Streicher, who was editor of the anti-Semitic journal *Der Stürmer*, was indicted and hanged for crimes against humanity.

Walther Funk, Minister of Economic Affairs, strongly protested his innocence at the trial, claiming that he had simply implemented the plans of the party leadership. Found guilty of war crimes, crimes against peace, and crimes against humanity, he was sentenced to life imprisonment. Fritz Sauckel, Plenipotentiary-General for Labour Mobilization, was instrumental in conducting slave raids into Soviet Russia and other territories. Found guilty on counts three and four, he was sentenced to hang. Alfred Jodl, Chief of Operations Staff of the High Command of the Armed Forces, was Hitler's closest military advisor. In his defence, he claimed that it was not the task of a soldier to act as judge over the supreme commander. Nonetheless, because he had condoned a variety of illegal acts, he was found guilty on all four counts and sentenced to death by hanging. Arthur Seyss-Inquart, Reich Governor of Austria and subsequently Reich Commissioner of the Netherlands, was also sentenced to hang.

In the case of Albert Speer, Reich Minister for Armaments and War Production, the Tribunal found him guilty of war crimes against humanity, but he was one of the few men who had the courage to inform Hitler that the war was lost and to take steps to prevent the destruction of production facilities. He was sentenced to twenty years imprisonment. Karl Doenitz, Commander in Chief of the German Navy, was similarly given a 10-year sentence for war crimes and crimes against peace. Baldur von Schirach, Reich Youth Leader and Governor of Vienna, was also given a limited sentence of twenty years for crimes against humanity. Erich Raeder who served as Grand Admiral was sentenced to life imprisonment, but released after ten years. Finally, the Tribunal convicted Hjalmar Schacht,

President of the *Reichsbank* and Minister without Portfolio, who was acquitted of the charges but found guilty of complicity in the murder of Russian prisoners of war and sentenced to six years' imprisonment. Franz von Papen, Reich Chancellor and later Hitler's Deputy Chancellor, was acquitted on all charges as was Hans Fritzsche, Head of Radio Broadcasting in the Reich Ministry of Broadcasting.

Discussion: War criminals

Following World War I, two conferences at Geneva and the Hague stipulated rules of conduct during warfare. During World War II, the President of Czechoslovakia and later representatives of other nations reported Nazi crimes, particularly towards inhabitants of eastern Europe. In response to these reports, the United Nations War Crimes Commission was established in October 1943, and representatives from a range of countries drew up lists of Nazi war criminals. After the war, the London Agreement established an International Military Tribunal to deal with these individuals. The Tribunal's charter laid down the terms of reference and the rules of procedure as well as indictable categories: crimes against peace, war crimes, and crimes against humanity.

As we have seen, the issue of the Nazis' crimes against humanity was a central aspect of the International Military Tribunal which opened in Nuremberg on 20 November 1945. In accordance with the London Charter, indictments were submitted by the four main prosecutors representing the United States, the Soviet Union, Britain and France. For nearly a year the proceedings took place: twelve defendants were sentenced to death, three to life imprisonment and three were acquitted. Having dismissed the plea that the accused were simply following orders, the Tribunal stressed that warfare did not rule out individual moral obligation.

Following the Nuremberg Trials, later trials – known as Subsequent Nuremberg Proceedings – took place in the American Zone. Yet by 1949 these trials were stopped. Nonetheless, some countries which had been under Nazi rule continued to hold trials, largely of Nazi collaborators. Of over 100,000 known criminals, fewer than 10,000 were ever tried. One reason why the desire to punish Nazi criminals diminished was that the political climate

251

dramatically changed following the war. The Soviet Union, which had been a supporter of the Allies during wartime, was increasingly perceived as an enemy of the West. Because Germany was partitioned at the end of the war, the Western Allies were determined to strengthen the western sector against the Communist threat.

In the wake of these changes, a number of former Nazi officials were retained in official positions to ensure social stability and the efficient running of society. Anxiety about Soviet supremacy deterred the Allies from weakening German society; as a result, many Germans were protected from prosecution and imprisonment. In addition, the Western Allies were committed to the view that the mistakes of Versailles should not be repeated – Germany was not to be weakened and disgraced, as occurred after World War I. Hence, Western fears about a potential German reaction created conditions favourable to economic recovery.

Israel, on the other hand, was committed to punishing Nazi criminals, and in 1961 held a trial of Adolf Eichmann, Chief of the Jewish Office of the Gestapo. Seized by the Israeli Secret Service in Argentina, Eichmann was flown to Israel and tried in public over several months. Found guilty of crimes against the Jewish people and humanity, he was hanged in an Israeli prison. Although questions were raised about the jurisdiction of Israel to act in this way, John Demjanjuk was recently arrested and accused of being Ivan the Terrible of Treblinka.

Despite the determination of many Jews to bring Nazi criminals to trial, questions have recently been raised about whether it makes sense to put ageing Nazis on trial for war crimes and crimes against humanity. Some have argued that the crimes committed by these former Nazis were so horrific that the perpetrators must be punished. Opponents, however, have stressed that it is nearly impossible to provide reliable witnesses. In addition, they have pointed out the inconsistency involved in hunting down Nazi war criminals while allowing others who have committed equally monstrous crimes at other times to go free. In some cases, these individuals have even been protected by Western countries or the United Nations.

Whatever the answer to this particular problem, there is arguably a pressing need to establish a new International Tribunal – like that which existed at Nuremberg – invested with the responsibility of bringing war criminals to trial. Since the end of the war, other genocides have taken place, such as the onslaught against the Bengalis in 1971 with the loss of between 1½ million and 3 million victims, the murder of approximately 150,000 Hutu of Burundi in 1972, the murder of about 1000 Ache Indians in Paraguay between 1968 and 1972, the death of approximately 2 million Kampucheans between 1975 and 1979, and the massacre of about 200,000 East Timor Islanders from 1975 to the present. Like the Holocaust, these atrocities need to be exposed and the perpetrators brought to justice.

Notes

1 Ann and John Tusa, *The Nuremberg Trial*, London, 1995, p. 13.
2 *Ibid.*, pp. 154–5.
3 *Ibid.*, p. 160.
4 *Ibid.*, p. 166.
5 *Ibid.*, p. 201.
6 *Ibid.*, p. 237.
7 *Ibid.*, pp. 238–9.
8 *Ibid.*, p. 239.

25. Denying the Holocaust

Despite the mass of contrary evidence, a number of revisionist historians have been adamant that the Holocaust never took place. In their view the attempt to annihilate the Jewish people did not occur. Further, they insist that if either side was guilty during World War II, it was not the Germans; rather the real crimes against humanity were committed by the Americans, Russians, British and French. In their view, the Jewish community has perpetrated the myth of the Holocaust for their own purposes. In the view of Holocaust deniers, the Jews were not victims of the Nazis – instead they stole billions of dollars in reparations, destroyed Germany's reputation, and gained world-wide support for the creation of a Jewish state.

Holocaust denial

One of the earlier proponents of Holocaust denial was Maurice Bardèche who was highly critical of Allied War Propaganda. In his book, *Letter to François Mauriac*, he defended the policy of collaboration. This was followed by *Nuremberg or the Promised Land* in which he argued that some of the evidence regarding the concentration camps was falsified. In his view, many of the deaths that took place in the camps were the result of starvation and illness. Further, he maintained that the term 'Final Solution' referred to the transfer of Jews to ghettos in the east. According to Bardèche, the Jews were responsible for the war by supporting the Treaty of Versailles. In addition, he maintained that German soldiers were not culpable for following orders – Nazi Germany was intent on overcoming the Communist threat. Further, he alleged that the Nuremberg Trials were a scandal since they punished Germany for seeking to defeat Stalin. Finally, in his view, the Allied bombing policy was the major crime of the war.

A second figure who contributed to this early debate was Paul Rassinier, a former Communist who had been deported to Buchenwald. In *Le Passage de la Ligne*, he attempted to demonstrate that survivors' claims about the Nazis were not reliable. In this and subsequent works Rassinier maintained that survivors exaggerated what had occurred to them. It was not the SS who were responsible for atrocities in the camps, but rather inmates who were in charge of the camps. Although he admitted that exterminations did take place, he alleged that this was not the official policy of the Nazis. According to Rassinier, the Nazis were not evil; rather, they acted as benefactors of those who had been deported. Their intention in rounding up Jews and transferring them to the east was to protect such individuals by removing them from areas where they could be attacked. Although life in the camps was difficult, this was due to those in the lower ranks of the SS who disobeyed orders. In general, he argued, the SS were humane.

In a later work, *The Drama of European Jewry*, he asserted that the alleged genocide of European Jewry was a myth. The gas chambers, he claimed, were an invention of Zionists. Further, he maintained that former Nazis falsely claimed that they had committed crimes against Jews so that they would receive lenient treatment. He also stressed that the testimonies of Nazi leaders tried of war crimes should be discounted because they were testifying under the threat of death, and they therefore confessed what might most likely save their lives.

In Rassinier's view, those responsible for such falsification were the Zionists who were aided by Jewish historians and institutions that conducted research on the Holocaust. Such fraud was motivated by the Jewish desire for gain. Those who perpetrated the genocide hoax wished to ensure that Germany would pay remunerations to Israel. In this way Israel has swindled Germany with the assistance of Jewish scholars and researchers. In presenting this diatribe against Zionism, Rassinier was bitterly critical of Raul Hilberg's *The Destruction of the European Jews*. Hilberg, Rassinier stated, was deliberately dishonest in manipulating information for his own purposes.

Turning to Hitler, Rassinier was intent on demonstrating that, despite contradictory evidence, the Führer had no intention of destroying the Jewish population of Europe. All seeming references to such annihilation, he argued, were hyperbolic declarations. There was, he believed, no explicit evidence which could prove the Nazis' intention to murder Jewry. In this connection, he stressed that Hitler's speeches were not used as evidence at the Nuremberg Trials. It has been the media, controlled by Zionists, which has fostered this falsification of the Nazi past.

In the United States, a number of writers argued along similar lines. In 1952, for example, W. D. Herrstrom stated in *Bible News Flashes* that 5 million illegal aliens including many Jews who resided on American soil were survivors of the Holocaust who were reported as having perished under the Nazi regime. In 1949 James Madole, writing in *National Renaissance Bulletin* alleged that it is a lie that Nazi Germany cremated 6 million Jews. At the same time Benjamin H. Freedman argued thousands of Jews were living in the United States who had allegedly perished in the camps; for this reason, the American Jewish community is reluctant to indicate religious affiliation on census reports. Another figure of this period, George Lincoln Rockwell, also contended that the Holocaust was a profitable fraud. In *The Cross and the Flag*, L. K. Smith similarly asserted that the 6 million who allegedly died in the camps were actually residing in the United States.

Another writer of this era, Harry Elmer Barnes, claimed that the Allies were responsible for World War II. In his view Hitler's actions were necessary to rectify the injustices of the Versailles Treaty. It was not Hitler's inhumanity, but rather his benevolence that led to his downfall. Hitler did not launch an aggressive attack on Poland; rather he sought to avoid war. It was the British instead who were responsible for the outbreak of war on the Eastern and Western fronts. Hitler did not initiate the conflict, but was forced into war by the actions of the British. In this connection, Barnes was instrumental in the publication of *The Forced War* by David Leslie Hoggan in which he asserted that the British and the Poles had provoked the war against Germany. In this work Hoggan also maintained that Poland's treatment of the Jews was far harsher than that of Germany. Nazi Germany's attitude towards the Jews, he believed, was generally tolerant. Attempting to illustrate that the Jews had not been the target of discrimination, Hoggan stressed that in early 1938 Jewish doctors and dentists were still participating in the German national compulsory insurance programme.

Later Barnes became increasingly absorbed by claims about German atrocities. In *Revisionism and Brainwashing*, he was critical of the lack of opposition to atrocity stories. In this regard, he was anxious to demonstrate that the Allies had waged a brutal and inhumane assault against Germany. Supportive of Rassinier's writing, he believed that such accounts were fabrications produced by Jews for their own aims. Following the Eichmann trial, Barnes attacked the media for its sensationalism about the Nazis. In his view, the actions of the Allies were criminal, particularly the bombing of Hamburg, Tokyo and Dresden. The gas chambers, he stated, were post-war inventions, concocted by historians and others. For Barnes, the *Einsatzgruppen* were simply acting as guerrilla forces behind the lines.

Arguing along similar lines, Austin J. App argued in the late 1950s that less than 6 million Jews died during the Nazi regime. A defender of Nazi Germany, he later formulated eight axioms in *The Six Million Swindle* which have served as the guiding principles of Holocaust denial:

1. Emigration, never annihilation, was the Reich's plan for solving Germany's Jewish problem. Had Germany intended to annihilate all the Jews, a half million concentration camp inmates would not have survived and managed to come to Israel, where they collect 'fancy indemnities from West Germany'.
2. 'Absolutely no Jews were gassed in any concentration camps in Germany, and evidence is piling up that none were gassed in Auschwitz.' The Hitler gas chambers never existed. The gassing installations found in Auschwitz were really crematoria for cremating corpses of those who had died from a variety of causes, including the 'genocidic' Anglo-American bombing raids.
3. The majority of Jews who disappeared and remain unaccounted for did so in territories under Soviet, not German, control.
4. The majority of Jews who supposedly died while in German hands were, in fact, subversives, partisans, spies, saboteurs, and criminals or victims of unfortunate but internationally legal reprisals.
5. If there existed the slightest likelihood that the Nazis had really murdered 6 million Jews, world Jewry would demand subsidies to conduct research on the topic and Israel would open its archives to historians. They have not done so. Instead they have persecuted and branded as an anti-Semite anyone who wished to publicize the hoax. This persecution constitutes the most conclusive evidence that the 6 million figure is a 'swindle'.

6. The Jews and the media who exploit this figure have failed to offer even a shred of evidence to prove it. The Jews misquote Eichmann and other Nazis in order to try to substantiate their claims.

7. It is the accusers, not the accused, who must provide the burden of proof to substantiate the 6 million figure. The Talmudists and Bolsheviks have so browbeaten the Germans that they pay billions and do not dare to demand proof.

8. The fact that Jewish scholars themselves have 'ridiculous' discrepancies in their calculations of the number of victims constitutes firm evidence that there is no scientific proof to this accusation.[1]

Neo-facists groups were also anxious to promote Holocaust denial. In 1974 a short pamphlet, *Did Six Million Really Die? The Truth at Last* was published by Richard Harwood, the pseudonym of Richard Verrall of the National Front. Based on *The Myth of Six Million*, this work contended that Jews have used the Holocaust myth to protect the Jewish faith and weaken other people's quest for self-preservation. According to Harwood, the Jewish people have manipulated historical events to serve their own ends. Any time anyone challenges the Jewish presentation of historical events, he contended, such individuals are branded as anti-Semitic. Like previous writers, Harwood argued that the aim of the Nazis was to encourage Jewish emigration, rather than bring about the annihilation of the Jewish race.

Holocaust denial was promoted later in the 1970s by Arthur Butz, a professor of electrical engineering at Northwestern University. In his *The Hoax of the Twentieth Century*, Butz argued that the Jewish people had perpetrated The hoax of the Holocaust to further Zionism. In Butz's opinion, the Holocaust myth was promoted by a conspiratorial group of Zionists who were intent on gaining sympathy and support for Israel. Banding together, Jews world-wide had used their considerable power to foster the belief that millions of Jews died at the hands of the Nazis. In pursuit of this aim, masses of documents were forged as evidence of the Nazi crime against the Jewish people. Such forgeries included reports by *Einsatzgruppen* commanders, official communiqués by high-ranking members of the Third Reich and speeches by Nazi leaders. Butz also cast doubt on the testimony of those accused of war crimes by insisting that such declarations were less reliable than documentary evidence. Further, he claimed that such testimonies were extracted through torture, or that defendants fabricated statements in the hope of saving their lives.

In 1979 the Institute for Historical Review held a conference for Holocaust deniers which attracted a wide range of participants. Anxious to gain academic support, this organization sponsored annual convocations and published the *Journal of Historical Review*. Focusing primarily on World War II, the Institute has been concerned to dismiss the Holocaust as a myth which has been perpetrated on the public. In line with previous theories about the Holocaust, the Institute has been concerned to demonstrate the pernicious influence of those who have sought to distort historical events for their own ends.

In the early 1980s the Canadian government accused Ernst Zundel, a German citizen living in Canada, of promoting anti-Semitism through false documents about the Holocaust. During the trial, the prosecution maintained that Zundel was an ardent racist and anti-Semite. Found guilty in 1985, he was sentenced to fifteen months in prison, but this was overturned on appeal. This was followed by a second trial in 1988. Anxious to be of assistance, Robert Faurisson, infamous for his views about the gas chambers, went to Canada to help Zundel and his lawyers. According to Faurisson, the apparatus in the camp was too small and primitive to have functioned as gas chambers.

Joining in Zundel's defence, the historian David Irving together with Faurisson solicited the help of Fred A. Leuchter who, as we have noted, believed that it was impossible for the Germans to have gassed the Jews. After visiting Auschwitz and Majdanek, Leuchter argued on the basis of fragments from these sites that execution chambers did not exist during the Nazi era. According to Leuchter, the contention that 6 million victims were gassed in the camps is a myth. His findings are contained in *The Leuchter Report: An Engineering Report on the Alleged Execution Gas Chambers at Auschwitz, Birkenau and Majdanek, Poland* which was widely publicized.

More recently, Holocaust deniers have sought to influence public opinion on American college campuses. Bradley Smith, who had been involved in a range of activities connected with the Holocaust, put a two-page advertisement in college newspapers claiming that the Holocaust was a hoax. This provoked a fierce debate. While many defended his right to free speech, Holocaust denial was bitterly criticized in courses dealing with the Nazi onslaught against the Jews. Previously courses dealing with the Holocaust had recruited few students – this controversy aroused considerable attention, and Holocaust studies became a major feature of academic life.

In line with the views of Holocaust deniers, Smith's advertisement claimed that the gas chambers did not exist, the Nuremberg Trials were a scandal, and that those deported to the camps were well nourished until the Allies destroyed the infrastructure of Germany through bombing raids. Further, the advertisement claimed that the Nazis never intended to exterminate the Jews. Declaring that those who placed the advertisement were only interested in ascertaining the truth about the events of World War II, Smith accused mainline historians of distortion. Due to the arguments of Holocaust deniers, the advertisement continued, it was now admitted that the number of Jews killed at Auschwitz was smaller than originally claimed, and that Jewish bodies had not been used to make soap.

Events at the University of Michigan stimulated further controversy. After the advertisement was published in the *Michigan Daily*, the newspaper subsequently ran an apology for printing it. This was followed by the decision of the editorial board to express its belief that although the editors disapproved of Smith's text, they did not consider it right to censor unpopular views. The next day a campus rally attacked Holocaust denial and the paper's policy. The president of the university then condemned the advertisement, but supported the editorial policy of free speech. Similarly at Duke University, the *Duke Chronicle* declared that it was the paper's responsibility to allow freedom of expression, a view upheld by the president of the university. At Cornell, the editors of the *Cornell Daily Sun* echoed the same sentiment. So, too, did the newspaper at the University of Montana as well as other institutions across the country.

In 1992 Smith ran a second advertisement which was a reprint of an article from the *Journal of Historical Review* entitled *Jewish Soap*. This advertisement blamed Simon Wiesenthal and Stephen Wise for the falsehood that the Nazis made Jews into soap. Like the first advertisement, it stated that historians had abandoned this myth to salvage the Holocaust hoax. In a covering letter, Smith asserted that this advertisement was fully documented. However, unlike the first advertisement, many college newspapers refused to print it.

More recently a historians' debate has taken place in Germany which has sought to provide a revisionist interpretation of the past. While accepting that the Holocaust took place, they nonetheless seek to minimize German guilt for the Third Reich. In the view of these scholars, the Allies should share a greater sense of responsibility for the atrocities of the war; further, they assert that it has been a mistake to point to the Holocaust as the sole manifestation of human evil in the modern world. Repeatedly they emphasize that other tragedies have taken place in this century such as Stalin's gulags, the Armenian massacre, and the actions of the United States in Viet Nam.

Discussion: Rebutting Holocaust denial

As we have seen, there are serious difficulties with the arguments presented by Leuchter and others concerning the existence of the gas chambers. Yet these are not the only problems with the range of allegations made by those who dispute that the Holocaust occurred. The most glaring difficulty is the Holocaust deniers' refusal to accept the mass of evidence about the evils of the Nazi regime. Given that similar testimonies were given by both Jews and non-Jews, such eye-witness accounts appear to constitute incontrovertible evidence about the victimization of those deported to the camps.

With regard to the gas chambers, Holocaust deniers repeatedly call for proof of the existence of such facilities. Yet they systematically dismiss the reliability of all accounts, whether given by Jews who claim to have witnessed such killing operations or first-hand testimony by the SS. Such refusal is based on the paradoxical conviction that because these accounts corroborate one another, they are likely to be fabrications. Further, Holocaust deniers refuse to accept extensive research such as that undertaken by Jean-Claude Pressac. On a research trip to Auschwitz in 1979, Pressac examined photographs, documents and work orders regarding the construction of gas chambers. On further visits he discovered additional documents. Since the publication of his study of the gas chambers in 1989, he has investigated archives in the former Soviet Union where he has discovered additional material.

Pressac's findings demonstrate the falsehood of the Holocaust deniers' claim that there is no documentary evidence regarding the existence of the gas chambers. His investigation revealed that an inventory of equipment for Crematorium III included one gas-tight door and fourteen showers. The drawings for these showers revealed that the shower heads were not connected to water pipes. Further, a letter of 29 January 1943 from SS Captain Bischoff, head of the Auschwitz *Waffen-SS*, to an SS major general in Berlin, referred to the gassing cellar. Added to this evidence was a time sheet in which a civilian worker had recorded that a room in the western part of Crematorium IV was a *Gaskammer*.

Pressac also discovered an order made in February 1943 by the *Waffen-SS* and Police Central Construction Management for twelve gas-tight doors for Crematoria IV and V. In March a time sheet submitted by the contractors referred to a concrete floor in a gas chamber. Moreover, a telegram of 26 February 1943 sent by an SS officer to one of the firms hired for the construction of a gas chamber requested the use of ten gas detectors. In the same month a civilian employee working on Crematorium II referred to modifying the air extraction system of the undressing cellar II. In the same letter he asked about the possibility of preheating the areas to be used as the gas chamber. Another letter of March signed by SS Major Bischoff referred to an order for a gas door for Crematorium II. Finally, the inventory for Crematorium II contained a reference to a gas-tight door. All this material constitutes documentary evidence supporting the existence of gas chambers in the camps, the type of proof demanded by Holocaust deniers.

Given the existence of such material, it might be thought that Holocaust deniers, particularly those who describe themselves as historians of the Third Reich, would have abandoned their position. Yet this conclusion overlooks the fact that Holocaust denial is in many cases politically motivated. The founder of the Institute of Historical Research, Willis Carto, was the founder of Liberty Lobby, an ultra-right-wing organization. According to the Anti-Defamation League, the Liberty Lobby is at the helm of a publishing complex that has propagated anti-Jewish propaganda for decades. Willis Carto's political vision was based on contempt for Jews, the belief that the government needs to protect the racial heritage of the United States, and the conviction that there currently exists a conspiracy to undermine the Western world.

Other figures advocating Holocaust denial share similar ideas. In a variety of writings David Irving, a British historian, argued that Israel had swindled billions of Marks in voluntary reparations from West Germany. The gas chambers, he maintained, were a myth promulgated by Jews. Tracing the origins of this myth to the British

Psychological Warfare Executive, he stated that it was used in 1942 to spread false propaganda that the Germans were using gas chambers to kill Jews and others. Condemned by the British Houses of Parliament as a Nazi propagandist and apologist for Hitler, Irving's anti-Semitism is indicative of those who seek to distort historical reality for their own ends. Such attitudes are one of the greatest dangers in the modern world, as the historian Deborah Lipstadt has noted:

> If Holocaust denial has demonstrated anything, it is the fragility of memory, truth, reason and history. The deniers' campaign has been carefully designed to take advantage of these vulnerabilities. ... Right-wing nationalist groups in Germany, Italy, Austria, France, Norway, Hungary, Brazil, Slovakia and a broad array of other countries, including the United States, have adopted Holocaust denial as a standard facet of their propaganda. Whereas these groups once justified the murder of the Jews, now they deny it. Once they argued that something quite beneficial to the world happened at Auschwitz. Now they insist nothing did. Their anti-Semitism is often so virulent that the logical conclusion of their argument is that though Hitler did not murder the Jews, he should have.[2]

Notes

1 Lipstadt, *op. cit.*, pp. 99–100.
2 *Ibid.*, pp. 216–17.

26. The Holocaust and religious belief

In the decades following the Holocaust, the Jewish community was preoccupied with a variety of issues: the creation of a Jewish state, rebuilding Jewish communities in Europe, revitalizing Jewish life throughout the world. It was not until some time later that Jewish theologians began to struggle with the religious perplexities raised by the deaths of millions of Jews. The Third Reich's system of murder squads, concentration camps and killing centres challenged traditional assumptions about the nature of God and brought about a re-evaluation of the Jewish understanding of God's action in the world.

The Jewish response

Pre-eminent among modern Jewish writers who have wrestled with the theological implications of the Holocaust is the novelist Elie Wiesel. At the concentration camp Birkenau, Wiesel came close to death as he marched towards a pit of flaming bodies only to stop a few feet from the edge. 'Never shall I forget those flames which consumed my faith forever,' he wrote.[1] For Wiesel the Holocaust is inexplicable with God, but also it cannot be understood without him. Auschwitz made it impossible for Wiesel to trust God's goodness, but it also made questions about God more important.

In this regard, Wiesel has been heard to remark, 'If I told you I believed in God, I would be lying; if I told you I did not believe in God, I would be lying'.[2] Wiesel is thus at odds with God because the only way he can be for God after Auschwitz is by being against him. This stance is eloquently portrayed in Wiesel's play *The Trial of God* which touches on the central theological dilemma posed by the death camps. As Wiesel explained in the foreword to the play and elsewhere, he witnessed a trial of God at Auschwitz where three rabbis who conducted the proceedings found God guilty and then participated in the daily prayer. In staging his case for and against God, Wiesel emphasizes that there was no need for God to allow the Holocaust to occur; it was an event that produced only death and destruction. Yet Wiesel asserted to be Jewish is 'never to give up – never to yield to despair'.[3] It is in this spirit that Wiesel conducted his dispute with God. As a survivor of the horrors of the death camps, Wiesel refuses to let God go. His struggles serve as a testimony that the religious quest was not incinerated in the gas chambers of the Nazi period.

Unlike Wiesel, some Jewish thinkers have found it impossible to sustain a belief in the traditional understanding of God after the Holocaust. According to Richard Rubenstein, Auschwitz is the utter and decisive refutation of the traditional affirmation of a providential God who acts in history and watches over the Jewish people whom he has chosen from all nations. In *After Auschwitz*, published in 1966, he wrote:

> How can Jews believe in an omnipotent, beneficent God after Auschwitz? Traditional Jewish theology maintains that God is the ultimate, omnipotent actor in historical drama. It has interpreted every major catastrophe in Jewish history as God's punishment of a sinful Israel. I fail to see how this position can be maintained without regarding Hitler and the SS as instruments of God's will. ... To see any purpose in the death camps, the traditional believer is forced to regard the most demonic, anti-human explosion of all history as a meaningful expression of God's purposes.[4]

In this study Rubenstein insisted that the Auschwitz experience has resulted in a rejection of the traditional theology of history; this must be replaced by a positive affirmation of human life in and for itself without any special theological relationship. Hence Rubenstein stated that we should attempt to establish contact with those powers of life and death which animated ancient Caananite religion. According to Rubenstein, God is the ultimate nothing, and it is to this divine source that human beings and the world are ultimately to return. There is no hope of salvation for humankind; one's destiny is to return to divine nothingness. In this context, Auschwitz fits into the archaic religious consciousness and observance of the universal cycle of death and rebirth. The Nazi slaughter of European Jewry was followed by the rebirth of the Jewish people in the land of Israel.

Unlike Wiesel and Rubenstein, a number of Jewish thinkers have sought to adopt a more positive theological stance. In *Tremendum*, published in 1981, Arthur A. Cohen addressed the religious dilemmas raised by the Holocaust. In his view, the Holocaust was the human tremendum,

> the enormity of an infinitized man, who no longer seems to fear death, more to the point, fears it so completely, denies death so mightily, that the only patent of his refutation and denial is to build a mountain of corpses to the divinity of the dead.[5]

Like Rubenstein, Cohen recognized that the Holocaust presents insurmountable difficulties for classical theism and for the Jewish understanding of God's relationship with the Jewish people. For Cohen, post-Holocaust theology must take account of three elements: (1) God must abide in a universe in which God's presence and evil are both seen as real; (2) the relationship of God to all creation must be seen as meaningful and valuable; and (3) the reality of God is not isolated from God's involvement with creation. Embracing kabbalah as well as the philosophy of Franz Rosenzweig, Cohen argued that God was initially all in all, but God overflowed absolute self-containment in a moment of love. For Cohen the world is God's created order, lovingly formed by the divine word without the surrender of human freedom.

Human beings, Cohen asserted, have the capacity to respond to God since they partake of God's speech and freedom. For Cohen, such freedom was intended to be tempered by reason, but this did not occur and therefore human freedom became the basis of the horrific events of the Holocaust. In advancing this view, Cohen criticized those who complain that God was silent during events of the Holocaust. Such an assessment is, he believed, a mistaken yearning for a non-existent interruptive God who is expected to interfere with earthly life. But if there were such a God, the created order would be an extension of the divine realm, and there would be no opportunity for freedom.

Since Cohen did not believe that God acts in history, he dismissed the view that God was responsible for Auschwitz. Instead he asserted that God acts in the future. God's role is not to act as a direct agent in human affairs, but as a teacher. His intention is to instruct human beings so as to limit their destructive impulses. For Cohen, divine teaching is manifest in Jewish law. In this way, human freedom is granted within the framework of the tradition.

A number of theologians have been unwilling to alter the traditional understanding of God in the way that Cohen recommended. According to Eliezer Berkovits in *Faith after the Holocaust*, the modern Jewish response to the destruction of 6 million Jews should be modelled on Job's example. At Auschwitz, God was hidden, yet according to Berkovits in his hiddenness he was actually present. As hidden God, he is Saviour. In the apparent void he is the redeemer of Israel.

How this is to be understood is shrouded in mystery. Berkovits wrote that if Jewish faith is to be meaningful in the post-Holocaust age, the Jew must make room for the impenetrable darkness of the death camps without religious belief:

The darkness will remain, but in its 'light' he will make his affirmation. The inexplicable will not be explained, yet it will become a positive influence in the formulation of that which is to be acknowledged ... perhaps in the awful misery of man will be revealed to us the awesome mystery of God.[6]

Another attempt to provide a biblically-based explanation for God's activity during the Nazi regime was proposed by Ignaz Maybaum in *The Face of God After Auschwitz*. In this study Maybaum argued that God has an enduring relationship with Israel, that he continues to act in history, and that Israel has a divinely sanctioned mission to enlighten other nations. According to Maybaum, the Holocaust is a result of God's intervention, but not a divine punishment. In explaining this view, he used the crucifixion of Jesus as a model for understanding Jewish suffering during the Holocaust. Just as Jesus was an innocent victim whose death provides a means of salvation for humanity, so the deaths of the victims of the Holocaust were sacrificial offerings. Maybaum asserted that the Jews were murdered by the Nazis because they were chosen by God for this sacrifice.

Maybaum contended that Jewish history was scarred by three major disasters which he designates by the Hebrew word *churban*, an event of massive destructiveness. For Maybaum each *churban* was a divine intervention which has decisive significance for the course of Jewish history. The first was the destruction of Jerusalem in 586 BCE; the second was the Roman devastation of the second Temple in Jerusalem; the third was the Holocaust, an event in which the Jewish people were sacrificial victims in an event of creative destructiveness. In Maybaum's view, God used the Holocaust to bring about the end of the Middle Ages, and usher in a new era of modernity. For Maybaum, Hitler was sent by God to bring about this transformation of Jewish life; God used the Holocaust as a means to bring about the modern world.

Paralleling this conception, Bernard Maza in *With God's Fury Poured Out* argued that in the Holocaust God's fury was poured out upon the Jewish people. The righteous martyrs of the Holocaust proclaimed their trust in God's will, and through their death God was able to accomplish his divine purposes. By means of their suffering the Jewish people were rescued from the oppression of their exile and Torah-Judaism was able to prevail.

Maza explained that most survivors of the concentration camps saw no hope anywhere but Palestine. After the establishment of a Jewish state the Jewish community was able to overcome its previous defencelessness. No longer were Jews homeless; the world had consented to return them to their ancient homeland. They had fought for their survival against all odds and prevailed. It was now possible for them to discover their religious identity.

Many Jews who survived the Holocaust were religiously observant. These individuals joined with Torah-committed Jews in Palestine – new *yeshivot* were created, old *yeshivot* expanded, and Torah elementary schools were strengthened. In the United States a similar efflorescence of Torah-based Judaism took place. As the flood of European Jews sought refuge in America after the Holocaust, they joined with American Jews to build new institutions. In other parts of the Jewish world there have been similar developments – Torah Judaism has become increasingly important in contemporary society. For Maza this was the goal of God's providential plan in which the Holocaust was an indispensable element.

Another traditional approach to the Holocaust is to see in the death camps a manifestation of God's will that his chosen people survive. Such a paradoxical view is most eloquently expressed by Emil Fackenheim in a series of publications in which he contends that God revealed himself to Israel out of the furnaces of Auschwitz.

For Fackenheim the Holocaust was the most disorienting event in Jewish history, a crisis which requires from the Jewish community a reassessment of God's presence in history.

Through the Holocaust, he believed, God issued the 614th commandment: Jews are forbidden to grant posthumous victories to Hitler. According to Fackenheim, Jews are here instructed to survive as Jews. They are commanded to remember in their very guts and bowels the martyrs of the Holocaust, lest their memory perish. Jews are forbidden, furthermore, to deny or despair of God, however much they may have to contend with him or with belief in him. They are forbidden finally to despair of the world as the place which is to become the Kingdom of God lest we make it a meaningless place.

In his later work, Fackenheim stressed that the Holocaust represents a catastrophic rupture with previously accepted views of Judaism, Christianity and western philosophy. According to Fackenheim, the process of mending this rupture (*tikkun*) must take place in the scheme of life rather than of thought. The resistance to the destructive logic of the death camps constitutes the beginning of such repair. As Fackenheim explained: some camp inmates were willing to become *muselmänner*, those who were dead while still alive. Such resistance was exhibited by pregnant mothers who refused to abort their pregnancies hoping that their offspring would survive and frustrate the plans of the National Socialist Party to eliminate every Jew.

Such resistance was more than self-protection. Since the Holocaust was a *novum* in history, this resistance was also a novum. As emphasized by Pelagia Lewinska, a Polish Roman Catholic:

> They had condemned us to die in our own filth, to drown in mud, in our own excrement. They wished to abuse us, to destroy our human dignity. From the instant in which I grasped the motivating principle ... it was as if I had been awakened from a dream. .... I felt under orders to live and if I did die in Auschwitz, it would be as a human being. I would hold on to my dignity.[7]

Fackenheim views this statement as evidence of the ontological dimension of resistance and of a commanding voice. In the past when Jews were threatened, they bore witness to God through martyrdom but Fackenheim believes that such an act would have made no sense in the concentration camps. Such death was what the Nazis hoped to accomplish. This resistance served as a new kind of sanctification, the refusal to die as a holy act. For Fackenheim those who heard God's command during the Holocaust were the inmates of camps who felt under an obligation to resist the logic of destruction. Among the most significant Jewish acts of *tikkun* in the post-Holocaust world was the decision of the survivors of the Nazi period to make their homeland in Israel. Though Israel is continually endangered, the founding of a Jewish state represents a monumental attempt to overcome the events of World War II.

Discussion: The Holocaust and Jewish theology

These varied attempts to come to terms with the Holocaust all suffer from serious defects. As we have seen, Rubenstein rejected the traditional Jewish understanding of God's activity. For Jewish traditionalists seeking to make sense of the horrors of the Holocaust, Rubenstein's discussion offers no consolation or promise of hope. Cohen's conception of deism is also so remote from mainstream Jewish thought that it cannot resolve the religious perplexities posed by the death of 6 million Jews in the camps. Wiesel's agonizing struggle with religious doubt illuminates the theological problems connected with the events of the Nazi period but plunges the believer deeper into despair.

At the other end of the spectrum the views of writers who have attempted to defend the biblical and rabbinic concept of God are beset with difficulties. Maybaum's view that God used Hitler as an instrument for the redemption of humankind is a monstrous conception, as is Maza's belief that the Holocaust was providentially planned so that Torah Judaism would be strengthened. Fackenheim's assertion that God issued the 614th commandment through the ashes of the death camps will no doubt strike many as wishful thinking. Finally, Berkovits' view that God was hidden during the Nazi period offers no theological solution to the problem of suffering. These major Holocaust theologians have therefore not provided satisfactory answers to the dilemmas posed by the death camps.

One element is missing from all these justifications of Jewish suffering: there is no appeal to the Hereafter. Though the Bible only contains faint references to the realm of the dead, the doctrine of life after death came into prominence during the Maccabean period when righteous individuals were dying for the faith. Subsequently the belief in the World to Come was regarded as one of the central tenets of the Jewish faith. According to rabbinic scholars, it was inconceivable that life would end at death. God's justice demanded that the righteous of Israel enter into a realm of eternal bliss where they would be compensated for their earthly travail.

Because of this belief, generations of Jews have been able to reconcile their belief in a benevolent God with the terrible tragedies they endured. Through the centuries the conviction that the righteous would inherit eternal life has sustained generations of Jewish martyrs who suffered persecution and death. As Jews were slaughtered, they glorified God through dedication to the Jewish faith. Such an act is referred to as *Kiddush ha-Shem*. These heroic Jews who remained steadfast in their faith did not question the ways of God. Rather, their deaths testify to their firm belief in a providential Lord of history who would reserve a place for them in the Hereafter.

In Judaism this act of sanctification was a task for all Jews if the unfortunate circumstances arose. Thus through centuries of oppression, *Kiddush ha-Shem* gave meaning to the struggle of Jewish warriors, strength of endurance under cruel torture, and a way out of slavery and conversion through suicide. In the Middle Ages, repeated outbreaks of Christian persecution strengthened the Jewish determination to profess their faith. *Kiddush ha-Shem* became a common way of confronting missionary coercion. If Jews were not permitted to live openly as Jews, they were determined not to live at all. When confronted by force, Jews attempted to defend themselves, but chose death if this proved impossible.

During the Middle Ages Jews also suffered because of the accusation that they performed ritual murders of Christian children, defamed Christianity in the Talmud, desecrated the Host, and brought about the Black Death. As they endured trials and massacres, they were fortified by the belief that God would redeem them in a future life. Repeatedly they proclaimed their faith in God and witnessed to the tradition of their ancestors. In later centuries, *Kiddush ha-Shem* also became part of the history of Spanish Jewry. Under the fire and torture of the Inquisition chambers and tribunals, Jews remained committed to their faith.

271

In the concentration camps as well many religious Jews remained loyal to the tradition of *Kiddush ha-Shem*. Joining the ranks of generations of martyrs, they sanctified God with unshakeable faith. As they awaited the final sentence, they drew strength from one another to witness to the God of Israel. In the camps many Jews faced death silently. When their last moments arrived they died without fear. They neither grovelled nor pleaded for mercy since they believed it was God's judgement to take their lives. With love and trust they awaited the death sentence. As they prepared to surrender themselves to God, they were convinced that their deaths would serve as a prelude to redemption.

What is absent from current Holocaust theology is this traditional conviction about the Hereafter. Yet, without this belief, it is simply impossible to make sense of the world as the creation of an all-good and all-powerful God. Without the eventual vindication of the righteous in Heaven, there is no way to sustain the belief in a providential God who watches over his chosen people. The essence of the Jewish understanding of God is that he loves his chosen people. If death means extinction, there is no way to make sense of the claim that he loves and cherishes all those who died in the concentration camps – suffering and death would ultimately triumph over each of those who perished.

But if there is eternal life in a World to Come, then there is hope that the righteous will share in a divine life. Moreover, the divine attribute of justice demands that the righteous of Israel who met their deaths as innocent victims of the Nazis will reap an everlasting reward. Here then is an answer to the religious perplexities of the Holocaust. The promise of immortality offers a way of reconciling the belief in a loving and just God with the nightmare of the death camps. As we have seen, this hope sustained the Jewish people through centuries of suffering and martyrdom. Now that Jewry stands on the threshold of the twenty-first century, it must again serve as the fulcrum of religious belief. Only in this way will the Jewish people who have experienced the Valley of the Shadow of Death be able to say in the ancient words of the Psalmist, 'I shall fear no evil for thou art with me'.

Notes

1 E. Wiesel, *Night* in R. Rubenstein and J. Roth, *Approaches to Auschwitz*, London, 1987, p. 283.
2 *Ibid.*, p. 255.
3 E. Wiesel, *A Jew Today*, New York, 1978, p. 164.
4 R. Rubenstein, *After Auschwitz*, New York, 1966, p. 153.
5 A. Cohen, *Tremendum* in Rubenstein and Roth, *op. cit.*, p. 330.
6 E. Berkovits, *Faith After the Holocaust*, New York, 1973, pp. 5–6.
7 E. Fackenheim, *To Mend the World*, New York, 1982, p. 250.

Bibliography

Autobiographies and memoirs

Benes, E., *From Munich to New War and New Victory*, Boston, 1954.

Bormann, Martin, *The Bormann Letters: The Private Correspondence between Martin Bormann and his Wife*. Ed. H. R. Trevor-Roper, London, 1954.

Gilbert, G. M., *Nuremberg Diary*, New York, 1947.

Goebbels, Joseph, *The Early Goebbels Diaries: 1925: 1925–1926*. Ed. Helmut Heiber, New York, 1963.

Goebbels, Joseph, *Final Entries: 1945: The Diaries of Joseph Goebbels*. Ed. H. R. Trevor-Roper, New York, 1979.

Goebbels, Joseph, *The Goebbels Diaries*. Ed. Louis P. Lochner, New York, 1948.

Göring, Hermann, *The Political Testament of Hermann Göring: A Selection of Important Speeches and Articles by Field-Marshal Hermann Göring*. Ed. H. W. Blood-Ryan, London, 1939.

Hanfstaengl, Ernst, *Unheard Witness*, New York, 1957.

Himmler, Heinrich, *Diaries of Heinrich Himmler's Early Years*. Ed. W. T. Angress and B. F. Smith, *Journal of Modern History 31*, 1959.

Hitler, Adolf, *Blitzkrieg to Defeat: Hitler's War Directives, 1939–1945*. Ed. H. R. Trevor-Roper, New York, 1964.

Hitler, Adolf, *Hitler's Secret Book*, trans. Salvator Attanasio, New York, 1961.

Hitler, Adolf, *Mein Kampf*, London, 1996.

Hitler, Adolf, *The Speeches of Adolf Hitler: April 1922-August 1939*. Ed. Norman H. Baynes, 2 Vols, London, 1942.

Hoess, Rudolf, *Kommandant of Auschwitz*. Ed. Martin Broszat, New York, 1961.

Kersten, Felix, *The Kersten Memoirs*, London, 1956.

Kubizek, August, *The Young Hitler I Knew*, trans. E. V. Anderson, New York, 1955.

Papen, Franz von, *Franz von Papen: Memoirs*, London, 1952.

Reck-Malleczewen, Friedrich Percyval, *Diary of a Man in Despair*, trans. Paul Rubens, New York, 1970.

Ribbentrop, Joachim, *The Ribbentrop Memoirs*, London, 1962.

Riefenstahl, Leni, *A Memoir*, New York, 1993.

Rommel, Erwin, *The Rommel Papers*. Ed. B. H. Liddell Hart, London, 1953.

Schacht, Hjalmar Greeley, *Account Settled*, London, 1949.

Schacht, Hjalmar Greeley, *Confessions of the Old Wizard*, Boston, 1956.

Schuschnigg, Kurt, *Austrian Requiem*, trans. Franz von Hildebrand, London, 1946.

Shirer, William, *Berlin Diary: The Journal of a Foreign Correspondent 1934–1941*, New York, 1941.

Speer, Albert, *Infiltration*, trans. Joachim Neugroschel, New York, 1981.

Speer, Albert, *Memoirs*, trans. Richard and Clara Winston, New York, 1981.

Strasser, Otto, *Hitler and I*, Boston, 1940.

Thyseen, Fritz, *I Paid Hitler*, London, 1941.

Warlimont, Walter, *Inside Hitler's Headquarters*, London, 1954.

General studies

Baumont, Maurice, *The Third Reich*, New York, 1955.

Bracher, Karl Dietrich, *The German Dictatorship: The Origins, Structure and Effects of National Socialism*, New York, 1970.

Broszat, Martin, *The Hitler State*, New York, 1981.

Buchheim, H., *The Third Reich: Its Beginning, Its Development, Its End*, Munich, 1961.

Childers, Thomas, and Caplan, Jane (eds), *Re-evaluating the Third Reich*, New York, 1993.

Frei, Norbert, *National Socialist Rule in Germany: The Führer State 1933–1945*, trans. Simon B. Steyne, Oxford, 1993.

Gilbert, Martin, *The Holocaust*, London, 1987.

Grunberger, Richard, *The Twelve-Year Reich: A Social History of Nazi Germany, 1933–1945*, New York, 1979.

Kershaw, Ian, *The Nazi Dictatorship: Problems and Perspectives of Interpretation*, Baltimore, 1985.

Maltitz, Horst von, *The Evolution of Hitler's Germany: The Ideology, the Personality, the Moment*, New York, 1973.

Peterson, Edward N., *The Limits of Hitler's Powers*, Princeton, 1969.

Rhodes, James M., *The Hitler Movement: A Modern Millenarian Revolution*, Stanford, 1980.

Shirer, William, *The Rise and Fall of the Third Reich*, New York, 1959.

Waite, Robert G. L. (ed.), *Hitler and Nazi Germany*, New York, 1965.

The Nazis

Abel, Theodor, *Why Hitler Came to Power*, Cambridge, Mass., 1986.
Allen, William Sheridan, *The Nazi Seizure of Power: The Experience of a Single German Town 1930–1935*, New York, 1973.
Dornberg, John, *Munich 1923: The Story of Hitler's First Grab for Power*, New York, 1982.
Eyck, Erich, *A History of the Weimar Republic*, trans. Harlan P. Hanson, 2 Vols, Cambridge, Mass., 1962.
Friedrich, Otto, *Before the Deluge: A Portrait of Berlin in the 1920s*, New York, 1973.
Gay, Peter, *Weimar Culture: The Outsider as Insider*, New York, 1968.
Gordon, Harold J., Jr., *Hitler and the Beer Hall Putsch*, Princeton, 1972.
Halperin, William S., *Germany Tried Democracy: A Political History of the Reich from 1918–1933*, New York, 1965.
Hamilton, Richard, *Who Voted for Hitler?*, Princeton, 1983.
Hanser, Richard, *Putsch: How Hitler Made Revolution*, New York, 1971.
Jablonsky, David, *The Nazi Party in Dissolution: Hitler and the Verbotzeit, 1923–1925*, London, 1989.
Laqueur, Walter, *Weimar: A Cultural History, 1918–1933*, New York, 1974.
Merkl, Peter, *The Making of a Stormtrooper*, Princeton, 1975.
Mitchell, Otis C., *Hitler over Germany: The Establishment of the Nazi Dictatorship, 1918–1934*, Philadelphia, 1983.
Turner, Henry A., *German Big Business and the Rise of Hitler*, New York, 1985.
Wheaton, Eliot B., *The Nazi Revolution, 1933–35: Prelude to Calamity*, New York, 1969.

Hitler

Bezymenski, Lev, *The Death of Adolf Hitler*, New York, 1969.
Binion, Rudolf, *Hitler among the Germans*, New York, 1979.
Bromberg, Norbert, and Small, Verna Volz, *Hitler's Psychopathology*, New York, 1983.
Bullock, Alan, *Hitler: A Study in Tyranny*, New York, 1962.
Bullock, Alan, *Hitler and Stalin: Parallel Lives*, New York, 1992.
Carr, William, *Hitler: A Study in Personality and Politics*, New York, 1979.
Cross, Colin, *Adolf Hitler*, New York, 1973.
Fest, Joachim, *Hitler*, trans. Richard and Clara Winston, New York, 1973.
Harris, Robert, *Selling Hitler*, New York, 1987.
Hauner, Milan, *Hitler: A Chronology of His Life and Time*, New York, 1983.

Heiden, Konrad, *Der Führer: Hitler's Rise to Power*, Boston, 1944.
Infield, Glenn B., *Eva and Adolf*, New York, 1974.
Jenks, W. A., *Vienna and the Young Hitler*, New York, 1960.
Jetzinger, Franz, *Hitler's Youth*, trans, Lawrence Wilson, London, 1958.
Kershaw, Ian, *The 'Hitler Myth'. Image and Reality in the Third Reich*, New York, 1987.
Langer, Walter C., *The Mind of Adolf Hitler*, New York, 1972.
Maser, Werner, *Hitler*, trans. Peter and Betty Ross, London, 1973.
Payne, Robert, *The Life and Death of Adolf Hitler*, New York, 1973.
Rosenfeld, Alvin, *Imagining Hitler*, Bloomington, 1985.
Schramm, Percy, *Hitler: The Man and the Military Leader*, trans. Donald S. Detwiler, Chicago, 1971.
Toland, John, *Hitler*, 2 Vols, New York, 1976.
Trevor-Roper, H. R., *The Last Days of Adolf Hitler*, New York, 1947.

Nazi leaders

Adams, Henry M. and Adams, Robin K., *Rebel Patriot: A Biography of Franz von Papen*, Santa Barbara, 1987.
Bewley, Charles, *Hermann Göring and the Third Reich*, New York, 1962.
Black, Peter R., *Ernst Kaltenbrunner: Ideological Soldier of the Third Reich*, Princeton, 1984.
Bramsted, Ernest K., *Goebbels and National Socialist Propaganda*, East Lansing, Michigan, 1965.
Breitman, Richard, *The Architect of Genocide: Heinrich Himmler and the Final Solution*, New York, 1991.
Bytwerk, Randall L., *Julius Streicher*, New York, 1983
Calic, Edouard, *Reinhard Heydrich*, trans. Lowell Bair, New York, 1982.
Cecil, Robert, *The Myth of the Master Race: Alfred Rosenberg and Nazi Ideology*, New York, 1972.
Frankel, H. and Manvell, R., *Dr Goebbels: His Life and Death*, New York, 1960.
Frischauer, Willi, *The Rise and Fall of Hermann Göring*, New York, 1951.
Heiber, Helmut, *Goebbels*, trans. John K. Dickinson, New York, 1972.
Irving, David, *Göring: A Biography*, New York, 1989.
Lang, Jochen von, *The Secretary, Martin Bormann, the Man Who Manipulated Hitler*, trans. Christa Armstrong and Peter White, Athens, Ohio, 1981.
Leaser, James, *Rudolf Hess: The Uninvited Envoy*, London, 1962.
Manvell, Roger and Fraenkel, H., *Rudolf Hess: A Biography*, London, 1971.
Manvell, Roger and Fraenkel, H., *Himmler*, New York, 1968.
McGovern, J., *Martin Bormann*, New York, 1968.

Schmidt, Mathias, *Albert Speer: The End of a Myth*, trans. Joachim Neugroschl, New York, 1984.

Smith, B. F., *Heinrich Himmler: A Nazi in the Making 1900–1926*, Stanford, 1971.

Nazi terror and propaganda

Baird, J. W., *The Mythical World of Nazi Propaganda 1939–45*, Minneapolis, 1974.

Blackburn, Gilmer W., *Education in the Third Reich: A Study of Race and History in the Nazi Textbooks*, New York, 1985.

Bleuel, Hans Peter, *Sex and Society in Nazi Germany*, trans. J. Maxwell Brownjohn, New York, 1973.

Conway, John S., *The Nazi Persecution of the Churches, 1933–1945*, London, 1968.

Crankshaw, Edward, *Gestapo*, New York, 1956.

Furhammer, Leif and Folke, Isaksson, *Politics and Film*, trans. Kersti French, New York, 1971.

Hale, Oren J., *The Captive Press in the Third Reich*, Princeton, 1964.

Hamilton, Alastair, *The Appeal of Fascism: A Study of Intellectuals and Facism, 1919–1945*, New York, 1971.

Helmreich, Ernst Christian, *The German Churches under Hitler*, Detroit, 1979.

Höhne, Heinz, *The Order of the Death's Head*, trans. Richard Berry, New York, 1971.

Hull, David Steward, *Film in the Third Reich: Art and Propaganda in Nazi Germany*, New York, 1973.

Kirkpatrick, Clifford, *Nazi Germany: Its Women and Family Life*, New York, Bobbs-Merrill, 1938.

Koch, H. W., *The Hitler Youth: Origins and Development, 1922–45*, New York, 1975.

Koehl, Robert Lewis, *The Black Corps: The Structure and Power Struggles of the Nazi SS*, Madison, 1983.

Kogon, Eugen, *The Theory and Practice of Hell: The German Concentration Camps and the System behind them*, trans. Heinz Norden, New York, 1958.

Koonz, Claudia, *Mothers in the Fatherland: Women, the Family and Nazi Politics*, New York, 1987.

Laqueur, Walter, *Young Germany: A History of the German Youth Movement*, London, 1962.

Mosse, George L. (ed.), *Nazi Culture: Intellectual, Cultural and Social Life in the Third Reich*, New York, 1966.

Reitlinger, Gerald, *The SS: Alibi of a Nation, 1922–1945*, Englewood Cliffs, 1981.

Rempel, Gerhard, *Hitler's Children: The Hitler Youth and the SS*, Chapel Hill, 1989.

Snydor, Charles W., *Soldiers of Destruction: The SS Death's Head Division, 1933–1945*, Princeton, 1977.

Stein, George H., *The Waffen-SS*, Ithaca, 1966.

Stephenson, Jill, *The Nazi Organization of Women*, London, 1975.

Zeman, Z. A. B., *Nazi Propaganda*, Oxford, 1973.

Holocaust

Arad, Yitzhak, *The Pictorial History of the Holocaust*, New York, 1990.

Arendt, Hannah, *Eichmann in Jerusalem*, New York, 1963.

Botwinick, R., *A History of the Holocaust*, New Jersey, 1996.

Burleigh, M. and Wippermann, W., *The Racial State: Germany 1933–45*, Cambridge, 1996.

Dawidowicz, Lucy, *The War Against the Jews, 1933–1945*, New York, 1990.

Fischer, K., *The History of an Obsession*, London, 1998.

Fischer, K. P., *Nazi Germany*, London, 1995.

Fleming, Gerald, *Hitler and the Final Solution*, Los Angeles, 1982.

Friedlander, S., *Nazi Germany and the Jews*, London, 1997.

Gilbert, Martin, *The Holocaust: A History of the Jews of Europe during the Second World War*, New York, 1985.

Hilberg, Raul, *The Destruction of the European Jews*, 3 Vols, New York, 1985.

Klee, Ernst, *The Good Old Days: The Holocaust as Seen by Its Perpetrators and Bystanders*, trans. Deobrah Burnstone, New York, 1991.

Landau, R., *The Nazi Holocaust*, London, 1992.

Lifton, Robert J., *The Nazi Doctors: Medical Killing and the Psychology of Genocide*, New York, 1986.

Lipstadt, Deborah E., *Denying the Holocaust: The Growing Assault on Truth and Memory*, New York, 1993.

Marrus, Michael R., *The Holocaust in History*, Hanover, N. H., 1987.

Mendelssohn, John (ed.), *The Holocaust*, 18 Vols, New York, 1987.

Noakes, J. and Pridham, G. (eds), *Nazism 1919–1945*, 3 vols., 1919–1945, Exeter, 1995.

Reitlinger, Gerald, *The Final Solution: The Attempt to Exterminate the Jews of Europe*, New York, 1953.

Rubenstein, W. D., *The Myth of Rescue: Why the Democracies Could not Save more Jews from the Nazis*, London, 1997.

Sofsky, W., *The Order of Terror: The Concentration Camp*, Princeton, 1997.

Tusa, A. and J., *The Nuremberg Trial*, London, 1995.

Wistrich, R., *Who's Who in Nazi Germany*, London, 1995.

Yahil, Leni, *The Holocaust: The Fate of European Jews*, New York, 1990.

Index